Cognitive Therapy for
Depression and Anxiety

A PRACTITIONER'S GUIDE

Other titles of interest from Blackwell Science

Basic Child Psychiatry
Sixth Edition
P. Barker
0 632 03772 5

Basic Family Therapy
Third Edition
P. Barker
0 632 03227 8

Basic Forensic Psychiatry
Second Edition
M. Faulk
0 632 03321 5

Cognitive Therapy for Depression and Anxiety

A PRACTITIONER'S GUIDE

IVY-MARIE BLACKBURN
PhD, MA, DCP, Clin Psychol, FBPsS
Consultant Clinical Psychologist
Cognitive Therapy Course Director
Newcastle City Health NHS Trust
Visiting Professor of Clinical Psychology
University of Durham

KATE M. DAVIDSON
PhD, MA, MPhil, C Clin Psychol, AFBPsS
Consultant Clinical Psychologist
Department of Clinical Psychology
Stobhill Hospital, Glasgow

FOREWORD BY
R. E. KENDELL
FRCP, FRCPsych, DPM
Professor of Psychiatry and
Dean of the Faculty of Medicine
University of Edinburgh

Blackwell
Science

© 1990, 1995 by
Blackwell Science Ltd
Editorial Offices:
Osney Mead, Oxford OX2 0EL
25 John Street, London WC1N 2BL
23 Ainslie Place, Edinburgh EH3 6AJ
238 Main Street, Cambridge
    Massachusetts 02142, USA
54 University Street, Carlton
    Victoria 3053, Australia

Other Editorial Offices:
Arnette Blackwell SA
    1, rue de Lille, 75007 Paris
    France

Blackwell Wissenschafts-Verlag
GmbH
    Kurfürstendamm 57
    10707 Berlin, Germany

    Feldgasse 13, A-1238 Wien
    Austria

First published in hardback 1990
Reissued in paperback with
amendments 1995

Printed and bound in Great Britain
    at the University Press, Cambridge

DISTRIBUTORS
    Marston Book Services Ltd
    PO Box 87
    Oxford OX2 0DT
    (Orders: Tel: 01865 791155
              Fax: 01865 791927
              Telex: 837515)

North America
    Blackwell Science, Inc.
    238 Main Street
    Cambridge, MA 02142
    (Orders: Tel: 800 215-1000
                    617 876-7000
              Fax: 617 492-5263)

Australia
    Blackwell Science Pty Ltd
    54 University Street
    Carlton, Victoria 3053
    (Orders: Tel: 03 347-0300
              Fax: 03 349-3016)

A catalogue record for this title
is available from the British Library

ISBN 0 632 03986 8

Library of Congress
Cataloging-in-Publication Data

Blackburn, I. M. (Ivy-Marie)
    Cognitive therapy for depression
and anxiety: a practitioner's guide/
Ivy-Marie Blackburn, Kate M.
Davidson; foreword by R. E.
Kendell.
        p. cm.
    'First published in hardback
1990.'
    'Paperback reissue with updated
amendments.'
    Includes bibliographical
references and index.
    ISBN 0 632 03986 8 (pbk.)
    1. Depression, Mental—
Treatment.   2. Cognitive therapy.
3. Anxiety—Treatment.
I. Davidson, Kate M.   II. Title.
RC537.B52   1995
616.85'270651—dc20   95-22027
                              CIP

Contents

**Part 2 · Application of Cognitive Therapy
Illustrated by Case Studies**

Foreword

A generation ago two utterly different forms of psychotherapy dominated contemporary thinking and practice. On the one hand was psychoanalysis and its derivatives, fashionable, wielding great influence on the arts and the intelligentsia and powerfully entrenched in most North American and many European universities. On the other was the behaviour therapy of Skinner and Eysenck, stridently proclaiming its scientific credentials and contemptuous of the arcane mysteries and the high priests of psychoanalysis. Both were incapable of understanding or even respecting the other, for both were convinced that they and they alone understood the secret springs of human motivation.

Twenty-five years later psychoanalysis and behaviourism are both in retreat, the former fatally handicapped by its unscientific attitudes and procedures and the therapeutic impotence of its practitioners, the latter discredited by its associations with brainwashing and its failure to recognize the emotional and intellectual differences between a human patient and a Wistar rat. In their place Beck's cognitive therapy has started to blossom and it is easy to see why. Unlike psychoanalysis its techniques are straightforward, easily described and deliberately free of mystique. More importantly, Beck and his colleagues have been determined from the beginning to test the efficacy of their techniques by random allocation clinical trial and to subject every assumption to the risk of falsification. Moreover, unlike behaviourism, cognitive therapy is explicitly human both in its origins and its applications. It is primarily concerned with ideas rather than behaviours and its rationale is based on reasoned arguments and the persuasive power of evidence. The thinking man's psychotherapy, if you like.

This book by Professor Blackburn and Dr Davidson describes the antecedents and development of cognitive therapy and its application first to depressions and more recently to anxiety states and panic disorders. Every important study and every clinical trial of cognitive techniques since A. T. Beck first began experimenting with novel ways of treating depressions in Philadelphia in the 1960s is described and its findings discussed. The concepts, terminology and cognitive therapy are described in detail with a wealth of illustrative examples, for this book is, as its title says, a practitioner's guide. Of course, by reading a book one can no more become a psychotherapist than one can learn to ski or to ride a horse but, thanks to their extensive clinical experience and descriptive skills, Professor Blackburn and Dr Davidson do succeed in providing a convincing and life-like description of how cognitive therapy actually works. The second half of the book consists entirely of illustrative case histories and provides an excellent 'feel' for the framework, the course and the occasional vicissitudes of the treatment. Perhaps the authors draw too sharp a distinction between depressive illnesses and anxiety disorders, for most patients have both sets of symptoms simultaneously, but stereotypes can certainly be valuable in textbooks.

Because cognitive therapy is still in its development phase it is still possible to describe within one modest volume almost everything about it that needs to be known. The authors have succeeded in doing just this and I believe that this book will be invaluable to any psychiatrist, clinical psychologist, nurse therapist or general practitioner who is interested in cognitive therapy and already has some experience of 'talking treatments'. Almost certainly, many will be interested, for cognitive therapy has great potential. It is already evident that it is as effective as tricyclic antidepressants in non-psychotic unipolar depressions and if it proves to reduce the relapse rate as well it will have major advantages to offset its higher cost. Beyond the depressions and anxiety disorders, its sphere of applications remains largely unexplored. Even so, it looks likely to have an important and interesting future.

Edinburgh 1989   R. E. Kendell

Introduction

The proliferation of psychotherapies in the last three decades, estimated as exceeding 250 varieties with their own 'brand names', underscores the need for 'talking therapies' in the treatment of the emotional disorders. This vast array of choices can, however, be daunting for the would-be psychotherapist or lead to the misguided conclusion that it does not matter what one does — all pyscho-therapies are the same or of equal efficacy. Whilst research is now in progress to attempt to identify the common elements in the various psychotherapies which may constitute the *active ingredients* leading to effective emotional and behaviour change, little is yet known in this area. The immediate concern of the clinician is to have at his* disposal a systematic therapeutic approach of known efficacy. A second point of importance for the busy clinician is 'How do I develop the skills to apply this system of therapy?' and third, 'Who is it suit-able for?'

Our aim in this book is to provide the practising professional in mental health with a detailed guide to the application of one type of pyschotherapy, namely *cognitive therapy*. We have selected two areas of psychopathology, depression and anxiety, because, as will be described later, these are by far the most prevalent disorders encountered in the community and in the clinic and, importantly, cognitive therapy has already been demonstrated to be effective in the treatment of these disorders. Cognitive therapy is not specific to any one disorder and the techniques used to treat different disorders are often the same. The strategies for change, however, can be specific to a particular disorder in that they are inspired by the cognitive model of that disorder. Thus, with an understanding of the cognitive therapy approach and clinical experience in emotional disorders other than depression and anxiety, the reader should be able to extrapolate from the contents of this guide the cognitive therapy treatment of other disorders.

The guide is presented in two parts; the first part consists of four chapters dealing with the general background to cognitive therapy; the second part consists of four chapters which illustrate by means of case histories the therapeutic methods described in Part 1. In the first chapter we define the clinical syndromes which this book deals with,

*For simplicity, the masculine gender pronoun has been used throughout this book.

before describing the cognitive model of depression and of anxiety in the second chapter. We discuss the theoretical underpinning of cognitive therapy in these two emotional disorders without detailing the vast research literature which cognitive theories have fostered over the last 25 years, but interested readers will be able to follow this up from the selective references. On the other hand, we provide evidence for the efficacy of cognitive therapy from the results of controlled treatment trials, so that therapists can judge for themselves whether cognitive therapy has anything to offer them. The last two chapters of Part 1 give a full description, with examples, of cognitive therapy techniques for the treatment of depression and anxiety.

The main emphasis in the rest of the book is practical. The case studies will enable the reader to see how cognitive therapy is applied and how treatment develops from the first interview onwards. In the last chapter, we discuss methods for dealing with common problems which may arise during the course of treatment.

The book is aimed at psychiatrists, clinical psychologists, nurse therapists and general practitioners. However, we feel that any professional involved in mental health care can benefit from using the general techniques of cognitive therapy, as these will help him utilize his time with patients more fruitfully and more economically.

Part 1
The Cognitive Model and
its Application to Depression
and Anxiety

Chapter 1
The Syndromes of Depression and Anxiety

The aim of this chapter is to describe the current classificatory systems for depression and anxiety in order to delimit the disorders we will refer to in this book.

The extent of the problem

Both anxiety and depression are recognized as being common complaints among general and clinical populations. From studies in Europe and in the USA, it is estimated that 9–26% of women and 5–12% of men have had a major depressive illness in their lifetime. At any one time, it is estimated that between 4.5–9.3% of women and 2.3–3.2% of men will be suffering from this disorder. Thus, roughly twice as many women as men will be suffering from depression at any one point in time and this proportion is reflected in clinical populations. This disproportionate rate in the prevalence of depression applies particularly to younger age groups. Younger people are also more likely to recover from a depressive episode than the older groups and are less likely to experience a recurrence of illness (Robins *et al.*, 1984; Blacker & Clare, 1987). Several studies of general practice patient populations give estimates of prevalence for major depression around 5% (Hoeper *et al.*, 1979; Blacker & Clare, 1987), making depressive disorder one of the more common clinical problems in general practice. It is estimated that only around 10% of general practice patients suffering from depression are referred to psychiatric services.

Prevalence of depression

In the case of anxiety, Marks & Lader (1973), in a review of 22 studies, estimate that approximately 3% of the general population suffer from an anxiety state. In primary care settings, that is in general practice populations, the prevalence of anxiety states is reported to be higher than that of depression. Kedward & Cooper (1969) suggest that 27% of patients who present to their general practitioners (GPs) with psychiatric symptoms have an anxiety state. The prevalence of anxiety disorders decreases, however, in psychiatric practice. A reason given for this is that GPs have tended to treat anxious patients themselves, usually with benzodiazepines. Where patients with anxiety disorders are referred to psychiatric services, the disorders may be of a more chronic nature. The pattern of referral of anxiety disorders to psychiatric services may, however, be changing, as psychological treatments are now regarded as preferable to drug treatment and benzodiazepine dependence is

Prevalence of anxiety states

becoming increasingly recognized as an avoidable condition.

Weissman & Myers (1978) reported that over 80% of people with generalized anxiety disorder have had panic disorder and/or a phobia at some time in their lives and that 39% of those suffering from phobias have had panic disorder. Thus, like depression, anxiety, with or without panic attacks, is one of the commonest psychopathological conditions.

Diagnosis

Depressive disorders

The classification of depressive disorders has been a source of long-standing controversy, centring on the question of whether the different presentations of the illness differ quantitatively, in terms of severity, or qualitatively, in terms of different disease entities. Early controversies relied on detailed phenomenological descriptions of patients and then, with the advent of computers, on multi-variate analyses of symptom ratings from large populations of patients. The main argument can be schematically represented as in Figure 1.1.

Dimensional model

Discrete illnesses model

While both models shown in Figure 1.1 do not deny the existence of a typical psychotic and typical neurotic group, proponents of the dimensional model suggest that the majority of patients would be represented somewhere along the middle of the dimension, psychotic–neurotic, while the proponents of the discrete illnesses model would suggest a bimodal distribution, with only a few patients in the middle grey area. It would be inappropriate to go into the various debates here (see Kendell, 1976). Instead, we will define the main diagnostic criteria used in clinical and research studies, so that we can delimit the group of patients who have been shown to respond to cognitive therapy.

Table 1.1 indicates that depressive illness can affect many different functions to a greater or lesser extent. All depressed patients will have some or all of these symptoms in different degrees of severity, and, in addition, some depressed patients present with clear psychotic symptoms in the form of delusions and hallucinations.

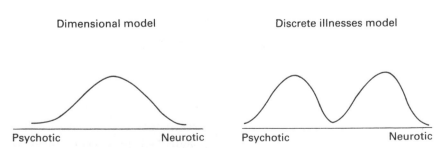

Dimensional model   Discrete illnesses model

Psychotic   Neurotic   Psychotic   Neurotic

Figure 1.1   Classification of depression illness

Table 1.1 Functional analysis of depressive illness

Psychological symptoms

Mood	Sadness, anxiety, irritability
Thinking	Loss of concentration, slow and muddled thinking, pessimistic outlook, self-blame, indecisiveness, low self-esteem
Motivation	Lack of interest in work and hobbies, avoidance of social or work activities, wish to escape, increased dependency
Behaviour	Inactivity, pacing, crying, complaining

Biological symptoms

Loss of appetite/increased appetite
Loss of libido
Disturbed sleep
Retardation/agitation

These are sometimes described as 'integrated delusions' in that they are understandable in the context of the patient's mood, unlike the 'disintegrated' delusions of schizophrenic patients. The delusions are generically called delusions of contrition, that is they relate to themes of guilt, illness, poverty and death. The hallucinations, which are rarer, refer similarly to accusatory and self-deprecatory themes.

In practice, the different diagnostic systems described below have

Table 1.2 ICD-10 depressive episode criteria

A 1 The depressive episode should last for at least 2 weeks
  2 There have been no hypomanic or manic symptoms sufficient to meet the criteria for hypomanic or manic episode at any time in the individual's life
  3 The episode is not attributable to psychoactive substance use or to any organic mental disorder

B 1 Depressed mood to a degree that is definitely abnormal for the individual, present for most of the day and almost every day, largely influenced by circumstances, and sustained for at least 2 weeks
  2 Loss of interest or pleasure in activities that are normally pleasurable
  3 Decreased energy or increased fatiguability

C 1 Loss of confidence or self-esteem
  2 Unreasonable feelings of self-reproach or excessive and inappropriate guilt
  3 Recurrent thoughts of death or suicide, or any suicidal behaviour
  4 Complaints or evidence of diminished ability to think or concentrate, such as indecisiveness or vacillation
  5 Change in psychomotor activity, with agitation or retardation (either subjective or objective)
  6 Sleep disturbance of any type
  7 Change in appetite (decrease or increase) with corresponding weight change

Subtypes: Somatic syndrome; Mild depressive episode; Moderate depressive episode; Severe depressive episode with or without psychotic symptoms

heuristic value as they indicate different treatment approaches. *The Manual of the International Statistical Classification of Diseases, Injuries and Causes of Death* (ICD-10, World Health Organisation, 1993) and the *Diagnostic and Statistical Manual of Mental Disorders* (DSM-IV, American Psychiatric Association, 1994) classificatory systems are described in Tables 1.2–1.4.

Table 1.3 DSM-IV criteria for major depressive episode

A Five (or more) of the following symptoms have been present during the same 2-week period and represent a change from previous functioning; at least one of the symptoms is either (1) depressed mood or (2) loss of interest or pleasure. *Note:* Do not include symptoms that are clearly due to a general medical condition, or mood-incongruent delusions of hallucinations
  1 Depressed mood most of the day, nearly every day, as indicated by either subjective report (e.g. feels sad or empty) or observation made by others (e.g. appears tearful). *Note:* In children and adolescents, can be irritable mood
  2 Markedly diminished interest or pleasure in all, or almost all, activities most of the day, nearly every day (as indicated by either subjective account or observation made by others)
  3 Significant weight loss when not dieting or weight gain (e.g. a change of more than 5% of body weight in a month), or decrease or increase in appetite nearly every day. *Note:* In children, consider failure to make expected weight gains
  4 Insomnia or hypersomnia nearly every day
  5 Psychomotor agitation or retardation nearly every day (observable by others, not merely subjective feelings of restlessness or being slowed down)
  6 Fatigue or loss of energy nearly every day
  7 Feelings of worthlessness or excessive or inappropriate guilt (which may be delusional) nearly every day (not merely self-reproach or guilt about being sick)
  8 Diminished ability to think or concentrate, or indecisiveness, nearly every day (either by subjective account or as observed by others)
  9 Recurrent thoughts of death (not just fear of dying), recurrent suicidal ideation without a specific plan, or a suicide attempt or a specific plan for committing suicide

B The symptoms do not meet criteria for a Mixed Episode

C The symptoms cause clinically significant distress or impairment in social, occupational, or other important areas of functioning

D The symptoms are not due to the direct physiological effects of a substance (e.g. a drug of abuse, a medication) or a general medical condition (e.g. hypothyroidism)

E The symptoms are not better accounted for by bereavement, i.e. after the loss of a loved one, the symptoms persist for longer than 2 months or are characterized by marked functional impairment, morbid preoccupation with worthlessness, suicidal ideation, psychotic symptoms, or psychomotor retardation

Subtypes: Severity/psychotic/remission; Chronic; With catatonic features; With melancholic features; With post-partum onset

---

ICD-10 is now more in line with DSM definitions, having got rid of the term manic-depressive which was still used in ICD-9 (World Health Organization, 1977) and differentiating between psychotic and non-psychotic depressive episodes, without using the term 'neurotic'. 'Somatic syndrome' in ICD-10 is very similar to the 'melancholic features' of DSM-IV (Table 1.4).

Table 1.4 DSM-IV criteria for melancholic features

Specify if:
With Melancholic Features (can be applied to the current or most recent Major Depressive Episode in Major Depressive Disorder and to a Major Depressive Episode in Bipolar I or Bipolar II Disorder only if it is the most recent type of mood episode)

A Either of the following, occurring during the most severe period of the current episode:
  1 Loss of pleasure in all, or almost all, activities
  2 Lack of reactivity to usually pleasurable stimuli (does not feel much better, even temporarily, when something good happens)

B Three (or more) of the following:
  1 Distinct quality of depressed mood (i.e. the depressed mood is experienced as distinctly different from the kind of feeling experienced after the death of a loved one)
  2 Depression regularly worse in the morning
  3 Early morning awakening (at least 2 hours before usual awakening time)
  4 Marked psychomotor retardation or agitation
  5 Significant anorexia or weight loss
  6 Excessive or inappropriate guilt

These definitions are too loose for use in any research study where groups need to be defined very carefully, for example, in treatment outcome studies. It is better to use DSM-IV, or research diagnostic criteria (RDC), particularly developed for research by some of the DSM-III contributors (Spitzer *et al.*, 1978). DSM-IV recognizes two depressive disorders: *major depression* in which there is one or more major depressive episodes; and *dysthymia* in which there is a nearly continuous depressed mood for at least 2 years, the criteria for major depression are not met over the first 2 years of the condition, and the depressed mood is accompanied by at least two depressive symptoms. Major depression can include psychotic symptoms and may or may not be the melancholic type. The term *melancholia* has been substituted for the endogenous sub-category of earlier versions, possibly to avoid the implied causal inferences of the term 'endogenous'. Tables 1.3 and 1.4 list the criteria for major depressive episodes and for the melancholic sub-type.

Major depression

Dysthymia

Melancholia

Most research in cognitive therapy, whether related to treatment outcome or the measurement of cognitive dysfunction, has been in depressed out-patients satisfying criteria for major depression, without psychotic symptoms, but with or without melancholic symptoms.

Anxiety disorders

Being anxious to some degree can be regarded as part of a normal coping response to everyday problems. However, when this is excessive and inappropriate to a situation it is regarded as a handicap and is recognized as a clinical problem. Definitions of anxiety as a clinical phenomenon vary. Some definitions emphasize physiological symptoms, others psychological. On the whole, there is little agreement as to whether both are required to be present or to what degree these symptoms should be represented in order to make a diagnosis of an anxiety state. Table 1.5 describes the various functions which can be affected in anxiety disorder.

Boundaries between the syndromes

The boundaries between the syndromes of anxiety and of depression are often blurred. Some clinical researchers view depression as resulting from long-standing anxiety (Wolpe, 1971). Anxiety is a common feature in depressive disorders and patients suffering from anxiety may also experience symptoms of depression. It is, therefore, important to recognize these features and to establish what is the

Primary and secondary diagnosis

primary and secondary diagnosis or whether both syndromes are present to the same degree of importance. In general, the distinction between primary and secondary diagnosis is made according to which disorder was manifest first. Any disorder appearing at a later stage is then considered secondary even though it may potentially be of a more life-threatening nature, such as in the case of secondary major depressive disorder where suicidal features may be present. As in the case of depression, the main classificatory systems used are ICD-10, DSM-IV and RDC. The definition of anxiety states from ICD-10 is described in Table 1.6.

Phobic states

Phobic states are described separately as neurotic states with abnormally intense dread of certain objects or of specific situations which would not normally have that effect. However, if the anxiety spreads from a specified situation or object to a wider range of circumstances, it is considered to be an anxiety disorder.

Table 1.5 Functional analysis of anxiety disorder

Psychological symptoms	
Mood	Anxiety, irritability, feeling keyed up
Thinking	Worrying, difficulty concentrating, mind going blank, overinterpretation of threat, view of self as vulnerable, low self-efficacy
Motivation	Avoidance of situations, increased dependency, wish to escape
Behaviour	Restlessness, jumpiness, excessive alertness
Biological symptoms	
	Autonomic arousal: for example, sweating, shaking, dizziness, palpitations, nausea, dry mouth

A There must have been a period of at least 6 months with prominent tension, worry, and feelings of apprehension about everyday events and problems

B At least four of the symptoms listed below must be present, at least one of which must be from items 1 to 4:

Autonomic arousal symptoms
   1 palpitations or pounding heart, or accelerated heart rate
   2 sweating
   3 trembling or shaking
   4 dry mouth (not due to medication or dehydration)
Symptoms involving chest and abdomen
   5 difficulty in breathing
   6 feeling of choking
   7 chest pain or discomfort
   8 nausea or abdominal distress (e.g. churning in stomach)
Symptoms involving mental state
   9 feeling dizzy, unsteady, faint, or light-headed
   10 feelings that objects are unreal (derealization), or that the self is distant or 'not really here' (depersonalization)
   11 fear of losing control, 'going crazy', or passing out
   12 fear of dying
General symptoms
   13 hot flushes or cold chills
   14 numbness or tingling sensations
Symptoms of tension
   15 Muscle tension or aches and pains
   16 Restlessness and inability to relax
   17 Feeling keyed up, on edge, or mentally tense
   18 A sensation of a lump in the throat, or difficulty in swallowing
Other non-specific symptoms
   19 Exaggerated response to minor surprises or being startled
   20 Difficulty in concentrating, or mind 'going blank', because of worrying or anxiety
   21 Persistent irritability
   22 Difficulty in getting to sleep because of worrying

C The disorder does not meet the criteria for panic disorder (F41.0), phobic anxiety disorders (F40.-), obsessive-compulsive disorder (F42.-), or hypochondriacal disorder (F45.2)

D Most commonly used exclusion clause. The anxiety disorder is not due to a physical disorder, such as hyperthyroidism, an organic mental disorder (F00–F09), or a psychoactive substance-related disorder (F10–F19), such as excess consumption of amphetamine-like substances or withdrawal from benzodiazepines

Panic Disorder (episodic paroxysmal anxiety)
A The individual experiences recurrent panic attacks that are not consistently associated with a specific situation or object and that often occur spontaneously (i.e. the episodes are unpredictable). The panic attacks are not associated with marked exertion or with exposure to dangerous or life-threatening situations

B A panic attack is characterized by all of the following:

1 It is a discrete episode of intense fear or discomfort

2 It starts abruptly

3 It reaches a maximum within a few minutes and lasts at least some minutes

4 At least four of the symptoms listed below must be present, one of which must be from items (a) to (d)

Autonomic arousal symptoms

(a)   Palpitations or pounding heart, or accelerated heart rate

(b)   Sweating

(c)   Trembling or shaking

(d)   Dry mouth (not due to medication or dehydration)

Symptoms involving chest and abdomen

(e)   Difficulty in breathing

(f)   Feeling of choking

(g)   Chest pain or discomfort

(h)   Nausea or abdominal distress (e.g. churning in stomach)

Symptoms involving mental state

(i)   Feeling dizzy, unsteady, faint, or light-headed

(j)   Feelings that objects are unreal (derealization), or that the self is distant of 'not really here' (depersonalization)

(k)   Fear of losing control, 'going crazy', or passing out

(l)   Fear of dying

General symptoms

(m) Hot flushes or cold chills

(n)   Numbness or tingling sensations

C Most commonly used exclusion clause. Panic attacks are not due to a physical disorder, organic mental disorder or other mental disorders such as schizophrenia and related disorders, mood disorders or somatoform disorders

---

Generalized anxiety disorder

As in the case of depressive illness, ICD-10 and DSM-IV are now more similar for anxiety disorder and panic than their predecessors ICD-9 and DSM-III-R (American Psychiatric Association, 1987) were. ICD-9 did not particularly differentiate panic disorder from the general anxiety states. Tables 1.7 and 1.8 give a list of DSM-IV criteria for generalized anxiety disorders and for panic disorder.

Panic disorder can exist with or without agoraphobia, that is fear of being in places or situations from which escape might be difficult or in which help might not be available. In this book, we shall consider only generalized anxiety disorder and panic disorder because there is no satisfactory evidence to date of the efficacy of cognitive therapy in the treatment of phobic states.

Table 1.7 DSM-IV diagnostic criteria for generalized anxiety disorder

A Excessive anxiety and worry (apprehensive expectation), occurring more days than not for at least 6 months, about a number of events or activities (such as work or school performance)

B The person finds it difficult to control the worry

C The anxiety and worry are associated with three (or more) of the following six symptoms (with at least some symptoms present for more days than not for the past 6 months). *Note:* Only one item is required in children
    1 Restlessness or feeling keyed up or on edge
    2 Being easily fatigued
    3 Difficulty concentrating or mind going blank
    4 Irritability
    5 Muscle tension
    6 Sleep disturbance (difficulty falling or staying asleep, or restless, unsatisfying sleep)

D The focus of the anxiety and worry is not confined to features of an Axis I disorder, e.g. the anxiety or worry is not about having a Panic Attack (as in Panic Disorder), being embarrassed in public (as in Social Phobia), being contaminated (as in Obsessive-Compulsive Disorder), being away from home or close relatives (as in Separation Anxiety Disorder), gaining weight (as in Anorexia Nervosa), having multiple physical complaints (as in Somatization Disorder), or having a serious illness (as in Hypochondriasis), and the anxiety and worry do not occur exclusively during Postraumatic Stress Disorder

E The anxiety, worry, or physical symptoms cause clinically significant distress or impairment in social, occupational, or other important areas of functioning

F The disturbance is not due to the direct physiological effects of a substance (e.g. a drug of abuse, a medication) or a general medical condition (e.g. hyperthyroidism) and does not occur exclusively during a Mood Disorder, a Psychotic Disorder, or a Pervasive Developmental Disorder

Table 1.8 DSM-IV diagnostic criteria for panic disorder with or without agoraphobia

A Both 1 and 2
    1 Recurrent unexpected Panic Attacks
    2 At least one of the attacks has been followed by 1 month (or more) of one (or more) of the following:
        (a) persistent concern about having additional attacks
        (b) worry about the implications of the attack or its consequences (e.g. losing control, having a heart attack, 'going crazy'
        (c) a significant change in behaviour related to the attacks

B Presence or absence of agoraphobia

C The Panic Attacks are not due to the direct physiological effects of a substance (e.g. a drug of abuse, a medication) or a general medical condition (e.g. hyperthyroidism)

D The Panic Attacks are not better accounted for by another mental disorder, such as Social Phobia (e.g. occurring on exposure to feared social situations), Specific Phobia (e.g. on exposure to a specific phobic situation), Obsessive-

Compulsive Disorder (e.g. on exposure to dirt in someone with an obsession about contamination), Postraumatic Stress Disorder (e.g. in response to stimuli associated with a severe stressor), or Separation Anxiety Disorder (e.g. in response to being away from home or close relatives)

Outcome

Although follow-up studies of anxiety and depression have been reported, it is difficult to assess the long-term outcome for these disorders. This is mainly due to the methodological problems encountered in studies of this nature. Some studies have only followed up in-patients, others only out-patients and it is, therefore, difficult to generalize the findings from one group to the other. As in all follow-up
Methodological problems
studies, there are problems in collecting adequate information about episodes of illness and symptoms across time and this often results in data being biased, perhaps towards more chronic cases. Definitions of outcome status vary across studies and are often not clearly defined, thus making direct comparisons difficult and inexact. Other factors that operate independently of morbidity also affect outcome status and cannot be easily controlled for in studies; for example, unemployment, economic recessions and hospital admission policies will vary from place to place as well as across time (Coryell & Winokur, 1982). Yet another difficulty in follow-up studies is how different treatments affect outcome. Since most studies select patients who have had psychiatric contact, many are likely to have received whatever treatment was considered effective at the time. This will obviously vary across time and individuals, thus affecting comparability of follow-up studies.

Depressive disorders

Despite the developments of modern pharmacotherapy for the treatment of depression, the chronicity and recurrence of many types
Chronicity and recurrence
of affective illness are becoming increasingly stressed in the research literature. Keller *et al.* (1984) reported that 21% of patients with an episode of major depression and no history of chronic minor depression (DSM-III-R dysthymia sub-type) had not recovered after 2 years of prospective follow-up, that is they still had major symptoms of depression. Murphy (1983) found that 48% of elderly depressed patients had had a poor outcome after 1 year, being still in treatment and/or showing major residual symptoms. Murphy *et al.* (1986) reported that an initial diagnosis of depression was predictive of an unfavourable prognosis, in terms of recurrence of illness, over a 17-year period. While 56% of their cohort of patients with an initial diagnosis of an affective disorder showed a poor outcome, patients with the full depressive syndrome, with or without anxiety, had the poorest outcome (79.2%). Comparable results have been reported by several other studies, e.g. Winokur & Morrison (1973), Schwab *et al.* (1979).

Of patients who do recover from a depressive episode, which typically lasts an average of 30 weeks, 36% have a recurrence of illness within a year (Keller & Shapiro, 1981). Controlled follow-up studies of maintenance treatment (see Chapter 2, p. 34) indicate that although medication does reduce relapse rate relative to placebo, recurrence of illness remains unacceptably high (Glen *et al.*, 1984). Attempts have been made to identify factors predicting relapse and chronicity. The most consistent psychosocial factor has been found to be the personality factor of neuroticism (Kerr *et al.*, 1972; Hirschfield *et al.*, 1986). Factors which predict recovery and relapse must be differentiated. Keller & Shapiro (1981) found that long duration of illness is a negative predictor of response to treatment, while number of previous episodes of illness predicts relapse.

Other factors predicting bad outcome have been listed as negative life events (Brown & Harris, 1978), lack of adequate treatment, continued physical illness, in-patient status, a positive family history, depression secondary to another disorder (e.g. alcoholism) and the presence of a non-endogenous pattern of symptoms.

Thus, psychosocial factors, illness characteristics, as well as quality of treatment have been implicated as predictors of poor long-term outcome in depressive illness. Whilst little control can be exercised by the clinician on psychosocial or illness factors, it is evident that more emphasis on type and quality of treatment may help to alleviate the unfortunate level of morbidity caused by depressive illness.

Anxiety disorders

There are many fewer long-term follow-up studies of anxiety states than of depressive disorders. Greer (1969), in a review of studies looking at the prognosis of anxiety states, found that between 41% and 58% of patients were rated as recovered or much improved in follow-ups of at least 1 year. Murphy *et al.* (1986), in the 17 year follow-up study mentioned above, found that 38.5% of their anxious cohort had a poor outcome in terms of chronic or recurrent illness.

The course of anxiety states has also been found to be complicated by secondary depression. Clancy *et al.* (1978) found that approximately 44% of anxious neurotics developed secondary depressions during a 4–9 year follow-up period.

Who is suitable for cognitive therapy? Indications and counterindications for cognitive therapy

A recent scale to assess suitability for short-term cognitive therapy (Segal & Safran, 1990) has been developed. It consists of 10 six-point scales which attempt to rate: Accessibility of automatic thoughts; awareness and differentiation of emotions; acceptance of personal responsibility for change; compatibility with cognitive rationale; alliance potential (In-session evidence); alliance potential (Out-of session evidence); chronicity of problems; security operations; focality; and patient optimism/pessimism regarding therapy.

These criteria are primarily based on clinical experience and remain to be tested for their predictive validity.

Depression

Whilst the literature supports the applicability of cognitive therapy to unipolar depression in general, few definite statements can be made in the current state of research about who would benefit most from cognitive therapy and who from antidepressant medication. Table 1.9 summarizes research and clinical findings.

In addition to the findings listed in Table 1.9, long duration of illness or chronicity has been found to be a negative predictor of response (Fennel & Teasdale, 1982; Blackburn, 1984). This variable has, of course, been found to be a negative predictor of response for all types of treatment, as discussed above. It is our clinical experience that such patients may have a better chance of response with a combination of cognitive therapy and vigorous drug treatment, possibly because chronicity induces a secondary process of 'being depressed about being depressed' which can be tackled in therapy. The psychological characteristic of 'learned resourcefulness' as a predictive factor is interesting in that it may indicate that the personal characteristics which patients bring to treatment may be important in determining choice of treatment.

Table 1.9 Indications and counterindications for cognitive therapy in depression

Indications	Counterindications
Unipolar illness	Psychotic symptoms (delusions and hallucinations)
Out-patient/general practice status	Bipolar illness
With or without endogenous symptoms	Extreme retardation or stupor
With or without medication	Concurrent treatment with electroconvulsive therapy (ECT)
High 'learned resourcefulness';* educational level is not relevant	Low 'learned resourcefulness'

*This predictive variable was identified by Simons *et al.* (1985) in a multiple regression analysis. It is measured by relative scores on the self-control schedule (Rosenbaum, 1980).

Generalized anxiety disorder and panic attacks

The current level of knowledge makes it impossible to state with any

Generalized anxiety disorder (with or without panic attacks)
Panic disorder (where symptoms are due to hyperventilation)
Anxiety as an accompanying symptom of depression
With or without medication

certainty who, in this group of disorders, would benefit from cognitive therapy. However, hints from the literature would suggest some general guidelines which are summarized in Table 1.10.

In contrast to the evidence in depressed patients, chronicity does not appear to be a counterindication to using cognitive therapy with anxious patients (Salkovskis *et al.*, 1986; Durham & Turvey, 1987).

There is evidence which suggests that a combination of pharmacological treatment (certain tricyclics and monoamine oxidase inhibitors) and psychological approaches which include graded exposure can be particularly therapeutic for patients with panic attacks (Telch, 1988). For generalized anxiety states, the long-term use of benzodiazepines is contraindicated (Committee on the Review of Medicines, 1980) and cognitive therapy appears to be a particularly useful alternative here.

References

American Psychiatric Association (1987). *Diagnostic and Statistical Manual of Mental Disorders*, 3rd revised edn. American Psychiatric Association, Washington DC.

American Psychiatric Association (1994). *Diagnostic and Statistical Manual of Mental Disorders*, 4th edn. American Psychiatric Association, Washington DC.

Blackburn, I. M. (1984). Setting relevant patient differences: a problem in phase IV research. *Pharmacopsychiatry*, **17**, 143–7.

Blacker, C. V. R. & Clare, A. W. (1987). Depressive disorder in primary care. *British Journal of Psychiatry*, **150**, 737–51.

Brown, G. W. & Harris, T. O. (1978). *Social Origins of Depression. A Study of Psychiatric Disorder in Women*. Tavistock, London.

Clancy, J., Noyes, R., Hoenk, P. R. & Slymen, D. J. (1978). Secondary depression in anxiety neurosis. *Journal of Nervous and Mental Disease*, **166**, 846–50.

Committee on the Review of Medicines (1980). Systematic review of the benzodiazepines. *British Medical Journal*, **280**, 910–12.

Coryell, W. & Winokur, G. (1982). Course and outcome. In Paykel, E. S. (ed) *Handbook of Affective Disorders*, pp. 93–106. Churchill Livingstone, Edinburgh.

Durham, R. C. & Turvey, A. A. (1987). Cognitive therapy vs behaviour therapy in the treatment of chronic general anxiety. *Behaviour Research and Therapy*, **25**, 229–34.

Fennel, M. J. V. & Teasdale, J. D. (1982). Cognitive therapy with chronic, drug-refractory depressed out-patients: a note of caution. *Cognitive Therapy and Research*, **6**, 455–9.

Glen, A., Johnson, A. & Shepherd, M. (1984). Continuation therapy with lithium and amitriptyline in unipolar illness: a randomised double-blind controlled trial. *Psychological Medicine*, **14**, 37–50.

Greer, S. (1969). The prognosis of anxiety states. In Lader, M. H. (ed) *Studies of Anxiety*, pp. 151–7. Royal Medico-Psychological Association, London.

Hirschfield, R. M., Klerman, G. L., Andreasen, N. C., Clayton, P. J. & Keller, M. B. (1986). Psychosocial predictors of chronicity in depressed patients. *British Journal of Psychiatry*, **148**, 648–54.

Hoeper, E. W., Nycz, G. R., Cleary, P. D., Regier, D. A. & Goldberg, I. D. (1979). Estimated prevalence of RDC mental disorder in primary medical care. *International Journal of Mental Health*, **8**, 6–15.

ICD-10 (1993) *The ICD-10 Classification of Mental and Behavioural Disorders.* World Health Organisation, Geneva.

Kedward, H. B. & Cooper, B. (1969). Neurotic disorders in urban practice: a three year follow-up. *Journal of the College of General Practitioners*, **12**, 148–63.

Keller, M. B., Klerman, G. L., Lavori, P. W., Coryell, W., Endicott, J. & Taylor, J. (1984). Long term outcome of episodes of major depression. *Journal of the American Medical Association*, **252**, 788–92.

Keller, M. B. & Shapiro, R. W. (1981). Major depressive disorder. Initial results from a one-year prospective naturalistic follow-up study. *Journal of Nervous and Mental Disorders*, **169**, 761–8.

Kendell, R. E. (1976). The classification of depression. A review of contemporary confusion. *British Journal of Psychiatry*, **129**, 15–28.

Kerr, T. A., Roth, M., Schapira, K. & Gurney, C. (1972). The assessment of prediction of outcome in affective disorders. *British Journal of Psychiatry*, **121**, 167–74.

Marks, I. & Lader, M. (1973). Anxiety states (anxiety neurosis): a review. *Journal of Nervous and Mental Disease*, **156**, 3–18.

Murphy, E. (1983). The prognosis of depression in old age. *British Journal of Pyschiatry*, **142**, 111–19.

Murphy, J. M., Olivier, D. C., Sobol, A. M., Monson, R. R. & Leighton, A. H. (1986). Diagnosis and outcome: depression and anxiety in a general population. *Psychological Medicine*, **16**, 117–26.

Robins, L. N., Helzer, J. E., Weissman, M. N., Orvaschel, H., Gruenberg, E., Burke, J. D. & Regier, D. A. (1984). Lifetime prevalence of specific psychiatric disorders in three sites. *Archives of General Pyschiatry*, **41**, 949–58.

Rosenbaum, M. (1980). A schedule for assessing self-control behaviors: preliminary findings. *Behavioural Therapy*, **11**, 109–21.

Safran, J. D. & Segal, Z. V. (1990). *Suitability for Full-term Cognitive Therapy Rating Scales (Appendix II) in Interpersonal Process in Cognitive Therapy.* Basic Books, New York.

Salkovskis, P. M., Jones, D. R. O. & Clark, D. M. (1986). Respiratory control in the treatment of panic attacks: replication and extension with concurrent measurement of behaviour and Pco_2. *British Journal of Psychiatry*, **148**, 526–32.

Schwab, J. J., Bell, R. A., Warheit, G. J. & Schwab, R. B. (1979). *Social Order and Mental Health: The Florida Health Study.* Brunner/Mazel, New York.

Simons, A. D., Lustman, P. J., Wetzel, R. D. & Murphy, G. E. (1985), Predicting response to cognitive therapy of depression: the role of learned resourcefulness. *Cognitive Therapy and Research*, **9**, 79–89.

Spitzer, R. L., Endicott, J. & Robins, E. (1978). *Research Diagnositic Criteria (RDC) for a Selected Group of Functional Disorders*, 3rd edn. Psychiatric Institute, Biometrics Research, New York State.

Telch, M. J. (1988). Combined pharmacological and psychological treatments for panic sufferers. In Rachman, S. & Maser, J. D. (eds) *Panic: Psychologiçal Perspectives,* pp. 167–87. Lawrence Erlbaum Associates, Hillsdale, New Jersey

Weissman, M. M. & Myers, J. K. (1978). Affective disorders in a US urban community: the use of research diagnostic criteria in an epidemiological survey. *Archives of General Psychiatry*, **35**, 1304–11.

Winokur, G. & Morrison, J. (1973). The Iowa 500. Follow-up of 225 depressives. *British Journal of Psychiatry*, **123**, 543–8.

Wolpe, J. (1971). Neurotic depression: experimental analog, clinical syndromes and treatment. *American Journal of Psychotherapy*, **25**, 362–8.

World Health Organisation (1977). *Manual of the International Statistical Classification of Diseases, Injuries and Causes of Death*, 9th revised edn. World Health Organisation, Geneva.

World Health Organisation (1993). *Manual of the International Statistical Classification of Diseases, Injuries and Causes of Death*, 10th revised edn. World Health Organisation, Geneva.

Chapter 2
Cognitive Therapy: Model and Efficacy

Definition

Cognitive therapy is a system of psychotherapy based on a theory of
the emotional disorders (Beck, 1967), a body of experimental and
clinical studies (Kovacs & Beck, 1978; Blackburn, 1988a) and well-
defined therapy techniques (Beck *et al.*, 1979). It is a structured form
of psychotherapy designed to alleviate symptoms and to help patients
learn more effective ways of dealing with the difficulties contributing
to their suffering. The therapeutic thrust of cognitive therapy is
problem-orientated. It is directed at correcting the combination of
psychological and situational problems which may be contributing to
the patient's distress. The label 'cognitive therapy' is used because the
techniques employed are directed at changing errors or biases in
patients' cognitions. This includes the way in which situations and
stresses are appraised, assumptions about self, world and future and
the beliefs and attitudes which are presumed to increase vulnerability
to emotional disorders. This approach to treatment is based, as
mentioned above, on historical, theoretical and experimental
grounds.

Structured

*Problem-
orientated*

Historical perspective

Philosophical antecedents

Cognitive theorists usually trace their philosophical ancestry to the
stoics of the first and second centuries AD, in particular to the slave
Epictetus and the emperor Marcus Aurelius. Epictetus is quoted as
saying 'Men are disturbed not by things but by the views they take of
them' and Marcus Aurelius wrote: 'If some external object distresses
you, it is not the object itself, but your judgement of it which causes
pain. It is up to you to change your judgement. If it is your behaviour
which troubles you, who stops you from changing it?' (author's
translation). Thus both Epictetus and Marcus Aurelius stressed the
importance of interpretations of events and our ability to change
these.

Stoics

   However, of later thinkers, it is the eighteenth century philo-
sopher Kant who reflects most closely the epistemiological standpoint
of modern-day cognitive theorists in his differentiation between
things-in-themselves (*noumena*) which are unknowable and subjec-

tive experiences (*phenomena*) which are filtered through *a priori* structures of knowledge. Simply, we cannot know things in themselves — we only know our interpretations of events and of ourselves. It could be surmised that these interpretations are influenced by our past experience, our genetic make-up and sociocultural background and by our prevailing mood.

Psychological and psychiatric antecedents

The dominance of classical psychoanalysis over the first half of the twentieth century brought about a complete neglect of cognition in psychiatry, stressing instead bodily needs and instinctive behaviour. Arieti (1985) wrote 'Freud stressed how we tend to suppress and repress ideas which elicit anxiety. But we psychiatrists and psychoanalysts have suppressed or repressed the whole field of ideas, that is cognition. We have repressed it apparently because it is anxiety provoking'. Alfred Adler, as a neo-Freudian, can, however, be viewed as the forerunner of modern cognitive theorists and therapists. He considered motivational urges as insufficient to account for human behaviour. The meaning that is attached to events determines behaviour according to Adler (1919) and, thus, Adlerian therapy involves re-educating the patient towards a more satisfactory lifestyle by changing his attitudes, his goals, his values and his behaviour. Murray & Jacobson (1978) rightly describe Adler as 'the forerunner of many modern cognitive therapists such as Albert Ellis, Julian Rotter, George Kelly, Eric Berne and Aaron Beck'.

*Classical
psychoanalysis*

Adler

The behavioural movement started by Watson (1913) and Skinner (1945) came as a direct reaction against the mentalistic approach of psychoanalysis. Early behaviour therapists wanted to apply learning theory and conditioning as researched in laboratory animals to the clinic. Only observable phenomena, in terms of stimuli and responses, were acceptable and any inferred phenomena, for example thoughts and emotions, were considered as unnecessary, soft, unscientific or unparsimonious in the understanding of behaviour. The behavioural approach created a vitalizing effect on therapy in general and, at first, appeared completely justified. Eysenck (1960) provided powerful evidence (since contested) against the efficacy of traditional psychodynamic psychotherapy, while evidence for the efficacy of behaviour modification for the neurotic disorders was being reported abundantly with revolutionary zeal.

*Behavioural
movement*

These early crusading attitudes of what has come to be called 'metaphysical behaviourism' were criticized, principally on the grounds that they ignored important clinical elements, such as cognitive and social variables. Eysenck's (1960) analysis was challenged by Bergin (1971) and the theoretical basis for behaviour therapy was rightly put in question (see Mahoney *et al.*, 1974 for a review of the arguments).

*Cognitive-
behavioural
therapies*

*Diverse
influences*

Piaget

After the behavioural revolution, some have hailed the 1960s as the age of a cognitive revolution. However, as argued by Blackburn (1986), there has not been a revolution, but a gradual evolution of ideas and techniques which has led to current cognitive or cognitive-behavioural therapies. This evolution was brought about through diverse influences.

1   Academic cognitive psychologists, e.g. Miller, Gallanter & Pribram (1960) in their influential book *Plans and the Structure of Behavior*, began to apply the scientific method to the study of mental phenomena.

2   Developmental psychologists, in particular Piaget (Flavell, 1963), through the study of the intellectual, social and moral development of the child, were able to describe the developing human organism as actively information-seeking, instead of being a passive receptacle for environmental stimuli. Piaget suggested mental structures or schemata as ways of organizing information and controlling behaviour. The concept of schemata will be described in a later section in this chapter.

3   Social learning theorists, for example Miller & Dollard (1941), Rotter (1954) and Kelly (1955), began to discuss cognitive concepts, such as attention, mediation between stimulus and response, expectation, planning, reclassifying and personal constructs.

4   Behaviour therapists themselves were revising their model, allowing a role for mediational or cognitive factors. Homme (1965) described thoughts as 'coverants' or the covert 'operants of the mind' which are important early elements in response chains before they ultimately become overt. These covert responses could be analysed and modified by using the principles of behavior change. Bandura (1969) in his influential *Principles of Behavior Modification* did not accept that behaviour is passively shaped by environmental factors, as proposed by the classical behavioural model. For him, behaviour depends on thought processes, on information acquired from previous experiences and on self-control processes. This is best exemplified in vicarious learning and in modelling — that is, acquiring new learning, for example that snakes can be handled with impunity, through watching somebody else handle snakes.

Depression

While the seeds of cognitive behaviour therapy were being sown through these different channels, two clinicians separately put cognitive therapy for depression on the map. Ellis (1962) developed rational emotive therapy (RET) where patients' basic rules and assumptions about the world and themselves (cognitive mediational variables) are deduced from their communications and challenged as the main therapeutic technique for alleviating distress and improving coping behaviour. Beck (1963), having started as a psychoanalyst, was finding clinical evidence from his depressed patients which seemed to contradict pyschoanalytical theory. In a content analysis of the dreams of depressed and non-depressed patients (Beck & Ward, 1961) and of psychotherapeutic interviews with 50 depressed patients (Beck, 1963), Beck found evidence for what was to become the core of his cognitive theory of depression — namely specific errors in the content and form of depressed thinking indicating a general negative cognitive bias. Psychoanalytic theory would have predicted that depressed patients would report a number of sado-masochistic themes in their dreams and free-associations which would differentiate them from other pathological groups. Instead, Beck found a strongly negatively toned self-concept, with pessimistic outlooks and a perception of the life situation as frustrating and unrewarding.

Beck's model of depression (general): Depressed patients show dysfunctions in the processing of information which lead to or maintain depressed affect and depressed behaviour. Clinically, it is these distortions which are even more striking than the evident changes in affect which have led to the categorization of depression as an affective disorder. In the processing of information, three classes of cognitive variables intervene between stimuli (events) and responses (mood and behaviour). These are schemata, cognitive processes and content of thoughts. Depressed individuals show negative biases at all three levels of thinking.

Beck's model of
depression

The cognitive model of depression is seen by Beck (1984) as one level of explanation which does not contradict *biological* approaches to the understanding of depression. Biological and cognitive dysfunctions are two sides of the same coin, that is depressed thinking is necessarily accompanied by dysfunction in the functional level of certain neurotransmitters in the brain and by dysfunction in the hypothalamic–pituitary axis and similarly, the converse is true.

Processing of
information

This mediational learning model differs from the simple S–R (stimulus → response) model of classical behaviour therapy, but has antecedents in early learning theories (e.g. Tolman, 1932). Behavioural and cognitive models of depression are represented schematically in Table 2.1.

Biological
approaches

The *behavioural* model of depression (see Blackburn, 1985) has closely followed Skinner's (1953) original definition of depression as an extinction phenomenon, with decrease in active behaviour because of lack of contingent positive reinforcement. This model was expanded by Lewinsohn (1974) who defined three groups of factors as determining the degree of response-contingent reinforcement. These are an individual's potential reinforcers (which will differ in quality and quantity), their availability and the individual's skills at providing these reinforcers for himself (that is, instrumental and social skills).

Behavioural model

Table 2.1 Behavioural and cognitive models of depression

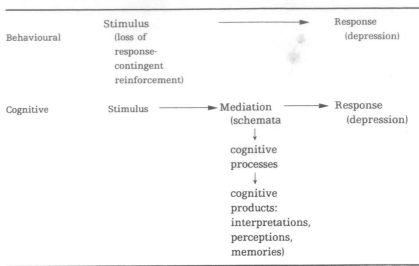

Anxiety

Cognitive behavioural approaches in anxiety have been developing over the past two decades and increasing attention has been given to this area as dissatisfaction with behavioural and drug treatments has grown.

Social learning theory

Bandura (1977) described how participant modelling was effective in reducing phobias and went on to develop his *social learning theory* of anxiety which emphasizes cognitive factors. He considered self-efficacy, an individual's estimate of his ability to cope with a situation, and outcome expectancy, an individual's estimate of the likelihood of certain consequences occurring, as being influential in moderating anxiety. Bandura argued that these are wholly conscious evaluations which an individual makes, and anxiety is seen as the outcome of these.

Primary and secondary appraisal

Lazarus (1966), in his essentially cognitive model of anxiety, made a distinction between two processes, namely *primary and secondary appraisal*. Primary appraisal is regarded as an individual's assessment of a situation as threatening, whereas secondary appraisal consists of his assessment of whether he has the necessary internal and external resources to deal with the situation. This combination of assessments of potential threat and coping resources determines how anxious an individual may become in a given situation.

Beck's model of anxiety

Beck's model of anxiety (general): The model which most clearly links emotions and thinking in anxiety disorders is that of Beck (Beck, 1976; Beck & Emery, 1985). In this model, anxiety disorders are conceptualized as being primarily thinking disorders. Beck *et al.* (1974a), in an investigation consisting of two studies designed to elicit

Thinking disorders

cognitions and visual imagery associated with anxiety, either directly or indirectly, found that anxious patients experience threatening types of thoughts or images which often precede attacks of anxiety. These thoughts relate to anticipated or visualized danger and extreme vulnerability.

It is assumed that anxiety disorders are derived from an organism's naturally selected survival mechanism when encountering objective threats and danger. The anxiety experienced in such circumstances cues an organism to take defensive action to avoid or minimize harm. Autonomic arousal, inhibition of behaviour and selective scanning of the environment for danger are naturally selected functions which increase an organism's chances of survival. However, in anxiety disorders, autonomic arousal, behaviour and cognitive processing do not correspond to an objective assessment of the degree of threat in a situation. Typically, anxious patients make appraisals which will overestimate the likelihood and severity of a feared event occurring and underestimate their coping ability and the rescue factors available.

The cognitive model of anxiety is represented schematically in Table 2.2. In this model, as in the model of depression, it is biases, at various levels of information processing, which influence an individual's response.

The cognitive model of panic disorder (Clark, 1986; Beck, 1988) proposes that panic results from the catastrophic misinterpretation of certain bodily sensations that are perceived as abnormal. During panic attacks, Beck asserts that the ability to process information, which could minimize or stop the attack, is lost. As a result, excessive focusing on bodily sensations leads to an increased likelihood that an individual will interpret these as being disastrous, which leads to yet further physiological arousal. A vicious circle then develops. Beck argues that this 'automatic reflexive processing' of impending disaster interferes with the ability to direct thinking and thus evaluate the sensations more objectively.

Panic disorder

Although there is now increasing emphasis on cognitive factors in anxiety, it should be noted that a more integrated approach, which takes into account the physiological or biological, cognitive and behavioural components of anxiety states would be desirable

Table 2.2 Cognitive model of anxiety

Stimulus ⟶ (anxiety-provoking situation)	Mediation ⟶ (schemata ↓ cognitive processes ↓ cognitive products: primary and secondary appraisal)	Response (subjective experience of anxiety, autonomic arousal, behavioural inhibition)

Table 2.3 Classical conditioning of fear responses

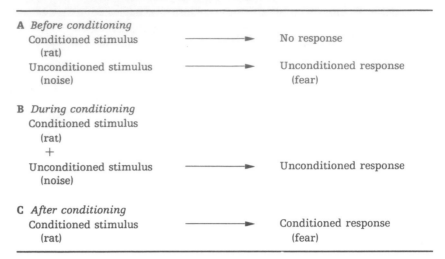

A *Before conditioning*		
Conditioned stimulus (rat)	⟶	No response
Unconditioned stimulus (noise)	⟶	Unconditioned response (fear)
B *During conditioning*		
Conditioned stimulus (rat) + Unconditioned stimulus (noise)	⟶	Unconditioned response
C *After conditioning*		
Conditioned stimulus (rat)	⟶	Conditioned response (fear)

Biological models

Behavioural models

(Mathews, 1985). *Biological* models have resulted from research aimed at finding specific biological pathology as a means of explaining the basis of anxiety disorders. Abnormal anxiety is seen as being the result of a biological event or dysfunction rather than as a psychological event. *Behavioural models* of anxiety, based on classical and operant learning theories have been use to explain the aetiology of phobic states in particular. Classical conditioning theories consider that any stimulus, whether complex or simple, when associated or paired with a situation which would usually elicit an overt fear response, will then trigger a fear response by itself (Table 2.3). These fear responses will consist of overt responses (flight, fight, avoidance, verbal expression) and covert responses (thoughts, images, physiological arousal). Any neutral stimulus can, therefore, come to elicit fear if it is paired with a threatening stimulus according to classical conditioning theory.

Operant or instrumental conditioning of fear responses was described by Skinner (1974). The crucial dependent variable in all behaviour, according to Skinner, is the response and its effect. In this model, avoidance behaviour will be reinforced as it reduces anxiety and if avoidance effectively reduces anxiety repeatedly, this learnt behaviour becomes permanent.

The role of cognitive events, processes and schemata in depression and anxiety

Cognitive events

An interview with a depressed patient will reveal immediately the predominant negative content of his thinking.

1 He uses a number of self-derogatory terms when describing

himself. He is lazy, cowardly, unworthy, dishonest, incapable, stupid, etc. Above all, he lacks the qualities which he feels are desirable or even necessary to attain the goals which he cherishes. Hence, he has a *negative view of self*.

2   He also sees his life situation or his world as generally unsatisfactory, frustrating and unrewarding. He sees his problems as insurmountable and inescapable. He may also see the rest of the world, not just his own circumstances, as full of misery and unhappiness. In other words, he has a *negative view of the world*.

3   Moreover, when he looks ahead into the future, he sees all his current difficulties as continuing for ever and as getting worse. He feels hopeless and helpless as he lacks the ability to make necessary changes. Therefore, he has *a negative view of the future* as well.

These three components have been labelled the *negative cognitive triad* by Beck (1976) and through them the other symptoms of depression can be understood at a cognitive level. Table 2.4 shows the cognitive model of depression. It must be stressed that this model explains depression at one level, without having to negate other levels of explanation, for example, biological or sociological. In our opinion, thinking can be regarded as a product of the brain and consequently the product of biochemical and physiological events. A human being lives in the world and is, therefore, under the influence of his environment and of social factors.

Beck (1967) may have overstated his theoretical position, leading to the inference that the negative cognitive triad *causes* the depressive syndrome. More recently (1984), he has clarified his position and taken a more ecumenical, and to our view, more reasonable, standpoint. Cognitive distortions are part and parcel of the depressive syndrome — they are symptoms and therefore cannot be conceptualized as causing themselves. They may, however, be seen as important entry points into the depressive system for therapeutic interventions. It could even be postulated that cognitions have hierarchical supremacy over some other symptoms of depression, but this would, in our current state of knowledge, be more a hypothetical statement open to verification than a statement of fact.

Table 2.4 Depressive content of thought and depressive symptoms

Negative view of self	Sadness, anxiety, irritability
	Lack of confidence
	Indecisiveness
	Lack of motivation and inactivity
Negative view of the world	Loss of interest
	Avoidance wishes
	Suicidal wishes and behaviour
	Loss of appetite
	Loss of libido
Negative view of the future	Sleep disturbance

There is an abundance of research studies (see Blackburn, 1988b) which have shown that the negative cognitive triad:

1 differentiates depressed patients from other psychiatric groups, that is, it is specific to depression;

2 differentiates depressed patients from normals, that is, it is sensitive to depression;

3 differentiates depressed patients from recovered depressed patients, that is, it reflects the state of depressive illness and is not a stable trait;

4 does not differentiate between sub-groups of depressed patients, that is, it is not sensitive to diagnostic sub-categories.

Anxious patients report thoughts and images relating to *themes of personal danger*. They react to situations as if they were dangerous or threatening, when in fact, there is little or no actual danger. Beck *et al.* (1974a) and Hibbert (1984) have described these themes in detail. They involve thoughts and images of vulnerability, inadequacy, lack of self control, social rejection and failure, disease, physical harm and death. In panic disorder, and when experiencing high levels of anxiety, patients are particularly likely to have thoughts relating to immediately impending physical injury or harm.

Anxiogenic cognitive triad

Anxious patients are more likely than non-anxious controls to interpret ambiguous situations as being personally threatening (Butler & Mathews, 1983), that is, they *view themselves as vulnerable*. They also tend to overestimate the amount of subjective risk to themselves in a situation. Their view of the *world as threatening* is, however, not necessarily that of a universally threatening or unpleasant place but rather they tend to regard themselves as especially at risk. They also view *the future as unpredictable*, treacherous and full of danger (Table 2.5).

Cognitive processes

Cognitive processes refer to the rules which are applied to stimuli in information processing. Perceptions, thoughts, mental images, associated memories are end-products or cognitive products after stimuli have been transformed through cognitive processes. Hollon & Kriss

Table 2.5 Anxious content of thought and anxiety symptoms

View of self as vulnerable	Anxiety, depression, Lack of self-confidence Avoidance Increased dependency
View of the world as threatening	Autonomic symptoms Disturbed sleep Loss of initiative Poor concentration
View of the future as unpredictable	Excessive alertness

(1984) make an analogy between cognitive processes and computer software. Distortions or errors in cognitive processing maintain the negative or anxious bias in the content of thought.

These distortions represent systematic logical errors which can easily be identified in the thoughts of depressed and anxious patients. Five types of generic errors have been identified as characteristic of information processing in depression and anxiety. These are summarized, with examples, in Table 2.6.

In an analysis of 200 thoughts collected during therapy from a sample of 50 depressed patients, Blackburn & Eunson (1988) found that the errors listed in Table 2.6 were sufficient to describe the cognitive processes of patients. One thought often contained more than one error, and individual patients had their own typical errors which tended to recur in different situations. These authors also found that 'selective abstraction' was most frequently associated with depressed mood, while 'arbitrary inference' was most frequently associated with anxious mood. Systematic errors occur in what are

Table 2.6 Examples of information processing errors in depression and anxiety

---

Situation: My boss laughed at two typing errors that I had made in a draft

1 *Selective abstraction*: the patient selects one aspect of a situation and interprets the whole situation on the basis of this one detail
    Interpretations: He dismissed 2 hours' hard typing with derision (*depression*)
                  I keep making mistakes (*anxiety*)

2 *Arbitrary inference*: the patient reaches a conclusion without enough evidence to support that conclusion or even in the face of contrary evidence
    Interpretations: He thinks I am a poor typist (*depression*)
                  I must be really clumsy (*anxiety*)

3 *Overgeneralization*: the patient draws a general conclusion on the basis of one aspect of a situation which has been arbitrarily selected from a whole context.
    Interpretations: Nobody appreciates me (*depression*)
                  I should never have become a secretary (*anxiety*)

4 *Magnification and minimization*: the patient exaggerates the negative aspect of a situation and minimizes the positive aspect
    Interpretations: What is wrong with me? I make nothing but mistakes
            (*depression*)
                  I can't cope with this. What if he gets angry? (*anxiety*)

5 *Personalization*: the patient relates to himself external events when there is no basis for making such a connection
    Interpretations: No wonder he looks so harassed all the time. He cannot
            even rely on me to type his work correctly (*depression*)
                  I am being ridiculed (*anxiety*)

---

called *automatic thoughts* or *self-talk*. These are the thoughts which occur as reflex actions and are the instant commentaries which we make about situations. They may not be at the forefront of our mind and may accompany more conscious mental activities. The secretary in the example in Table 2.6 could be taking notes or talking to her boss, but the running commentaries she makes at the back of her mind would be typical of her and causing or maintaining a dysphoric affect.

Normal and pathological processing

It is important to note that errors in the processing of information are not particular to depressed and anxious patients or other psychopathological groups. The difference between normal and pathological processing is likely to be in the extent, frequency and bias of the errors. Basic cognitive and social-cognitive researchers (Kahneman *et al.*, 1982; Nisbett & Ross, 1980) have highlighted processing errors in normal information processing, in particular when judgements have to be made under conditions of uncertainty, as they often are in the real world. Individuals use short-cuts or *heuristics* to process information, as under ordinary circumstances, human beings cannot possibly engage in deliberate, time-consuming information processing. Although these short-cuts or heuristics may lead to accurate inferences, more often than not they lead to inaccurate cognitive products because many aspects of information have to be ignored. Typically, heuristics will be influenced by an individual's affective state, past learning, beliefs and attitudes which will determine the judgements about probabilities of certain events, the classification of type of events and the evaluation of events. Piaget (1952) described two important universal cognitive processes: *assimilation* and *accommodation*. In the face of new information, assimilation occurs when an individual changes or assimilates the stimulus so that it fits his pre-existing *schema* (see next section) or he may accommodate by modifying his schema to fit the new information. Most of the literature suggests that assimilation occurs more often than accommodation and this is probably due to information processing heuristics which select aspects of stimuli and transform them in the ways described in Table 2.6.

Heuristics

Cognitive structures or schemata

Stable knowledge structures

These are stable knowledge structures which represent all of an individual's knowledge about himself and his world. They are made up of beliefs and theories about other people, oneself and the world in general. They will, therefore, affect what aspects of a situation we attend to, which we encode in our memory and how we interpret them. They will determine the processing short-cuts and errors in our thinking and finally the cognitive content or products. This aspect of thinking must be invoked to understand why and how the depressed or anxious person reaches the inferences he does about himself, his

Table 2.7 Schemata, information processing, thought content and depression

Stimulus	They did not speak to me
↓	
Schema	If people ignore you, it means they do not like you. If people do not like me, I am worthless
↓	
Information processing	They ignored me on purpose
↓	
Inference	They do not like me
↓	
Mood	Sad

Table 2.8 Schemata, information processing, thought content and anxiety

Stimulus	At a party
↓	
Set	Parties are difficult
Mode	People gathered together are threatening
↓	
Schema	If I do not behave correctly, I will not fit in and people will think I am peculiar
↓	
Information processing	No one is coming up to speak to me
↓	
Inference	They think I am strange
↓	
Mood	Anxious

world and his future — because it is by processing information through a schema that he goes beyond the information given. The two sketches in Tables 2.7 and 2.8 illustrate the role of the schema in depressive and anxious thinking.

Some of the typical schemata which have been elicited from depressed patients in the course of therapy or from questionnaire data (the Dysfunctional Attitude Scale, Weissman & Beck, 1978, see Appendix 1) are listed in Table 2.9.

Typical schemata, depressed patients

Beck (1967, 1976) has proposed that depressed patients have a negative schema, while anxious patients have a schema of the world as threatening and of themselves as lacking the self-efficacy to deal with the threat. Typical schemata elicited from anxious patients are shown in Table 2.10.

Typical schemata, anxious patients

Beck & Emery (1985) refer to schemata which are situationally specific as *cognitive sets* and to those which are global or general as *modes*. In anxiety disorders, the fear or danger mode appears to be overactive and still operates when danger is no longer present. This overactivation then leads to excessive mobilization of the autonomic

Table 2.9 Typical schemata of depressed patients

1 I must be loved by everybody
2 Either I am 100% successful or I am a total flop
3 My value as a person depends on what others think of me
4 I should always be a nice person
5 If people disagree with me, it means I am no good
6 I should always perform as best as I possibly can
7 I should be able to do everything by myself. To ask for help is to be weak

Table 2.10 Typical schemata of anxious patients

1 I should always be on the alert if I am to avoid something awful happening
2 If I do not behave correctly, I will be ridiculed and my position will be threatened.
3 If I do not show competence people will think I am a fool
4 If I feel anxious, this means I have no control of myself
5 If I continue to be anxious, I will die
6 If people look at me, they will criticize me
7 The world is full of dangers and threats which I cannot cope with

nervous system and to the environment being interpreted as danger-ous. They have suggested that certain neurochemical imbalances or fatigue may be responsible to some extent for the persistence of the danger mode.

The schemata considered to be depressogenic or anxiogenic (Tables 2.9 and 2.10) are self-referrent and have certain formal

Overstrict rules

characteristics, such as rigidity and undifferentiation. They are over-strict rules which appear child-like and have probably been learnt in early childhood, without modification through the process of accom-modation, as described above. They are influenced by an individual's sociocultural background and they become pre-potent during depres-sive or anxiety episodes.

According to research findings, basic schemata become dormant or latent during periods of remission and are reactivated by certain events which act as cues. Once reactivated, they are applied to more and more situations leading to increasingly distorted thinking. Schemata which are frequently used are very difficult to alter. In cognitive therapy, much effort is put into eliciting contradictory information to weaken or introduce some plasticity into these belief systems. It is our opinion that since these theories about the self are culture-bound, it is not possible, nor desirable, to alter them com-pletely. The therapeutic effort is aimed only at weakening the strength of the belief (see Chapter 4) and perhaps at making alternative belief systems available.

Research findings

Several research findings (see Blackburn, 1988b for a review) have shown that the schemata elicited from depressed patients using validated scales, for example the Dysfunctional Attitude Scale (DAS, Weissman & Beck, 1978; see Appendix 1), differentiate depressed patients from normal controls and other psychiatric groups. Some studies have also shown that recovered depressed patients cannot be differentiated from normal controls whether they have been treated with drugs or with cognitive therapy. It must, therefore, be concluded that depressogenic schemata reflect a state and not a stable personality trait. It seems that, during recovery, these schemata become inactive as proposed by Beck (Kovacs & Beck, 1978), but are reactivated under certain circumstances which constitute threatening situations for some individuals.

Mathews & MacLeod (1985), using a version of the Stroop colour naming test found that individuals suffering from anxiety were more disrupted in naming colours of words associated with possible danger than in naming those of neutral or positive words. They argued that anxious patients may allocate extra processing resources to threatening stimuli or alternatively that the emotional arousal arising from the perception of relevant words may indirectly interfere with colour naming. This experiment and others (see Brewin 1988 for a review) suggests that anxious patients specifically attend to threatening stimuli in a way which non-anxious controls do not. Individuals are presumed to possess 'danger' schemata in memory which are innately acquired or learnt from experience. In anxious patients, a preconscious bias to register threatening stimuli relating to these schemata operates, such that certain stimuli or events will capture an individual's attention. These stimuli may then be preferentially encoded into schemata in memory. They may then be easily accessed from memory should an individual confront an ambiguous situation in which potential threat or danger has to be determined.

Recent research (Beck *et al.*, 1983) indicates that there are supraordinate structures which are more stable than the schemata described above. These are *personality types* described as *autonomy* and *sociotropy*. The autonomous individual gets his satisfaction from independence, freedom and personal achievement, while the sociotropic individual is dependent on social gratifications, such as affection, company and approval. Thus an autonomous person's schemata would relate to needs of being alone, of independence, of achievement and of entitlement. A sociotropic person's schemata would relate to needs of love and affection, intolerance of solitude and needs of social approval. It is useful, as we shall see later (Chapter 5), to have an understanding of what these two contrasting types involve to be able to understand the patient, formulate a case and decide about therapeutic strategies. It is also possible that these character types would help predict which schemata become activated and under what circumstances, so that individual patients' vulnerabilities can be determined. However, these issues rely only on clinical evidence so far, as they have not yet been investigated in research studies.

Personality types

Research evidence for the efficacy of cognitive therapy

Cognitive therapy in depression has been the most studied to date in short- and long-term outcome studies although a few outcome studies of the efficacy of cognitive therapy in anxiety have now been published. In this section we will briefly review efficacy studies using cognitive therapy as described by Beck *et al.* (1979) for depression and Beck & Emery (1985) for anxiety. Studies using only components of the cognitive therapy package will not be covered, as they do not provide evidence for the therapy described in this book and are difficult to evaluate in view of the idiosyncratic nature of the therapy used. In our view, one of the weaknesses of early psychotherapy research has been the lack of definition and systematization of the therapy used, so that outcome research became meaningless. For a more detailed review of the various types of studies, interested readers are referred to Blackburn (1988c).

Cognitive therapy and pharmacotherapy in depression

In treatment outcome studies in depression, the well-tried tricyclic antidepressants are considered as the gold standard with which newer treatments are compared. The first study of Rush *et al.* (1977) comparing cognitive therapy with imipramine was the first study ever to show that a psychological method of treatment could be at least as effective as a tricyclic antidepressant drug. Since then, a number of other outcome studies have been published comparing cognitive therapy with pharmacotherapy — either alone or in combination. These studies are summarized in Table 2.11.

Apart from all using the same type of cognitive therapy, these treatment studies deal with the same sub-categories of depressed patients, namely out-patients satisfying diagnostic criteria (Spitzer *et al.*, 1978 or Feighner *et al.*, 1972) for unipolar major definite non-psychotic depression, including both endogenous and non-endogenous sub-types (see Chapter 1 for diagnostic criteria). In general, these studies are of adequate methodology, using random allocation and several standard outcome measures, but not always blind assessment. There is also no placebo group as such to control for time with therapist (unless relaxation treatment and insight therapy could be considered as placebo therapy!). The general conclusion is that cognitive therapy has not been found to be inferior to medication, except for the more severe depressions in the NIMH Study of 1989. In his meta-analytic study of 1989, Dobson analysed the results of eight studies and concluded that cognitive therapy patients, on average, did better than 70% of drug therapy patients.

The first comparative study of Rush *et al.* (1977) could be criticized on several methodological points. These researchers had tapered off medication at the end of treatment, so that at outcome

Table 2.11 Cognitive therapy and pharmacotherapy: relative efficacy in depression

Study	Outcome
Rush et al. (1977) (n: 41)	CT>imipramine
Beck et al. (1979) (n: 26)	CT=CT+amitriptyline
Dunn (1979) (n: 20)	CT+imipramine>supportive therapy and imipramine
McLean & Hakstian (1979) (n: 154)	CT>amitriptyline=relaxation>insight therapy
Blackburn et al. (1981) (n: 64)	Hospital clinic: Com>CT=antidepressants General practice: CT=Com>antidepressants
Rush & Watkins (1981) (n: 38)	Individual CT=individual CT+antidepressant>group CT
Murphy et al. (1984) (n: 70)	CT=nortriptyline=CT+nortriptyline= CT+placebo
Teasdale et al. (1984) (n: 34) GP	CT+treatment as usual>treatment as usual
Beck et al. (1985) (n: 33)	CT=CT+amitriptyline
Ross & Scot (1985) (n: 51) (GP)	CT (individual)=CT (group)>treatment as usual
Beutler et al. (1987) (n: 56) (elderly)	Group CT=CT+alprazolam=group CT+placebo=placebo
Covi & Lipman (1987)	Group CT=Group CT+imipramine>Psychodynamic
Elkin et al. (1989) (n: 239)	imipramine+clinical management=CT=IPT imipramine+clinical management>placebo+clinical management For HRSD>20, GAS<50 imipramine+clinical management>IPT>CT>placebo+ clinical management
Scott & Freeman (1992) (n: 121) GP	CT=Counselling=amitriptyline= treatment as usual
Hollon et al. (1992) (n: 154)	CT=imipramine=CT+imipramine

Com = Combination of antidepressants and cognitive therapy (CT)

evaluation at 12 weeks, contrary to usual clinical practice, the patients were off medication. Thus, an unfair advantage could have been given to cognitive therapy. On the other hand, an unfair advantage could be seen as having been given to medication, as they had rejected patients who had not responded to tricyclic antidepressants in previous episodes of illness. Other criticisms were that clinical ratings had not been done by assessors blind to the treatment modality; the patients were primarily middle class; and finally the study was done by the orginators of cognitive therapy at the centre for cognitive therapy in Philadelphia and could, therefore, have been biased in some way.

Later studies have answered most of these criticisms. All patients receiving drugs were still on medication at outcome assessments and patients were not excluded on the basis of their response to drugs. Three studies, Blackburn *et al.* (1981), Rush & Watkins (1981) and Teasdale *et al.* (1984) tried to circumvent this problem by allowing the prescribing physicians to choose the medication best suited to the individual patient, taking into consideration past history and presenting symptoms, as long as adequate dosages were adhered to. A variety of patients of different socioeconomic classes has now been included in the treatment trials and educational level has not been found to be a significant factor in outcome. Double-blind methodology is obviously impossible in treatment trials involving a psychotherapy alone group. The minimum precaution against bias taken in these studies has been that raters were not involved in the actual treatment and they were, as far as possible, single blind, although they might have detected medicated patients because of side-effects. The fact that research groups other than the cognitive therapy centre group in Philadelphia have been able to obtain results comparable to the Rush *et al.* (1977) study indicates that cognitive therapy can be mastered by any clinician through appropriate training and supervision and that it can be efficacious in different groups of patients.

Cognitive therapy is at least as effective as antidepressant medication

The conclusion from these treatment trials is that cognitive therapy is at least as effective as antidepressant medication in the treatment of unipolar non-psychotic major depression. The combination of cognitive therapy and medication appears to be superior to either treatment alone (Blackburn *et al.*, 1981) for hospital depressed out-patients who, compared to general practice patients, may have a longer course of illness, may have suffered more previous episodes of illness and may have more symptoms. For general practice patients or their equivalents (American studies) the combination of the two treatments has not been found to be superior to either treatment on its own, except in the Teasdale *et al.* (1984) study.

Cognitive therapy compared with other psychological treatments

Treatment outcome studies comparing cognitive therapy with other types of psychological treatment enable us to control for factors which comparisons with drug treatment cannot deal with methodologically. These include attention placebo effects and the specific effects of cognitive therapy. The attention placebo effect would postulate that cognitive therapy is effective primarily because of the relatively long time that patient and therapist spend together as compared to the time that pharmacotherapists typically spend with their patients. The non-

Table 2.12 Comparisons of cognitive therapy with other psychological treatments

Study	Outcome
Shaw (1977) (*n*: 32 self-referred students)	CT > BT = non-directive therapy > waiting list
Taylor & Marshall (1977) (*n*: 28 recruited depressed patients)	CT + BT > CT = BT > waiting list
Zeiss *et al.* (1979) (*n*: 44 media-recruited depressed patients)	CT = social skills training = increasing pleasant activities > waiting list
Wilson *et al.* (1983) (*n*: 25 media-recruited depressed individuals)	CT = BT > waiting list

BT = behaviour therapy; CT = cognitive therapy.

specificity effect would postulate that cognitive therapy is effective not because of the theory from which it is derived or because of its specific therapeutic methods, but because of the non-specific characteristics of structure, qualities of the therapist, credibility of the rationale and homework assignments. Table 2.12 summarizes the published studies to date comparing cognitive therapy with behaviour therapy and non-directive supportive therapy.

These studies are not of the same methodological standard as the studies described in the previous section for several reasons. The subjects were student volunteers or media-recruited depressed individuals and not clinic patients; the dependent measures were not uniform; the groups were small and the type of cognitive therapy given, although derived from the Beck *et al.* (1979) model, were not always systematized as in the pharmacotherapy trials. The indications are that cognitive therapy is superior to supportive non-directive therapy and to waiting-list controls, and either of equal efficacy or superior to behaviour therapy.

Equal efficacy or superior to behaviour therapy

As shown in Table 2.11, the multi-centre study carried out by the National Institute of Mental Health in the USA (Elkin *et al.*, 1989) describes a comparison of cognitive therapy with interpersonal psychotherapy (IPT, Klerman & Weissman, 1986), imipramine and placebo in 239 patients satisfying RDC for major unipolar depression. The results indicated that the three active treatments were equally effective and superior to placebo, although the patients in active treatment had been more severely depressed at the beginning of treatment. Moreover, there were more drop-outs from treatment in the placebo group. Imipramine effected a quicker response and, as IPT, was more effective in more severe depression.

Two studies have looked at the efficacy of *cognitive therapy in the elderly*. Gallagher & Thompson (1982) compared cognitive therapy, behaviour therapy and psychodynamic psychotherapy in three groups of elderly depressed patients. As assessed on the HRSD at the end of 12 weeks, all three treatments were of equal efficacy. However, at the end of 1 year, cognitive therapy and behaviour therapy proved superior to psychodynamic therapy, as improvement was better maintained. Steuer *et al.* (1984) compared group cognitive therapy with group psychodynamic psychotherapy in four groups of elderly patients. After 9 months of treatment, there was no difference between groups on observer rating scales of depression, but on a self-rating scale, the BDI, the groups receiving CT obtained significantly lower scores.

Thus, although the attention placebo argument can be refuted, especially as previous studies using non-directive or psychodynamic therapy have shown no effect in the treatment of depression (Whitehead, 1979), the 'non-specific argument' has not yet been answered adequately. Better planned studies of more adequate methodology are needed. The conclusions of Zeiss *et al.* (1979) remain a hypothesis to be tested, namely that successful psychological treatments have three important non-specific factors in common: (a) they provide the therapist and the patient with a clear rationale and a vocabulary for defining problems and describing change processes; (b) they are highly structured, so that treatment progresses in a planned manner; (c) they provide feedback and support, so that progress can be monitored realistically and become reinforcing.

Prevention of relapse in depression with cognitive therapy

The problem of relapse and long-term morbidity in depressive illness is becoming more and more highlighted by recent research (Editorial, *The Lancet* 1986; Keller *et al.*, 1984). The relapse rates on a placebo following active treatment appear to follow a linear regression over time ranging from 59% at 6 months (Mindham *et al.*, 1973) to 89% at 3 years (Glen *et al.*, 1984). Prophylactic maintenance medication does have a beneficial effect, but the rate of relapse remains disappointingly high. Glen *et al.* (1984) found relapse rates of 45%, 59% and 70% at 1, 2 and 3 years respectively for patients maintained on lithium or amitriptyline.

If cognitive therapy was shown to have an impact on the rate of relapse, it would indeed be of immense importance in our armamentarium — as it would then be not only of theoretical and of clinical interest, but also economically viable. To date, six studies have looked at relapse and the results have been consistently of great promise. These are summarized in Table 2.13.

All six studies indicate a marked improvement in relapse rates over a period of 1 year or 2 years in patients treated with cognitive

Table 2.13 Follow-up studies of cognitive therapy in depression. Percentage relapse

Cognitive therapy (CT)	12 months	18 months	24 months
Kovacs *et al.* (1981)			
(*n*: 35) CT	33	—	—
TCA	59	—	—
Beck *et al.* (1985)			
(*n*: 33) CT	42	—	—
CT + TCA	9	—	—
Simons *et al.* (1986)			
(*n*: 70) CT	20	—	—
TCA	66	—	—
CT + TCA	43	—	—
CT + P	18	—	—
Blackburn *et al.* (1986)			
(*n*: 36) CT			23
TCA			78
CT + TCA			21
Shea *et al.* (1992)			
(*n*: 61) CT	—	41	—
TCA + CM	—	61	—
IPT	—	57	—
Evans *et al.* (1992)			
(*n*: 44) TCA (no continuation)	—	—	50
TCA (continuation)	—	—	32
CT	—	—	21
CT + TCA	—	—	15

TCA = Tricyclic antidepressant

therapy alone or in combination with antidepressant medication as compared with patients treated with antidepressant medication. In the Blackburn *et al.* (1986) study, over the 2 year follow-up, the relapse rate for cognitive therapy alone was 23%, for the combined treatment 21% and for medication alone 78%. Thus, although the relapse rate on medication was equivalent to that reported by Glen *et. al.* (1984) for their placebo maintenance group, the two cognitive therapy groups suffered considerably less relapse than their patients maintained on medication for 2 years (50%).

These promising results can only be taken as tentative evidence, at this point, that cognitive therapy provides long-term protection against recurrence of depression, as the studies reported have been naturalistic rather than controlled and the numbers concerned in each individual study are small. As cognitive therapy aims to teach coping skills, and is particularly focused on the attitudes and thinking style which are deemed to maintain depression, it is possible that patients can apply this learning at the beginning of a recurrence of depression and hence prevent a full episode of depression from recurring. Another possibility is that the changes made during therapy bring about a permanent shift in a patient's cognitive style, so that he becomes less vulnerable to depression following treatment than he was at the onset of the depressive episode. It is known that medication, as well as cognitive therapy, changes thinking (Simons *et al.*, 1984; Blackburn & Bishop, 1983), as the groups recovered on the two types of treatment do not differ on scales measuring negative thinking at the end of treatment. Therefore, the difference in relapse cannot be attributed to residual negative thinking at the end of treatment in patients treated by drugs alone. More empirical research is needed to determine to what extent cognitive therapy reduces relapse in depression and what processes of change predict a good outcome.

Controlled trials of cognitive therapy for generalized anxiety

Some case studies using Beck's model have been published (Hollon, 1982; Last *et al.*, 1983; Waddell *et al.*, 1984) indicating that modifying the cognitive components in general anxiety can be effective. Other studies have used various methods of cognitive restructuring in the treatment of generalized anxiety. Woodward & Jones (1980) compared cognitive restructuring (using rational emotive therapy, Ellis & Grieger, 1977), systematic desensitization, the combination of both treatments and a no-treatment control group in 22 randomly assigned patients. The combined treatment was found to be superior to no treatment or either treatment on its own in the reduction of general anxiety (as measured by the Fear Survey Schedule, Wolpe & Lang, 1964). Systematic desensitization and the combined treatment were more effective than cognitive restructuring in reducing daily anxiety scores. Barlow *et al.* (1984) randomly assigned 11 patients with generalized anxiety disorder and nine patients with panic disorder to combined treatment consisting of biofeedback, relaxation and cognitive restructuring (stress inoculation, Meichenbaum & Turk, 1973) and to a waiting list control condition. The combined active treatment was superior on several dependent variables and gains were maintained at 3 months' follow-up.

Controlled trials

Cognitive therapy and behaviour therapy in anxiety

A selection of the best controlled trials is presented in Table 2.14. The term cognitive behavioural therapy (CBT) is used, as the various studies have not always used the same treatment package, although they all use a combination of cognitive and behavioural techniques. For more detailed reviews, the reader is referred to Durham & Allan (1993) and Chambless & Gillis (1993). In general, CBT has been found to be effective in generalized anxiety, but its specificity, relative to other active treatments, is ambiguous. More studies, using standard cognitive therapy techniques are needed. Studies which have looked at the long-term effect of cognitive treatment indicate that gains are maintained or augmented over 6–12 months follow-up (Blowers *et al.*, 1987; Butler *et al.*, 1987; Butler *et al.*, 1991).

Table 2.14 Controlled trials of cognitive therapy for generalized anxiety

Study	Outcome
Durham & Turvey (1987) (n: 41)	CBT = BT
Lindsay et al. (1987) (n: 40)	CBT = Anxiety Management Training = Benzodiazepine > waiting list
Butler et al. (1987) (n: 45)	CBT > waiting list
Butler et al. (1991) (n: 38)	CBT > behaviour therapy > waiting list
Power et al. (1989) (n: 31)	CBT > placebo CBT = diazepam
Power et al. (1990) (n: 101)	CBT = CBT + Diazepam CBT + placebo > Diazepam = placebo
Blowers et al. (1987) (n: 66)	CBT = non-directive therapy > waiting list
Borkovec et al. (1987) (n: 30 College students)	CBT + relaxation > non-directive therapy and relaxation
Borkovec & Matthews (1988) (n: 30 Community sample)	CBT + relaxation = non-directive therapy and relaxation
Borkovec & Costello (1993) (n: 55)	CBT = applied relaxation and non-directive therapy
Durham (1994) (n: 80)	CBT > analytic psychotherapy

Controlled trials of cognitive therapy for panic attacks

Treatment evaluation of cognitive therapy in panic disorder has been accumulating since the mid-1980s. Several uncontrolled case series indicated that cognitive-behavioural treatments may be effective in panic (Barlow et al., 1984; Clark et al., 1985; Salkovskis et al., 1986; Shear et al., 1991; Welkowitz et al., 1991). Clark et al. (1985) and Sokol et al. (1989) also reported that improvement at the end of treatment was maintained at 1–2 years follow-up.

Five controlled trials have since been published and these are summarised in Table 2.15.

Shear et al. (1994) also reported that at 6-months follow-up, subjects in the CBT group continued to improve while subjects receiving the non-prescriptive treatment showed slight worsening. Clark et al. (1994) reported 6 months and 15 months follow-up. At 6 months CT did not differ from imipramine, both treatments being superior to applied relaxation. However, at 15 months, CT was superior to both imipramine and relaxation.

The conclusion from these studies is that cognitive treatment for panic disorder is an effective method of treatment, that the re-interpretation and decatastrophising of bodily sensations associated

Table 2.15 Efficacy of cognitive therapy for panic attacks

Study	Outcome
Beck *et al.* (1992) (n: 33)	CT > supportive therapy
Barlow *et al.* (1989) (n: 46)	Panic Control (CT) = Cognitive restructuring + exposure > relaxation > waiting list
Klosko *et al.* (1990) (n: 57)	Panic Control (CT) > placebo, waiting list Alprazolam = CT = waiting list
Shear *et al.* (1994) (n: 65)	CBT = non-prescriptive treatment
Clark *et al.* (1994) (n: 64)	CT > relaxation, imipramine > waiting list

CBT = Cognitive-behavioural therapy

with hyperventilation provide quick relief of symptoms and that treatment gains are maintained over the follow-up period.

Overall summary

The cognitive models of depression and of anxiety describe biases at three levels of information processing — in the content of thought, the processing of stimuli and in basic cognitive structures.

Cognitive therapy has been developed to correct these biases and has been shown to be effective in the treatment of depression and of anxiety. Research evidence is stronger in the case of unipolar non-psychotic depression than it is for anxiety and panic disorders. This is due to historical reasons, in that cognitive therapy was first applied to depression and as such, there have been more rigorous studies of its efficacy in this disorder than in anxiety disorders. Controlled studies in general anxiety and panic disorders are promising, but further larger-scale treatment trials are needed. The clear evidence for the efficacy of cognitive therapy in the treatment of depression and the accumulating evidence for its ability to reduce relapse rates in this disorder raise the expectation that the same may be true for general anxiety with or without panic disorder.

References

Adler, A. (1919). *Problems of Neurosis*. Kegan Paul, London.
Arieti, S. (1985). Cognition in psychoanalysis. In Mahoney, M. J. & Freeman, A. (eds) *Cognition and Psychotherapy*, pp. 223–41. Plenum Press, New York.
Bandura, A. (1969). *Principles of Behaviour Modification*. Holt, Rhinehart & Wilson, New York.

Bandura, A. (1977). Self efficacy: toward a unifying theory of behavioural change. *Psychological Review,* **84,** 191–215.

Barlow, D. H., Cohen, A. S., Waddell, M. T., Vermilyea, B. B., Klosko, J. S., Blanchard, E. B. & DiNardo, P. A. (1984). Panic and generalized anxiety disorders: nature and treatment. *Behaviour Therapy,* **15,** 431–49.

Barlow, D. H., Craske, M. G., Cerny, J. A. & Klosko, J. S. (1989). Behavioural treatment for panic disorder. *Behaviour Therapy,* **20,** 261–82.

Beck, A. T. (1963). Thinking and depression. I. Idiosyncratic content and cognitive distortions. *Archives of General Psychiatry,* **9,** 324–33.

Beck, A. T. (1967). *Depression: Clinical, Experimental, and Theoretical Aspects.* Hoeber, New York.

Beck, A. T. (1976). *Cognitive Therapy and the Emotional Disorders.* International Universities Press, New York.

Beck, A. T. (1984). Cognition and therapy. *Archives of General Psychiatry,* **41,** 1112–14.

Beck, A. T. (1988). Cognitive approaches to panic disorder: theory and therapy. In Rachman, S. & Maser, D. (eds) *Panic: Psychological Perspectives.* pp. 91–109. Lawrence Erlbaum, Hillsdale, New Jersey.

Beck, A. T. & Emery, G. (1979). *Cognitive Therapy of Anxiety and Phobic Disorders.* Unpublished treatment manual of the Center for Cognitive Therapy, 133 South 36th Street, Philadelphia 19104.

Beck, A. T. & Emery, G. (1985). *Anxiety Disorder and Phobias: a Cognitive Perspective.* Basic Books, New York.

Beck, A. T., Epstein, N. & Harrison, R. (1983). Cognitions, attitudes and personality dimensions in depression. *British Journal of Cognitive Psychotherapy,* **1,** 1–11.

Beck, A. T., Hollon, S. D., Young, J. E., Bedrosian, R. C. & Budenz, D. (1985). Treatment of depression with cognitive therapy and amitriptyline. *Archives of General Psychiatry,* **42,** 142–8.

Beck, A. T., Laude, R. & Bohnert, M. (1974a). Ideational components of anxiety neurosis. *Archives of General Psychiatry,* **31,** 319–26.

Beck, A. T., Rush, A. J., Shaw, B. F. & Emery, G. (1979) *Cognitive Therapy of Depression: a Treatment Manual.* Guilford Press, New York.

Beck, A. T. & Ward, C. H. (1961). Dreams of depressed patients: characteristic themes in manifest content. *Archives of General Psychiatry,* **5,** 462–7.

Beck, A. T., Weissman, A. N., Lester, D. & Trexler, L. (1974b). The measurement of pessimism. The hopelessness scale. *Journal of Consulting and Clinical Psychology,* **42,** 861–5.

Bergin, A. E. (1971). The evaluation of therapeutic outcomes. In Bergin, A. E. & Garfield, S. L. (eds) *Handbook of Psychotherapy and Behaviour Change,* pp. 217–70. John Wiley & Sons, New York.

Beutler, L. E., Scogin, F., Kirkish, P. *et al.* (1987). The efficacy of cognitive therapy in depression: a treatment of depression in older adults. *Journal of Consulting and Clinical Psychology,* **55,** 550–56.

Blackburn, I. M. (1985). Depressions. In Bradley, B. P. & Thompson, C. (eds) *Psychological Applications in Psychiatry,* pp. 61–93. John Wiley & Sons, Chichester.

Blackburn, I. M. (1986). The cognitive revolution: an ongoing evolution. *Behavioural Psychotherapy,* **14,** 274–7.

Blackburn, I. M. (1988a). Psychological processes in depression. In Miller, E. & Cooper, P. J. (eds) *Adult Abnormal Psychology*, pp. 128–68. Churchill Livingstone, Edinburgh.

Blackburn, I. M. (1988b). Cognitive measures of depression. In Perris, C. Blackburn, I. M. & Perris, H. (eds) *Cognitive Psychotherapy: Theory and Practice*, pp. 98–119. Springer-Verlag, Heidelberg.

Blackburn, I. M. (1988c). An appraisal of comparative trials of cognitive therapy. In Perris, C. Blackburn, I. M. & Perris, H. (eds) *Cognitive Psychotherapy: Theory and Practice*, pp. 160–78. Springer-Verlag, Heidelberg.

Blackburn, I. M. & Bishop, S. (1983). Changes in cognition with pharmacotherapy and cognitive therapy. *British Journal of Psychiatry*, **143**, 609–17.

Blackburn, I. M., Bishop, S., Glen, A. I. M., Whalley, L. J. & Christie, J. E. (1981). The efficacy of cognitive therapy in depression: a treatment trial using cognitive therapy and pharmacotherapy, each alone and in combination. *British Journal of Psychiatry*, **139**, 181–9.

Blackburn, I. M. & Eunson, K. M. (1988). A content analysis of thoughts and emotions elicited from depressed patients during cognitive therapy. *British Journal of Medical Psychology*, **62**, 23–33.

Blackburn, I. M., Eunson, K. M. & Bishop, S. (1986). A two-year naturalistic follow-up of depressed patients treated with cognitive therapy, pharmacotherapy and a combination of both. *Journal of Affective Disorders*, **10**, 67–75.

Blowers, C., Cobb, J. & Mathews, A. (1987). Generalized anxiety: a controlled treatment study. *Behaviour Research and Therapy*, **25**, 493–502.

Borkovec, T. D. & Costello, E. (1993). Efficacy of applied relaxation and cognitive-behavioral therapy in the treatment of generalized anxiety disorder. *Journal of Consulting and Clinical Psychology*, **61**, 611–19.

Borkovec, T. D. & Mathews, A. (1988). Treatment of nonphobic anxiety disorders: a comparison of nondirective, cognitive and coping desensitization therapy. *Journal of Consulting and Clinical Psychology*, **56**, 877–84.

Borkovec, T. D., Mathews, A., Chambers, A., Ebrahim, S., Lytles, R. & Nelson, R. (1987). The effects of relaxation training with cognitive therapy or nondirective therapy and the role of relaxation-induced anxiety in the treatment of generalized anxiety. *Journal of Consulting and Clinical Psychology*, **55**, 883–8.

Brewin, C. R. (1988). *Cognitive Foundations of Clinical Psychology*. Lawrence Erlbaum Associates, London.

Butler, G., Cullington, A., Hibbert, G., Kumes, I. & Gelder, M. (1987). Anxiety management for persistent generalised anxiety. *British Journal of Psychiatry*, **151**, 535–42.

Butler, G. & Mathews, A. (1983). Cognitive processes in anxiety. *Advances in Behaviour Research and Therapy*, **5**, 51–62.

Butler, G., Fennell, M., Robson, P. & Gelder, M. (1991). Comparison of behaviour therapy and cognitive behaviour therapy in the treatment of generalized anxiety disorder. *Journal of Consulting and Clinical Psychology*, **59**, 167–75.

Chambless, D. L. & Gillis, M. M. (1993). Cognitive therapy of anxiety disorders. *Journal of Consulting and Clinical Psychology*, **61**, 248–60.

Clark, D. M. (1986). A cognitive approach to panic. *Behaviour Research and Therapy*, **24**, 461–70.

Clark, D. M., Salkovskis, P. & Chalkley, A. (1985). Respiratory control as a treatment for panic attacks. *Journal of Behaviour Therapy and Experimental Psychiatry*, **16**, 23–30.

Clark, D. M., Hackmann, A., Middleton, H., Anastasiades, P. & Gelder, M. (1994). A comparison of cognitive therapy, applied relaxation and imipramine in the treatment of panic disorder. *British Journal of Psychiatry*, **164**, 759-69.

Covi, L. & Lipman, R. S. (1987). Cognitive behavioural group psychotherapy combined with imipramine in major depression. *Psycopharmacol. Bull.* **23**, 173-6.

Dempsey, P. (1964). An undimensional depression scale for the MMPI. *Journal of Consulting and Clinical Psychology*, **28**, 364-70.

Dunn, R. J. (1979). Cognitive modification with depression-prone psychiatric patients. Cog. Ther. Res. **3**, 307-17.

Durham, R. C. & Allan, T. (1993). Psychological treatment of generalised anxiety disorder. A review of the clinical significance of results in outcome studies since 1980. *British Journal of Psychiatry*, **163**, 19-26.

Durham, R. C. & Turvey, A. A. (1987). Cognitive therapy vs behaviour therapy in the treatment of chronic general anxiety. *Behaviour Research Therapy*, **25**, 229-34.

Durham, R. C., Murphy, T. J. C., Allan, T., Richard, K., Treliving, L. R. & Fenton, G. W. (1994). A comparison of cognitive therapy, analytic psychotherapy and anxiety management training in the treatment of generalised anxiety disorder. *British Journal of Psychiatry*, **165**, 315-23.

Editorial, The Lancet (1986). Predicting chronicity in depression. *The Lancet*, **2**, 897-8.

Elkin, I., Shea, M. T., Watkins, J. T. *et al.* (1989). NIMH treatment of depression collaborative research program: general effectiveness of treatments. *Archives of General Psychiatry*, **46**, 971-82.

Elkin-Waskow, I. (1986). Two psychotherapies as effective as drugs. *Psychiatric News*, **21**, 1 and 24-25.

Ellis, A. (1962). *Reason and Emotion in Psychotherapy*. Lyle Stuart, New York.

Ellis, A. & Grieger, R. (1977). *Handbook of Rational Emotive Therapy*. Springer-Verlag, New York.

Evans, M. D., Hollon, S. D., DeRubeis, R. J. *et al.* (1992). Differential relapse following cognitive therapy and pharmacotherapy for depression. *Archives of General Psychiatry*, **49**, 802-808.

Eysenck, H. J. (1960). *Behavior Therapy and the Neuroses*. Pergamon, New York.

Feighner, J. P., Robins, E., Guze, S. B., Woodruff, R. W., Winokur, G. & Munoz, R. (1972). Diagnostic criteria for use in psychiatric research. *Archives of General Psychiatry*, **26**, 57-03.

Flavell, J. H. (1963). *The Developmental Psychology of Jean Piaget*. Van Nostrand, Princeton, New Jersey.

Gallagher, D. E. & Thompson, L. W. (1982). Treatment of major depressive affective disorder in older adult outpatients with brief psychotherapies.

Glen, A., Johnson, A. & Shepherd, M. (1984). Continuation therapy with lithium and amitriptyline in unipolar illness: a randomised double-blind controlled trial. *Psychological Medicine*, **14**, 37-50.

Hibbert, G. A. (1984). Ideational components of anxiety: their origin and content. *British Journal of Psychiatry*, **144**, 618-24.

Hollon, S. D. (1982). Cognitive-behavioural treatment of drug-induced pansituational anxiety states. In Emery, G., Hollon, S. D. & Bedrosian, R. C. (eds) *New Directions in Cognitive Therapy: a Casebook*, pp. 120-38. Raven Press, New York.

Hollon, S. D. & Kriss, M. (1984). Cognitive factors in clinical research and practice. *Clinical Psychology Review,* **4**, 35–76.

Homme, L. E. (1965). Perspectives in psychology: XXIV control of coverants, the operants of the mind. *Psychological Record,* **15**, 501–11.

Kahneman, D., Slovic, P. & Tversky, A. (eds) (1982). *Judgement Under Uncertainty: Heuristics and Biases.* Cambridge University Press, Cambridge.

Keller, M. B., Klerman, G. L., Lavori, P. W., Coryell, W., Endicott, J. & Taylor, J. (1984). Long-term outcome of episodes of major depression. *Journal of the American Medical Association,* **252**, 788–92.

Kelly, G. A. (1955). *The Psychology of Personal Constructs.* Norton, New York.

Klerman, G. & Weissman, M. (1986). The interpersonal approach to understanding depression. In Millon, T. & Klerman, G. (eds) *Contemporary Directions in Psychopathology. Toward the DSM-IV,* pp. 429–56. Guilford, New York.

Klosko, J. S., Barlow, D. H., Tassinari, R. & Cerny, J. A. (1990). A comparison of alprazolam and behaviour therapy in the treatment of panic disorder. *Journal of Consulting and Clinical Psychology,* **58**, 77–84.

Kovacs, M. & Beck, A. T. (1978). Maladaptive cognitive structures in depression. *American Journal of Psychiatry,* **135**, 525–35.

Last, C., Barlow, D. & O'Brien, G. T. (1983). Comparison of two cognitive strategies in treatment of a patient with generalised anxiety disorder. *Psychological Reports,* 53, 19–26.

Lazarus, R. S. (1966). *Psychological Stress and the Coping Process.* McGraw Hill, New York.

Lewinsohn, P. (1974). Clinical and theoretical aspects of depression. In Calhoun, K., Adams, H. & Mitchell, K. (eds) *Innovative Treatment Methods in Psychopathology,* pp. 63–120. John Wiley & Sons, Chichester.

Lindsay, W. R., Gamsu, C. V., McLaughlin, E., Hood, E. M. & Espie, C. A. (1987). A controlled trial of treatments for generalized anxiety. *British Journal of Clinical Psychology,* **26**, 3–15.

Mahoney, M. J., Kazdin, A. E. & Lesswing, N. J. (1974). Behavior modification: delusion or deliverance? In Franks, C. M. & Wilson, G. T. (eds). *Annual Review of Behavior Therapy and Practice,* Vol. 2, pp. 11–40. Brunner/Mazel, New York.

Mathews, A. (1985). Anxiety states: a cognitive-behavioural approach. In Bradley, B. P. & Thompson, C. (eds) *Psychological Applications in Psychiatry,* pp. 41–59. John Wiley & Sons, Chichester.

Mathews, A. M. & MacLeod, C. (1985). Selective processing of threat uses in anxiety states. *Behaviour Research and Therapy,* **23**, 563–9.

Mathews, A. M. & MacLeod, C. (1988). Current perspectives of anxiety. In Miller, E. & Cooper, P. (eds) *Adult Abnormal Psychology,* pp. 169–93. Churchill Livingstone, Edinburgh.

McLean, P. D. & Hakstian, A. R. (1979). Clinical depression: comparative efficacy of out-patient treatments. *Journal of Consulting and Clinical Psychology,* **47**, 818–36.

Meichenbaum, D. (1974). *Therapists' manual for cognitive behaviour modification.* Unpublished manuscript, University of Waterloo, Ontario N2L 3GI, Canada.

Meichenbaum, D. H. & Turk, D. (1973). *Stress inoculation: a skills training approach to anxiety management.* Unpublished manuscript, University of Waterloo, Ontario N2L 3GI, Canada.

Miller, G. A., Galanter, E. & Pribram, K. (1960). *Plans and the Structure of Behavior*. Holt, Rinehart & Winston, New York.

Miller, N. E. & Dollard, J. (1941). *Social Learning and Imitation*. Yale University Press, New Haven, Connecticut.

Mindham, R. H. S., Howland, C. & Shepherd, M. (1973). An evaluation of continuation therapy with tricyclic antidepressants in depressive illness. *Psychological Medicine*, **3**, 5–17.

Murphy, G. E., Simons, A. D., Wetzel, R. D. & Lustman, P. J. (1984). Cognitive therapy and pharmacotherapy, singly and together in the treatment of depression. *Archives of General Psychiatry*, **41**, 33–41.

Murray, E. J. & Jacobson, L. T. (1987). Cognition and learning in traditional and behavioural therapy. In Garfield, S. L. & Bergin, A. E. (eds) *Handbook of Psychotherapy and Behavior Change*, pp. 661–87. John Wiley & Sons, New York.

Nisbett, R. E. & Ross, L. (1980). *Human Inference: Strategies and Shortcomings of Social Judgement*. Prentice Hall, Englewood Cliffs, New Jersey.

Piaget, J. (1952). *The Origins of Intelligence in Children*. International Universities Press, New York.

Power, K. G., Jerrom, D. W. A., Simpson, R. J., Mitchell, M. J. & Swanson, V. (1989). A controlled comparison of cognitive-behaviour therapy, diazepam and placebo in the management of generalized anxiety. *Behavioural Psychotherapy*, **17**, 1–14.

Power, K. G., Simpson, R. J., Swanson, V., Wallace, L. A., Feistner, A. T. C. & Sharp, D. (1990). A controlled comparison of cognitive-behaviour therapy, diazepam, and placebo, alone and in combination for the treatment of generalized anxiety disorder. *Journal of Anxiety Disorders*, **4**, 267–92.

Rotter, J. B. (1954). *Social Learning and Clinical Psychology*. Prentice Hall, Englewood Cliffs, New Jersey.

Rush, A. J., Beck, A. T., Kovacs, M. & Hollon, S. D. (1977). Comparative efficacy of cognitive therapy versus pharmacotherapy in out-patient depression. *Cognitive Therapy and Research*, **1**, 17–37.

Rush, A. J. & Watkins, J. T. (1981). Group versus individual cognitive therapy: a pilot study. *Cognitive Therapy Research*, **5**, 95–103.

Salkovskis, P. M., Jones, D. R. O. & Clark, D. M. (1986). Respiratory control in the treatment of panic attacks: replication and extension with concurrent measurement of behaviour and PCO_2 *British Journal of Psychiatry*, **148**, 520–32.

Scott, A. I. F. & Freeman, C. L. (1992). Edinburgh primary care depression study: treatment outcome, patient after 16 weeks. *British Medical Journal*, **304**, 883–7.

Shaw, B. F. (1977). Comparison of cognitive therapy and behaviour therapy in the treatment of depression. *Journal of Consulting and Clinical Psychology*, **45**, 543–51.

Shea, M. T., Elkin, I., Imber, S. D. *et al.* (1992). Course of depressive symptoms over follow-up. *Archives of General Psychiatry*, **49**, 782–7.

Shear, M. K., Pilkonis, P. A., Cloitre, M. & Leon, A. C. (1994). Cognitive behavioral treatment compared with nonprescriptive treatment of panic disorder. *Archives of General Psychiatry*, **51**, 395–401.

Shear, M. K., Ball, G., Fitzpatrick, M., Josephson, S., Klosko, J. & Frances, A. (1991). Cognitive-behavioural therapy for panic: an open study. *Journal of Nervous and Mental Disease*, **179**, 468–72.

Simons, A. D., Garfield, S. L. & Murphy, G. E. (1984). The process of change in cognitive therapy and pharmacotherapy for depression. Changes in mood and cognition. *Archives of General Psychiatry*, **41**, 45–51.

Skinner, B. F. (1945). The operational analysis of psychological terms. *Psychological Review*, **52**, 270–7.

Skinner, B. F. (1953). *Science and Human Behaviour*. Macmillan, New York.

Skinner, B. F. (1974). *About Behaviourism*. Jonathan Cape, London.

Sokol, L., Beck, A. T., Greenberg, A. L., Wright, F. D. & Berchick, R. J. (1989). Cognitive therapy of panic disorder: A nonpharmacological alternative. *Journal of Nervous and Mental Disease*, **177**, 711–16.

Spitzer, R. L., Endicott, J. & Robins, E. (1978). *Research Diagnostic Criteria (RDC) For a Selected Group of Functional Disorders*, 3rd edn. Psychiatric Institute, Biometrics Research, New York State.

Steuer, J. L., Mintz, J., Mammen, C. L., Hill, M. A., Jarvik, L. F., McCarley, T., Motoike, P. & Rosen, R. (1984). Cognitive-behavioural and psychodynamic group psychotherapy in treatment of geriatric depression. *Journal of Consulting and Clinical Psychology*, **52**, 180–9.

Suinn, R. M. & Richardson, F. (1971). Anxiety management training: a non-specific behaviour therapy programme for anxiety control. *Behaviour Therapy*, **2**, 498–511.

Taylor, F. G. & Marshall, W. L. (1977). Experimental analysis of cognitive-behavioural therapy for depression. *Cognitive Therapy and Research*, **1**, 59–72.

Teasdale, J. D., Fennell, M. J. V., Hibbert, G. A. & Amies, P. L. (1984). Cognitive therapy for major depressive disorder in primary care. *British Journal of Psychiatry*, **144**, 400–6.

Tolman, E. C. (1932). *Purposive Behavior in Animals and Men*. Appleton-Century-Crofts, New York.

Waddell, M. T., Barlow, D. H. & O'Brian, G. T. (1984). A preliminary investigation of cognitive and relaxation treatment of panic disorder: effects on intense anxiety vs 'background' anxiety. *Behaviour Research and Therapy*, **22**, 393–402.

Watson, J. B. (1913). Psychology as the behaviourist views it. *Psychological Review*, **20**, 158–77.

Weissman, A. N. & Beck, A. T. (1978). Development and validation of the dysfunctional attitude scale. *Paper presented at the Annual Meeting of the Association for Advancement of Behavior Therapy*, Chicago, Illinois.

Welkowitz, L. A., Papp, L. A., Cloitre, M., Liebowitz, M. R., Martin, L. & Gorman, J. M. (1991). Cognitive-behaviour therapy for panic disorder delivered by psychopharmacologically oriented clinicians. *Journal of Nervous and Mental Disease*, **179**, 473–7.

Whitehead, A. (1979). Psychological treatment of depression. *Behaviour Research and Therapy*, **17**, 495–509.

Wilson, P. H., Goldin, J. C. & Charbonneau-Powis, M. (1983). Comparative efficacy of behavioural and cognitive treatments of depression. *Cognitive Therapy and Research*, **7**, 111–24.

Wolpe, J. & Lang, P. J. (1964). A fear survey schedule for use in behaviour therapy. *Behaviour Research and Therapy*, **2**, 27–30.

Woodward, R. & Jones, R. B. (1980). Cognitive restructuring treatment: a controlled trial with anxiety patients. *Behaviour Research and Therapy*, **18**, 401–7.

Zeiss, A. M., Lewinsohn, P. M. & Munoz, R. F. (1979). Non-specific improvement effects in depression using interpersonal, cognitive and pleasant events focused treatments. *Journal of Consulting and Clinical Psychology*, **47**, 427–39.

Chapter 3
Basic Skills Required for
Cognitive Therapy

Introduction

In this chapter and the next, we describe the techniques which have been developed for the treatment of depression and anxiety, whilst the following chapters in Part 2 show the application of these techniques. It must, however, be pointed out that cognitive therapy does not consist of a series of *techniques* which can be applied by a therapist in an automatic and uniform manner to every patient. Cognitive therapy is guided by the *conceptualization* of the individual case which begins in the first interview. Each case must be carefully conceptualized within a cognitive theoretical framework and it is this formulation or conceptualization which will lead the therapist to choose appropriate treatment strategies and techniques for each individual patient. In addition to skills in cognitive conceptualization, strategies and techniques, cognitive therapists must master a thera-peutic style which is specific to cognitive therapy, as well as becoming experienced in the recognized non-specific therapeutic skills. These skills will be described in the following sections.

Cognitive therapy was developed in clinical practice by Professor A. T. Beck and his group in Philadelphia. It has evolved over a period of 25 years and has been described in detail by Beck *et al.* (1979) for the treatment of depressive disorders and in Beck & Emery (1985) for the treatment of anxiety disorders and phobias. Three self-help manuals for the treatment of depression have also been published, Burns (1980), Rush (1983) and Blackburn (1987).

General skills required in cognitive therapy

Knowledge of clinical syndrome

To carry out cognitive therapy for depression and anxiety effectively, the therapist must have a detailed knowledge of both these disorders. Not only should he be able to recognize and diagnose the disorders, but he needs an in-depth understanding of their phenomenology. The *Diagnostic skills* diagnostic criteria for depressive and anxiety disorders were speci-fied in Chapter 1. As noted there, anxiety and depression can concur in the same individual. The therapist needs to establish which disorder is primary not only to make an accurate diagnosis, but also to understand the history of the illness and to set up priorities in terms of which symptoms or problems to treat first. Implicit in the above is the necessity for the therapist to have a good working knowledge of the range of psychiatric disorders. Only by having this knowledge can he respond in an appropriate way clinically. He would then be able to distinguish between disorders and to recognize when symptoms do not fit into a syndrome which may respond to cognitive therapy and, therefore, requires a different form of treatment: for example, when paranoid ideas become evident in patients in whom the diagnosis was originally that of social phobia.

In addition to diagnostic skills, the clinician needs to have the clinical experience which will allow him to gauge the severity of the illness as accurately as possible. Clinical scales for assessing severity of illness, for example the Hamilton Rating Scale for Depression (Hamilton, 1960) and the Hamilton Rating Scale for Anxiety (Hamilton, 1959), can only help to systematize and quantify clinical assessment for which a pre-existing knowledge of the variety of presentations and severities of these disorders is required.

Interviewing skills

Skills in clinical interviewing are essential to elicit important and relevant signs and symptoms. In depression, in particular, the therapist must be able to assess the presence of suicidal wishes and/or ideation and behaviour. It is preferable to ask direct and detailed *Direct questioning* questions, as the patient may be ashamed or embarrassed to acknowledge these symptoms or, because of worthlessness, he may think that it is not worth volunteering this information. If the interviewer does not pursue a series of questions relating to suicidal thoughts or behaviour in a matter of fact but sympathetic way, he may miss vital information and focus on less important aspects of the illness. The therapist will need to be skilled in ascertaining the presence of psychotic symptoms which, again, can be difficult to obtain and are sometimes concealed from the therapist. As pointed out in Chapter 1, the presence of psychotic features is a contra-indication, in our current state of knowledge, to using cognitive therapy.

General therapeutic skills

These refer to the personal characteristics which have been found to be desirable, that is to be conducive to more successful outcomes, in all therapists, whatever particular brand of therapy they use (Truax & Carkuff, 1967). Research has shown that even relatively untrained psychotherapists can have a degree of effectiveness in therapy if they display empathy, warmth, genuineness and understanding. These have been considered as necessary conditions arising from research developed within client-centred therapy (Rogers, 1951). *Empathy* requires that the therapist experiences an accurate and empathic understanding of the patient's experience. That is, he senses the patient's private world as if it were his own, but without losing his objectivity. The patient must, in his turn, perceive the therapist's acceptance and empathy. *Genuineness* indicates that the therapist should be, within the confines of the therapeutic relationship, a congruent, genuine and integrated person, that is, he must be able to reflect accurately to the patient how he experiences the patient's situation. *Warmth* is expressed not only empathically, but also through unconditional positive regard and *understanding* for each aspect of the patient's experience.

In our view, and according to large treatment outcome studies, for example, the three National Institute of Mental Health (NIMH) studies in the USA (Covi *et al.*, 1974; Klerman *et al.*, 1974; Friedman, 1975), these techniques in themselves are not sufficient to bring about important therapeutic changes in disorders such as depression and anxiety.

Specific skills required in cognitive therapy

Knowledge of cognitive model

In addition to the general characteristics described above, the 'would-be' cognitive therapist could not be competent unless he had a sound knowledge and understanding of the cognitive model of psycho-pathology as described in Chapter 2. Some familiarity with the research literature in this area would also be found helpful. We have found that in therapy, it is often useful to be able to explain some phenomenon that the patient is describing or to back some explanation that the therapist is giving, with well established research findings. For example, if a patient maintains that when he looks back on his life he can see only failures and unhappy incidents, the therapist can help the patient to re-attribute this phenomenon to depressive illness rather than to factual person history, as it has been consistently shown in studies of memory that, in depression, sad memories are not only more frequently but also more readily recalled (for example Clark & Teasdale, 1982). Discussions of such findings help in establishing the validity of the cognitive model and may also suggest appropriate therapeutic techniques. Moreover, patients find such information reassuring, as they can then regard the problem in the context of their illness and not as a permanent characteristic.

Apart from the therapeutic approach and techniques of cognitive therapy which this practical guide, as well as Beck *et al.* (1979, 1985), describe and with which the would-be cognitive therapist should be familar, there is also a style of therapy which is particular to cognitive therapy. The main features of the cognitive therapy style are as follows:

1 *Collaboration.* From the very beginning of therapy, the therapist establishes a collaborative relationship with the patient. This is achieved by being open and explicit, by reciprocal feedback and by establishing an agenda for treatment sessions in a collaborative fashion. The model the therapist wants to convey is that of two scientists working together to define what the problems are, to set hypotheses and to test ways of solving problems.

2 *Gentleness.* Since the key tool of cognitive therapy is questioning, the cognitive therapist must be particularly gentle, warm and appropriately empathic in his questioning, if he is to avoid being confrontative or persecutory. He must avoid appearing critical or as a prosecuting lawer.

3 *Ability to listen.* The therapist should be able to listen attentively to what the patient says, not only in the explicit content of his replies and discourse, but also in his implied meanings and sub-themes, as reflected by the particular words that he uses, the accompanying emotions, hesitations and silences. The cognitive therapist is aware not only of the content of what the patient says but also of the characteristics of the thoughts which are expressed. Such awareness directs the therapist's questions both for eliciting further information and for therapeutic interventions.

4 *Professional manner.* The therapist must always be professional and business-like in his manner. By this, we mean that he is problem orientated, he can provide empirical backing when necessary, he keeps to an agenda which is agreed with the patient, he portrays his understanding of the patient's communication by giving accurate feedback, and he takes responsibility for using the patient's time in an effective way.

5 *Flexibility.* One challenge which faces the cognitive therapist is the ability to be flexible in his choice of techniques in each individual case. It is sometimes necessary to go beyond the well tried techniques which are decribed in text books and to choose instead a strategy or technique appropriate to a particular problem or a particular hypothesis/conceptualization which the therapist may have from his current understanding of the case. Flexibility is also needed in the structure within sessions and over the course of therapy, in that although we will describe the general format of therapy, the sequencing of therapy goals may actually vary from patient to patient.

6 *Humour.* Last, but not least, we have observed that the judicious use of humour is useful and effective for several reasons. With depressed patients in particular, this may bring about a sudden change in their perspective of a situation. It is reassuring to patients that they have kept some ability for amusement; it relieves low mood temporarily and creates a special bridge between the patient and therapist in terms of sharing an understanding.

Training

One of the methodological advances of cognitive therapy is that right from the start its creators have insisted on systematizing the therapeutic techniques in treatment manuals and on the training of therapists. This is essential if a treatment method is to be evaluated in a reliable and valid manner. One of the weaknesses of psychotherapy research in the past has been that the various psychotherapies were not well defined, so that it was impossible to draw conclusions about their relative efficacies. Apart from the careful reading of cognitive therapy treatment manuals, a training in cognitive therapy requires

Supervision

supervision by a trained cognitive therapist for *at least* three cases. Teaching material in the form of audio and videotapes is usually available from teaching centres and these are of invaluable use in that

Cognitive therapy scale

they provide appropriate models. There is also a cognitive therapy competence scale, the Cognitive Therapy Scale (CTS) (Young & Beck, 1980; Vallis *et al.*, 1986; see Appendix 2) which is of help to trainers and trainees. This is an 11 item scale which assesses both the general psychotherapeutic qualities which are discussed above and skills in the application of specific cognitive therapy, strategies and techniques, as described later in this chapter and in the next two chapters.

Multicentre NIMH treatment trial

In the recent multicentre NIMH treatment trial comparing the relative efficacies of cognitive therapy, interpersonal psychotherapy and antidepressant medication (which was discussed in Chapter 2, p. 33), the CTS was used as the main training tool for the cognitive therapists (Shaw & Wilson-Smith, 1988). Therapists were trained to an extremely high standard for the requirements of an evaluation study. Although they were already experienced psychotherapists, they received an intensive 2 week training at the end of which they sat for an examination which included a written and a practical part. This showed that, compared to their previous 'usual' interview techniques, all the trainees had acquired cognitive therapy skills. Following this, each therapist received intensive supervision over a year for a minimum of four patients with a diagnosis of major unipolar depression. At the end of that year, eight of the ten trainees were considered competent enough to take part in the treatment outcome trial. For everyday clinical practice, such a level of training and competence would be impractical. However, we would recommend cognitive therapy trainees to attend regular workshops, if possible, in addition to the minimum training described above.

General characteristics of cognitive therapy

Cognitive therapy is a short-term, structured form of therapy which provides patients with a rationale for understanding their problems, a vocabulary for expressing themselves and training in techniques for

Table 3.1 Main characteristics of cognitive therapy

51

Basic skills

1	Time limited	15–22 sessions over 3–4 months
2	Structure	Each session lasts 1 hour
3	Agenda	Each session is structured by the use of an agenda to optimize the use of time
4	Problem-oriented	Therapist and patient focus on defining and solving presenting problems
5	Ahistorical	It deals with the here and now without recourse to the distant past history of the patient
6	Learning model	It does not use psychodynamic hypothetical constructs to explain the patient's behaviour. Rather dysfunctional behaviour is attributed to maladaptive learning. Relearning more functional behaviour is the goal
7	Scientific method	An experimental method is adopted, therapy involving collecting data (problems, thoughts, attitudes), formulating hypotheses, setting up experiments and evaluating results
8	Homework	The patient is given assignments for data collecting, verification of hypotheses and practice of cognitive skills
9	Collaboration	Patient and therapist work together to solve problems
10	Active and directive	The therapist adopts an active and directive role throughout treatment. He can be didactic sometimes but his main role is to facilitate the definition and resolution of problems
11	Socratic questioning	The principal therapeutic method is socratic questioning, which is to ask a series of questions aimed at bringing the patient to identify his underlying thought, to perceive alternative solutions or to modify his opinions
12	Openness	The therapeutic process is not clouded in mystique. Rather, it is explicit and open, therapist and patient sharing a common understanding of what is going on in therapy

surmounting distressful affective states and solving problems. Table 3.1 describes the main characteristics of cognitive therapy.

Table 3.1 makes it evident that cognitive therapy and behaviour therapy have many features in common, in particular the short-term format, the learning model and the use of homework to complement within-session therapy. However, the learning models differ (see Chapter 2) in that cognitive therapy is based on a mediational model and behaviour therapy on a stimulus–response model. Both therapies are ahistorical, do not refer to unconscious mechanisms, are time-

Comparison of cognitive and behaviour therapy

limited and problem centred, and the therapist is active and directive in both approaches. The differences, however, lie not only in the learning model but also in the main targets of therapy: cognitive therapy focusing primarily on cognitions and behaviour therapy on overt behaviours. The main difference is, of course, that cognitive therapy uses both cognitive and behavioural techniques to effect change, whereas behaviour therapy uses only behavioural techniques.

Structure of treatment sessions

The structure of treatment sessions was mentioned in Table 3.1 as an essential characteristic of cognitive therapy. Structure within treatment sessions and across sessions is important for several reasons. It allows the patient and the therapist to be effective in dealing with problems within the time available; it fosters a business-like, problem-solving attitude; it ensures that the current important topics are covered; it provides a convenient way of monitoring progress during therapy and ensures that the cognitive therapy model is adhered to. As can be seen in Appendix 2, the structure of sessions is considered an important point in the evaluation of the competence of cognitive therapists.

Typical session format

In Table 3.2, we describe a typical session format in cognitive therapy. Although the therapist would, on the whole, follow this format, he is not obliged to adhere to it rigidly, as the format will also be dictated by each individual patient and the stage of therapy. However, setting an *agenda* is to be considered essential.

Reviewing the patient's state

When *reviewing* the patient's state since the previous session, the particular skill needed is how to keep this part of the session to a minimum length of time to allow the rest of the session's work to be completed. A danger is that patients who have had experience of other styles of psychotherapy may tend to take the prompt 'How have you been since we last met?' as an indication to talk at length to a passive therapist. The therapist need not feel inhibited in interrupting the flow with a comment such as 'I see that things have not gone well for you this past week. I would like to hear more about this. Would you like to put these problems on *our agenda* for today?' Another comment may be 'Did you record this in the homework which we discussed?' Thus, a review of the homework is scheduled in and relevant problems pinpointed.

Agenda

If the *homework* involved the recording of thoughts, some patients bring back an enormous number of recorded sheets which would obviously take the full hour to review. As it is necessary to review homework for the patient to appreciate its importance and for mutual feedback, the therapist can explain that there will not be time to review everything. Together they can select a sample of the thoughts by deciding on the most important ones. If the homework was

Table 3.2 Session format of cognitive therapy   **53**

Basic skills

1 Review of patient's state	A general enquiry which may prompt the targets for the day's agenda
2 Set agenda	Each session lasts 1 hour Comments on last session Review of homework set at last session Establish the sessions target problem(s)
3 Homework review	Discuss outcome, difficulties and conclusions Determine further action
4 Session target(s)	Define problem Identify associated negative thoughts Answer negative thoughts Evaluate effect of answers on belief in original thought and on emotion How can answers be pursued in action?
5 Homework	Assign a task relevant to session's target(s) Explain rationale for task Elicit anticipated difficulties, doubts, predictions of outcome Rehearse if necessary
6 Session feedback	Check whether anything you did or said has upset the patient Ask if anything was not clear Ask what was helpful or unhelpful Enquire how patient is feeling Invite other questions or comments If important topic is raised reschedule for next session

behavioural, for example, trying a new type of social behaviour or increasing level of activity, any difficulties encountered are checked out and the the effect on patient's mood and cognition verified.

The *session's target(s)* are the main focus of each session. From the *agenda*, therapist and patient have already agreed on the main topic(s) and problem(s) to be discussed. These may typically consist of problem situations (interpersonal problems at home or at work), symptoms (e.g. low or anxious mood, sleep difficulties, panic attacks, inactivity, indecision, etc.), events (e.g. family Christmas, leaking roof, debts, problem neighbours) or thoughts and attitudes (e.g. negative view of self and others, hopelessness about the future, helplessness in the face of real or perceived difficulties). Problems are broken down into components which will lead to possible solutions; thoughts are examined, challenged and alternative interpretations considered; the emotional impact of alternative thoughts is assessed. If necessary, rehearsal and role play are used to practise problem solving. Specific techniques are described in the following chapter.

This part of the session will lead to the choice of appropriate *homework* assignments. As Table 3.2 (above) indicates, the choice of a

Session's target(s)

Homework

homework assignment is a collaborative enterprise. Homework fulfils two functions: first, it creates a link between sessions ensuring that the patient continues to work on his problems; secondly, it enables him to collect data to verify some erroneous interpretation or assumption, to test out predictions or to experiment with new behaviours. Compliance is facilitated by ensuring that the patient understands the relevance and rationale of the task. Eliciting his doubts and predictions provides typical negative cognitions which can be tested out. The execution of behavioural assignments may reveal to the patient and the therapist, in a concrete fashion, maladaptive coping strategies which may then be reshaped in future assignments.

Feedback

Feedback is particularly important as the session itself may have provoked depressive or anxious cognitions which may not otherwise be revealed. We have found that failing to elicit feedback may cause additional problems to the patient, as he may go away with a number of misunderstandings or negative interpretations which increase dysphoric mood and/or feelings of anger.

First interview

Having described the basic skills required for the application of cognitive therapy, we illustrate these using the first interview as a model. From this follows the method used to arrive at a conceptualization of a case. We regard this as an essential basic skill. In the *first interview*, the cognitive therapist has several aims which are listed in Table 3.3 and described in the following section.

It is understood that a previous diagnostic interview would already have taken place. It is advisable to begin the interview by setting an agenda as described in Table 3.2. The therapist explains that in the hour which is available, he would like to have a general idea of the patient's problem and then go on to explain about the treatment he has in mind. He asks the patient if such an agenda would suit him.

Exploration of problems

In the *exploration of problems*, the therapist first makes a functional analysis of the patient's symptoms, as described in Chapter 1, pp. 5 and 8. Instead of searching for a diagnosis (which he has already arrived at from the first interview), he is interested in finding out which particular areas of functioning are affected — affective,

Table 3.3 Aims of the first interview

1 Get an idea of what problems are troubling the patient
2 Establish the beginnings of rapport
3 Explain the basics of the cognitive model
4 Get preliminary understanding and acceptance from patient
5 Encourage hope
6 Give the patient an immediate experience of the structure and flavour of the cognitive approach

behavioural, motivational, cognitive, and physical. At this point, he needs particular skill to assess the degree of hopelessness of the patient and the presence of suicidal risk. The presence of suicidal risk would lead the therapist to short-circuit the rest of the agenda and deal with this problem immediately (see Chapter 8 for specific techniques to deal with the suicidal patient). In the case of out-patients, if the therapist considers that his therapeutic intervention has not been successful enough in the case of a high suicidal risk, then he should consider admitting the patient to hospital, even if it is just for a few days.

Secondly, the therapist explores which aspects of the patient's life are particularly affected. These could be work, close relationships, or social and leisure activities. He notes the presence of particular problems, for example, work problems, relationship difficulties, social isolation, academic difficulties, financial difficulties or perhaps accommodation problems. Some patients present with realistic and severe life problems which they may not be tackling effectively because of a sense of helplessness and hopelessness. *The assumption of cognitive therapy is that problems can be realistic, but depression or excessive anxiety are not.* It is important to note the presence of precipitants, the timing of the onset of the illness and its duration. All the time, the therapist is looking for evidence of the cognitive triad and listening for particular themes in the patient's communications. These are essential for a conceptualization of the individual patient's case, as described in the next section.

The therapist *should not be too detailed* in this part of his agenda. He can only try to get a general map of the territory and, therefore, does not focus in great detail on the patient's developmental history. He may note that childhood experiences are relevant; in such a case he would communicate this opinion to the patient and schedule an op-portunity to explore this further in a future session.

Rapport is established throughout the session by the general and specific skills described previously (pp. 46–50). The therapist listens carefully and communicates his attention and understanding by reflecting back what the patient has said. He also makes summaries of what has been discussed at regular intervals to give feedback to the patient, to ask for reciprocal feedback and to clarify the definition of problems. For example, he may want to ensure that he has understood correctly by asking 'Have I got this right? You are saying . . . '. His style is open and explicit, while at the same time, conveying an attitude of genuineness, warmth and empathic understanding.

Rapport

Once the therapist judges that he has an adequate preliminary understanding of the patient's problems and complaints, that is after about 45 minutes, he makes a summary and explains how the treatment will proceed. He uses a didactic approach to explain the *cognitive therapy model* to ensure a basic *understanding* and future *collaboration* from the patient. The basic epistemological point that

Explain the cognitive therapy model

the therapist tries to put across is that *thoughts are not reality but interpretations of reality and that these interpretations colour our feelings and determine our behaviour*. Since the patient is feeling distressed, it follows that his thoughts are distressing, and the aim of cognitive therapy is to monitor and examine these thoughts. To illustrate how the same situation may be interpreted in different ways which would lead to different moods and behaviour, Beck *et al*. (1979) recommend the use of a vignette as a concrete and vivid example. The *use of concrete images* to illustrate apparently intellectual points is desirable in cognitive therapy, as Part 2 of this book will make clear in case studies. The therapist may use any illustration of his choice. A possible vignette might be:

Use of concrete images

T: You have a rendezvous with a friend and you are waiting there at the prearranged place and time. Your friend has not arrived 15 minutes later. You *say to yourself* 'He has stood me up. He doesn't care about me'. You may then *feel* sad or angry and *decide* to leave. On the other hand, you may *say to yourself* 'He has had an accident'. You may then *feel* anxious, and you may *decide* to ring the police or a hospital casualty department. Yet again, you may *say to yourself* 'Something unexpected may have happened to delay him. He will be here soon'. You would then probably feel neither angry, nor sad or anxious and *decide* to continue to wait.

The therapist would then, having given this general illustration, use examples from the patient's own communications to show how the model relates to him. The patient might have described feeling depressed or anxious in a certain situation and on questioning, describe an accompanying thought or interpretation. The therapist would indicate how the interpretation was congruent with the feeling but not necessarily the only interpretation possible. Such examples from the patient's own experiences would lead the therapist to demonstrate how cognitive therapy is relevant for the individual and might help to overcome his dysphoric moods. The therapist requests feedback from the patient to assess whether he understands and is willing to participate in the treatment. He then explains the structure of sessions and of treatment and its probable duration.

Hope

Hope has been described as an important element in all psychotherapies (Frank, 1973). In cognitive therapy, hope is fostered by the various techniques already described. In the summary at the end of the exploration of problems, the therapist breaks down what the patient has told him into a *list of problems* that are concretely and specifically defined and, therefore, open to intervention. This helps in reducing global problems into manageable components and, therefore, encourages hope. His general manner, which is active, business-like and professional from the beginning, will also create hope by inspiring a positive problem-solving approach to difficulties.

List of problems

Taking time to explain the model of cognitive therapy, as described above, gives face *validity* to the approach. It is also helpful to give some empirical backing to the model, especially as some patients who come for cognitive therapy may already have experienced some other treatment approach, without success. The therapist needs to ensure that, while fostering hope, he does not raise the expectation of a miracle cure. He aims to obtain at least a willingness to try on an experimental basis. Empirical backing would indicate that there is a good chance of a favourable outcome, but it can be pointed out that should the treatment not prove successful, there are other approaches which might be suitable for the individual patient.

Finally, hope is encouraged by focusing at this point on a *specific problem which may be amenable to an immediate resolution.* Such a success experience may not always be possible and a partial solution is then aimed for. For example, the patient may complain of poor concentration which stops him from engaging in potentially pleasurable activities, such as reading. This can be checked out by asking the patient to read a few pages of a magazine, then stopping him and asking him to give an account of what he has read. This would demonstrate that some ability to concentrate exists and illustrate the experimental approach. This type of experiment has to be chosen judiciously. Not only does it have to fit in with the rest of the session, but it has to be tailor-made for the individual and have a very high chance of success. With an anxious patient, instructing him to sit back in his chair and to try some brief relaxation exercises can bring about the experience of control and mastery over his anxiety symptoms, even if it is for a short period of time and only to some extent. The most common intervention in this first interview is seeking an alternative interpretation of a distressing situation and underlining the patient's success in doing this. This procedure would also indicate to the therapist whether the patient is able to consider alternatives to his automatic interpretations and hence be potentially responsive to cognitive therapy. With depressed patients, if it is at all possible to appeal to their sense of humour this can be pleasantly surprising for them.

This first interview will have given the patient an immediate *experience of the structure and style of cognitive therapy.* Agenda setting at the beginning, problem orientation, a collaborative relationship and homework assignments are going to be the common ingredients in all treatment sessions. Patient and therapist decide on a suitable homework assignment even at this early stage. This must be relevant for the individual patient, but will, as a rule, include reading the booklet *Coping with Depression* (Beck & Greenberg, 1973) or 'Coping with anxiety', Appendix 1 of *Anxiety Disorders and Phobias: A Cognitive Perspective* — Beck & Emery 1985) and a behavioural rather than cognitive task (see next chapter). Right at the end of the first session, the therapist asks the patient for general feedback as discussed on page 54.

Formulation

Conceptualization of a case

As early as the end of the first or second interview, the therapist has begun to have a *formulation* of the patient's condition within the cognitive model. This represents a tentative hypothesis which future interviews will help in validating, expanding and modifying. It cannot be emphasized enough how important this exercise is, if appropriate cognitive therapy strategies and techniques are to be used. Without a formulation, the therapist can be likened to a general engaging in battle without planned tactics to guide him in the deployment of his troops and in the timing of his offensive. Similarly, without a flexible conceptualization and formulation, the therapist would be dealing piecemeal with problems which present themselves, with no idea about whether he is tackling the main targets or making any progress. The questions to which the therapist is formulating answers at this point are:

1 Why is this patient depressed, anxious or panicky at this particular point in his life?
2 What particular stresses are present?
3 What are the prominent personality charactistics displayed?
4 What are the principal emotions?
5 What are the principal themes of the patient's communications?
6 What are the principal themes, threats and experiences from the past?
7 Is the patient likely to respond to cognitive therapy?

Familiarity with the clinical syndromes and the cognitive model, as described in Chapters 1 and 2, are an essential prerequisite for this step in cognitive therapy. A schematic description of the main ingredients in the conceptualization of a case is given in Figure 3.1 below.

Current stresses

The *current stresses* which the patient perceives in his life will lead to an understanding of the possible precipitants of his depression or anxiety. Are they related to work, home, family, friends, colleagues? Do they appear objectively realistic or grossly exaggerated?

Vulnerabilities

What *vulnerabilities* do they reflect? Do they indicate vulnerabilities to the loss of friends or social support, to loss of approval, loss of love, loss of status? Is it a threat of illness, a fear of not coping with a new situation? A perception of loss of control? Are there many or few stresses?

Social support

The presence or absence of *social support* gives an understanding of how the patient organizes his life and whether he has close confiding relationships. A knowledge of his occupation gives an insight into his life style, his financial security and network of relationships. The lack of a job outside the house and lack of confiding relationships have been found to be vulnerability factors for depression (Brown & Harris, 1978).

Past traumas

Information about *past traumatic events* in the patient's life,

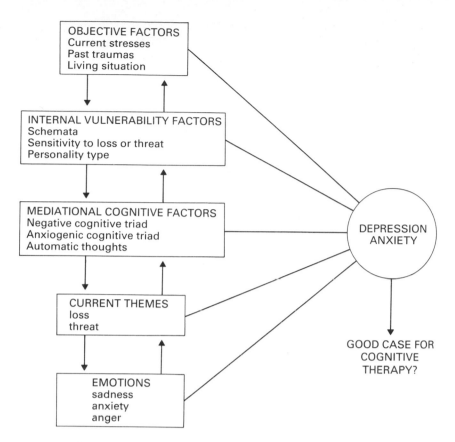

Figure 3.1 Schematic description of cognitive formulation.

without going into a detailed developmental history, will also shed light on current vulnerable areas as well as give some indication of his general coping style. Has the patient coped adequately with past problems or has he always shown poor coping skills? Are the current problems similar to past traumas and if so, why is the patient not coping now?

The cognitive model prompts the therapist to look for evidence of the *negative cognitive triad* in the content of the patient's communications and to register the preponderant *distressful emotions* and their intensity. He is particularly attentive to the themes of the *automatic thoughts* which the patient expresses and the implied rules which they may reflect. What does the patient admire in others, what does he castigate in others or in himself? Are certain cognitive errors made frequently? What 'musts' and 'shoulds' does he express?

Thus, from current and past history, as well as from the cognitive characteristics of the patient's communications, the therapist hypothesizes about the main themes of *loss* and *threat* for the individual patient, about his areas of vulnerabilities and his main *personality characteristics*. Does he appear to suffer from loss of social gratification (sociotropic/dependent personality?) or from loss of freedom,

Negative cognitive triad

Automatic thoughts

Loss and threat

Good case for
cognitive therapy

autonomy and successful achievement (autonomic/independent personality?). Has he shown a 'neurotic' pattern of coping over his life?

Finally, the therapist makes some decision about whether the patient is likely to be a *good case for cognitive therapy*. As was pointed out in chapter 1, pp. 12–14, indications from research are scarce up to now. However, a certain degree of self-reliance, the use of psychological language, access to emotions and some willingness to consider alternative views are considered positive indications. In our experience, patients who rely on somatic or concrete explanations, who cannot access their emotions and who cannot accept that their interpretations of events may be erroneous or only one of several possibilities, do not present an optimistic outlook for cognitive therapy. However, as for the general conceptualization, the judgement of suitability is only made tentatively at this stage.

Chapter 5 will illustrate how a conceptualization is made from the first interview.

References

Beck, A. T. & Emery, G. (1985). *Anxiety Disorders and Phobias: a Cognitive Perspective*. Basic Books, New York.

Beck, A. T. & Greenberg, R. L. (1973) *Coping with Depression*. Institute of Rational Living, New York.

Beck, A. T., Rush, A. J., Shaw, B. F. & Emery, G. (1979). *Cognitive Therapy of Depression*. Guilford Press, New York.

Blackburn, I. M. (1987). *Coping with Depression*. W. & R. Chambers Ltd, Edinburgh.

Brown, G. W. & Harris, T. O. (1978). *Social Origins of Depression*. Tavistock, London.

Burns, D. (1980). *Feeling Good: The New Mood Therapy*. William Morrow, New York.

Clark, D. M. & Teasdale, J. D. (1982). Diurnal variation in clinical depression and accessibility of positive and negative experiences. *Journal of Abnormal Psychology*, **91**, 87–95.

Covi, L., Lipman, R. S., Derogatis, L. R., Smith, J. E. & Pattison, J. H. (1974). Drugs and group psychotherapy in neurotic depression. *American Journal of Psychiatry*, **131**, 191–8.

Frank, J. O. (1973). *Persuasion and Healing*, 2nd edn. Johns Hopkins University Press, Baltimore, Maryland.

Friedman, A. (1975). Interaction of drug therapy with marital therapy in depressed patients. *Archives of General Psychiatry*, **32**, 619–37.

Hamilton, M. (1985). The assessment of anxiety states by rating. *British Journal of Medical Psychology*, **32**, 50–5.

Hamilton, M. (1960). A rating scale for depression. *Journal of Neurology, Neurosurgery and Psychiatry*, **23**, 56–61.

Klerman, G. L., Di Mascio, A., Weissman, M. M., Prusoff, B. A. & Paykel, E. S. (1974). Treatment of depression by drugs and psychotherapy. *American Journal of Psychiatry*, **131**, 186–91.

Rogers, C. (1951). *Client-Centered Therapy*. Houghton Mifflin Co., Boston, Massachusetts.

Rush, A. J. (1983). *Beating Depression*. Century Publishing Co., London.

Shaw, B. F. & Wilson-Smith, D. (1988). Training therapists in cognitive-behaviour therapy. In Perris, C. Blackburn, I. M. & Perris, H. (eds). *Cognitive Psychotherapy: Theory and Practice*. Springer-Verlag, Heidelberg.

Truax, C. B. & Carkhuff, R. R. (1967). *Toward Effective Counselling and Psychotherapy: Training and Practice*. Aldine, Chicago, Illinois.

Vallis, T. M., Shaw, B. F. & Dobson, K. S. (1986). The cognitive therapy scale: psychometric properties. *Journal of Consulting and Clinical Psychology*, **54**, 381–5.

Young, J. & Beck, A. T. (1980). *The cognitive therapy scale: rating manual* Unpublished manuscript, Center for Cognitive Therapy, Philadelphia.

Chapter 4
Cognitive Therapy Techniques
for Depression and Anxiety

Behavioural techniques

It is often appropriate to use behavioural techniques at the beginning of treatment as the problems which are best treated with these techniques can be extremely distressing for the patient and prevent therapy from progressing. It is also easier for the patient to master behavioural techniques at the beginning of therapy while training in cognitive techniques. The behavioural and situational problems in depression and anxiety which are the main targets of these techniques are listed in Table 4.1.

Behavioural and situational problems

Graded activities

Low levels of activity

Low levels of activity are a common complaint in depressed patients and also occur in anxious patients who may find that their agitation prevents them from completing tasks. The current level of activity is recorded by taking a detailed account of how the patient spends his time. This is best done by using the *Weekly Activity Schedule* (see

Table 4.1 Targets of behavioural techniques in depression and anxiety

Targets	Techniques
Inactivity	Graded activities
Indecisiveness and procrastination	Scheduling activities
Low mood	Distraction. Scheduling pleasurable activities
Anxious mood	Distraction, relaxation
Physical tension	Relaxation
Loss of pleasure or anhedonia	Scheduling pleasurable activities
Sleep difficulties	Stimulus control
Poor concentration	Graded tasks
Lack of motivation	Graded tasks. Scheduling for mastery and pleasure
Panic attacks	Respiratory control
Avoidance	Graded exposure
Problem situations	Rehearsal of coping techniques, for example, assertiveness training

Appendix 3), which the patient completes as part of his homework assignment.

Filling in an activity schedule may, in itself, increase activity as the patient gets an immediate feedback of what he is doing. In discussion with the patient, the desired or premorbid level of activity is ascertained and therapist and patient agree together on a list of activities for the coming week. These activities are graded in terms of amount and level of difficulty. The important point is to ensure that the desired outcome can be achieved. Some individuals may have set for themselves excessively ambitious targets to achieve within the context of an episode of depression or anxiety. The therapist would point this out and seek to modify the patient's goals. It must be emphasized that the task consists of *attempting* the planned activities and not necessarily of succeeding, for example, Beck suggests a time limit rather than a performance limit. The tasks are to be seen as experiments. If difficulties arise, these can be noted for discussion in the session and for rescheduling more appropriate activities. In the session the patient may express a number of negative automatic thoughts which disable him from carrying out activities, for example, 'What's the point?', 'I won't be able to do this', 'I can't cope'. The therapist can begin to challenge these thoughts using cognitive techniques (see Cognitive techniques below).

Experiments

Graded tasks to improve concentration are individually tailored, involving, for example, reading for differing lengths of time, reading materials of varying complexity, watching television programmes and working for increasing periods of time.

Graded tasks

Scheduling activities is used in the same way as graded tasks to tackle *indecisiveness and procrastination*. Depressed patients, because of their loss of self-confidence, often find it difficult to decide how best to organize their time or how to set priorities and thus end up procrastinating and blaming themselves for it. Anxious patients may be indecisive for other reasons such as poor concentration, fear of failing or of taking the wrong decision. Planning the weekly activities in advance alleviates some of these problems. It is useful to point out that the plan is only a guideline and not an inflexible prescription. Certain unforeseen circumstances may prevent the patient from keeping to his predetermined plan, for example, a neighbour may drop in when he planned to tidy up a room or it might be raining heavily when he planned to do some gardening. It is advisable to carry on with the predetermined schedule after the interruption has passed and reschedule the missed activity for another time.

Scheduling activities

Indecisiveness and procrastination

Weekly activities

Graded tasks and the scheduling of specific activities also help to deal with *motivational problems*, as the effort involved in deciding to carry out an activity is removed and, moreover, completing an activity and recording it are reinforcing in themselves. Depressed

Motivational problems

patients may have decreased or completely abandoned pleasurable activities or activities which would give a sense of mastery and achievement. In collaboration, therapist and patient schedule potentially pleasurable and purposeful activities from the patient's past repertoire which are then rated for *M (mastery)* and *P (pleasure)* on a scale of 0 to 5 (see Appendix 3). A score of 0 would indicate complete absence of pleasure and/or mastery and 5 would indicate high levels of pleasure or mastery. Patients often underestimate the degree of pleasure and/or mastery or do not show any discrimination between varying levels and rate every activity at the same low level. Such ratings would be discussed in the sessions to increase the patient's discrimination and to elicit related negative thoughts.

The specific *scheduling of pleasurable activities* is indicated for *relief of low mood* and *for loss of pleasure or anhedonia.* These may involve very simple activities which the patient is no longer carrying out or not carrying out often enough, either because he has lost the motivation or he may feel that it is somewhat self-indulging, weak or selfish to engage in purely pleasurable activities. A housewife may be encouraged to keep a little time to herself, away from continuous household chores. The professional man who says he is too busy to play golf may be asked to schedule in 2 hours' golf once a week. The office worker who says he used to enjoy long walks may be encouraged to restart this activity. The therapist does not, of course, prescribe activities which he himself thinks are pleasurable. The activities are selected, after careful questioning and prompting, in collaboration with the patient. It is also possible to use a questionnaire, the Schedule of Pleasant Activities (Brown & Lewinsohn, 1984), to ascertain which activities used to be rewarding for the patient.

With anxious patients, the Activity Schedule can additionally and importantly be used as a means of monitoring anxiety in relation to specific situations. This allows the therapist and patient to establish which types of situations are more anxiety provoking than others and to increase the patient's awareness of varying levels of anxiety.

Distraction or diversion activities can be used to alleviate *depressed or anxious mood,* even if the effect is only transient. For depression, listening to happy music has been found to be the most potent transient mood elevator (Pignatello *et al.*, 1986). Questioning would reveal what is a potentially effective distraction technique for each individual — these can be telephoning a friend, reading poetry, jogging, playing a game or gardening. We have found that asking a depressed patient to recall two or three happy memories from his past and writing these out in detail so that he can go back to them when needed is a useful technique as it is known from research evidence (Blaney, 1986) that depressed patients have difficulty in remembering pleasant events and tend to ruminate on unhappy memories which increase their dysphoria further. Some anxious patients need a quick technique that they can apply in any situation — this may involve counting specific objects around him, concentrating in detail on a pleasant mental image or working out a mental arithmetic problem.

Stimulus control techniques are used to alleviate *sleep difficulties* which are common in both depression and anxiety. These include decreasing stimuli which may interfere with sleep and increasing stimuli conducive to sleep. The patient is discouraged from cat-napping during the day, from drinking stimulants such as coffee or tea in the evening and from engaging in stimulating activities such as intellectual work or reading exciting books in the evening. In particular, ruminating about the day's problems while lying in bed is to be avoided by engaging in some distraction activity as described above. On the other hand, activities which are encouraged are winding down in the evening, engaging in relaxation exercises, going to bed at regular times, getting out of bed and doing something distracting if awake during the night and not looking at the clock when awake, as this increases wakefulness and anxiety further. Again, as we have stressed all along, the techniques which are chosen are dictated by each individual case from careful questioning and prompting.

Relaxation is a technique for coping with both *muscular and mental tension*. Systematic relaxation is taught by careful instructions about how to register tension in the various muscles and how to relax (Wolpe, 1958). In addition to training in the treatment session, the therapist can register the instructions on an audiotape which the patient uses at home. The patient is encouraged to practise the relaxation exercises (tensing and relaxing the muscles of the hands, arms, neck, shoulder, face, stomach, thighs and legs, taking deep breaths and exhaling slowly) daily, or twice daily if necessary, to the point where relaxation has become a new skill that he can apply in any situation, without instructions, whether he is driving his car, is engaged in social interactions or is at his place of work.

Graded exposure is a well tried technique in anxious patients who have previously usually used *avoidance as a coping technique*. Fearful situations are arranged in a hierarchy starting with the least anxiety-provoking and increasing gradually to the most feared situations. The patient is then encouraged to face these situations either alone or in the company of a relative or of the therapist. This technique is called *systematic desensitization* and is most useful with phobic patients. It is not always possible to elicit a hierarchy of fearful situations with generally anxious patients — so that exposure to situations which are not ranked for fearfulness is used. Patients may not experience anxiety in the clinic as they may regard the treatment environment as a relatively safe situation. They may also not experience anxiety outside treatment sessions, when accompanied by somebody they know well who may be seen as a protector. It is, therefore, important to agree with the patient in which situations he is likely to experience anxiety and to set these as homework assignments. By doing this in a graded way, the patient can be placed in increasingly anxiety-provoking situations, thereby countering his avoidance whilst putting into practice some of the coping techniques described in this section.

Respiratory control
Panic attacks

Overbreathing

Respiratory control has been found to be effective in the treatment of *panic attacks and somatic anxiety symptoms* (Clark *et al.*, 1985). These authors have developed a particular treatment programme which involves eliciting the physical symptoms present in panic attacks and verifying whether the same symptoms occur in a practice session of overbreathing for up to 2 minutes. Having brought on the symptoms, these can be relieved by asking the patient to breathe into a paper bag until he begins to feel calmer. The overbreathing reduces the amount of carbon dioxide in the lungs and blood and brings about the unpleasant physical sensations of panic — faintness, dizziness, tingling, headaches, tachychardia, chest pain, shakiness, nausea and others. By breathing in a paper bag held tightly over the mouth and nose, by breathing more slowly or by breathing with one's hands cupped over the mouth and nose, the amount of carbon dioxide in the lungs and blood is increased and the symptoms disappear quickly.

Behavioural test

Re-attribution

The similarity between the symptoms brought on by overbreathing and those present during panic attacks are noted in a behavioural test within the treatment session and lead to their re-attribution (a cognitive process) to overbreathing rather than to imminent heart attacks or other physical illnesses. Breathing control procedures are then taught as a coping technique to give the patient a pattern of breathing which is incompatible with hyperventilation and to test out that the symptoms are produced by hyperventilation rather than by the real catastrophes feared by the patient. The recommended breathing pattern which the patient must practise is either 12 breaths per minute or eight breaths per minute. He would then apply this pattern of breathing in potentially panicky situations or when he feels the symptoms coming on. A tape can be used or the patient can be asked to memorize a particular pattern of breathing in and out.

Rehearsal of coping techniques

Assertiveness training

Rehearsal of coping techniques may include training in *assertiveness*, *training in the control of anger* and *training in problem solving*. These are skills which the patient needs to develop to deal with problem situations.
Assertiveness training is useful for the patient who feels that he does not cope effectively with other people, such as being able to say 'no' to an inappropriate request, being able to express opinions, make

a request or ask a favour. This lack of coping often leads to feelings of anxiety or low self-esteem and a sense of lack of self-efficacy or helplessness. The first stage in assertiveness training is to establish what kinds of interpersonal difficulties the patient experiences. It is then essential to clarify exactly what the patient would like to be able to achieve in the situations he finds difficult. For example, he may wish to ask his manager at work to have his workload rationalized or a housewife may want more practical help at home from her husband. Having established reasonable goals, the therapist and the patient can engage in *role playing* a problem situation, which is then practised thoroughly using role reversal. For example, the patient will alternatively role play himself and then his manager and in the case of the housewife, herself and then her husband, while the therapist also plays alternate roles. This allows the patient to experience both roles, so that he can practise what he might say in the problem situation and understand how the other person may feel and react to his request. The rehearsed scenario is then set as a homework assignment and the results discussed at the next session. If the practice has been successful, the patient is congratulated and reinforced. For less successful outcomes, the situation is analysed again and a second, modified task assigned.

Role playing

Many patients find it difficult to tolerate anger in themselves or to express it in an appropriate and effective manner. It is often necessary to begin by explaining that anger is a *normal* emotion which is universally experienced. It fulfils useful functions in that it gives feedback to others about their behaviour and it provides a motivation for change. The problem is how to express the anger in a constructive manner. The appropriate expression of anger can be seen as an important part of assertiveness training. The skills taught to the patient within treatment sessions in role plays, as described above, are defining what the anger is about, pointing out to the other person what the difficulty or problem is, seeking agreement that this is a problem for both parties, stating what it is that has made them feel angry, listening to the other person's reply, and finding some mutual way of solving the problem. In dealing with an angry person, Burns (1980) recommends the following methods to reduce anger and to negotiate reasonable terms: *first*, instead of telling the person off, which will increase his anger, it is more appropriate to express *understanding* and *empathize* with his feelings; *secondly*, if he argues, agreeing with part of his statements will *disarm* him: *thirdly*, the way will then be open for the individual to clarify his point of view calmly and firmly and to negotiate in his favour.

Anger

Problem solving skills are taught to deal with *real life problems*. The therapist and the patient break down the problem into components and make a list of possible solutions. These are then tried out in homework assignments, the outcome is discussed in following treatment sessions and further solutions tested out, if necessary.

Problem solving skills

Cognitive techniques

Eliciting automatic thoughts

Automatic thoughts, as described in the theoretical section (Chapter 2) and the general description of cognitive therapy in this chapter, are the basic data of cognitive therapy. From the very first interview (see p. 54), the therapist stresses the relevance of cognitions to emotions and behaviour. Even if stress is put on behavioural techniques at the beginning of therapy, these techniques are used to elicit and modify cognitions, as well as to alleviate behavioural problems. The order in which we discuss cognitive therapy techniques in this chapter does not, therefore, indicate that the emphasis is solely on behaviour at the beginning of treatment. In fact, we find that behavioural assignments are very potent tools to elucidate and modify thinking patterns. Table 4.2 summarizes the main techniques which are used to elicit automatic thoughts.

Direct questioning

Direct questioning expressed as 'What was going through your mind?' rather than 'What were you thinking then?' is, evidently, the easiest method to direct the attention of the patient to his automatic information processing. Note that the former question is preferred to the latter because it is more *concrete* and *specific*. However, direct questioning is often unsuccessful in pinpointing automatic thoughts, especially at the beginning of therapy, when the monitoring of automatic thoughts is a new skill for the patient. It is worth noting that the registering of one's automatic thoughts is not an activity that people normally engage in in their day-to-day life. Automatic thoughts, by definition, are habitual and reflexive and, therefore, taken for granted. It demands a conscious effort to acquire the skill of increasing one's awareness of one's automatic thinking. For patients who are totally unaware of their automatic thoughts and who may insist that when they feel depressed or anxious, no thoughts cross their mind, it is comforting to point out that what is being asked of

Table 4.2 Techniques for eliciting automatic thoughts

1 Direct questions
2 'Guided discovery' or inductive questioning
3 The use of moments of strong emotion during treatment session
4 Using an increase in physical tension or the beginning of panic sensations
5 Mental imagery
6 Role plays
7 Ascertaining the meaning of events
8 Counting negative thoughts
9 Engaging in behavioural tasks and recording accompanying thoughts
10 Keeping a diary of mood changes and the concurrent automatic thoughts on dysfunctional thought forms (see Appendix 4)

them is difficult for everyone and that it is a new skill to learn which will prove useful. The skill consists of using moments of strong emotions or change of moods, distancing from the emotion for a while, becoming like an observer and registering what is going on at the back of one's mind.

If direct questions do not help in pin-pointing the key cognitions, the therapist uses *inductive questioning*, sometimes called *'guided discovery'* to help the patient trace the thoughts which maintain his dysphoric mood. This technique is probably the *key technique* of cognitive therapy and requires a great deal of skill. The therapist needs to be very attentive, so as to be able to ask a series of appropriate questions without actually putting words in the patient's mouth. The questions will lead the patient to recreate a situation in his mind and to gain an understanding of what was really going on. Moreover, this style of questioning constitutes a *model* for the patient which helps him to acquire the skills of monitoring his thoughts.

An example of inductive questioning would be:

*Inductive
questioning*

Key technique

Model

*Example of
inductive
questioning*

P: I felt terribly upset yesterday when I came back from work and I do not even know why.

T: What was going through your mind at the time? (*direct question*)

P: I don't know. Nothing in particular. I just felt this black cloud come over me.

T: Was this before you got home or after you got home?

P: I think I was beginning to be upset before I left work. But it just got worse and worse.

T: Had something happened at work?

P: Nothing much that I can remember. Nothing out of the ordinary, anyway.

T: What do you mean by 'nothing out of the ordinary'?

P: I was just doing my usual work; there were no classes to teach and I was marking some papers.

T: Is this when you started feeling bad?

P: Yes, that's right

T: Did anybody come into your office?

P: No, nobody came.

T: Was there any interruption, like a telephone call?

P: No, nothing at all.

T: Did it bother you that nobody called or telephoned?

P: No, I was relieved not to be interrupted for once and to be able to get on with the work.

T: While you were marking the papers, were you able to concentrate all the time?

P: No, you know what it's like. It's the same when I watch television. My mind is not really on it.

T: Did you have thoughts or images going through your mind?

P: Yes, I suppose so. I was beginning to think about going home.

*Create a
concrete image*

T: So here you were — sitting at your desk and it's getting near the time to go home. Is this what went through your mind? Did you have an image of your home? (*therapist tries to create a concrete image*)

P: Hmm, Hmm

T: Can you tell me what the image was?

P: Yes . . . I was thinking about the house being cold and no one being there — sitting by myself and forcing myself to eat some supper and the telephone not ringing. (*patient starts crying*)

T: OK—you created a very sad image in your mind and this made you feel depressed. You seem to have been painting a very black picture which made you feel low. Now, you could have had a very different image of going home. Let's try. Let us say you had a picture in your mind of going home, putting on the fire, making yourself a nice supper whilst listening to the radio and sitting down for the evening in front of a warm fire, watching a good film on T.V. You phone a friend and have an interesting chat. How do you think this picture would have made you feel?

P: I guess I would not have felt so low.

T: Yes, it is sometimes difficult to trace the pictures that go *through our mind* which colour our mood. Here, I think you have succeeded in tracing what started your black mood. It seems to me that what you did was *jump to conclusions* about how your evening would turn out and you managed to persuade yourself that the image was a reality. Do you see that?

P: Yes, maybe I did get carried away there.

T: Now let us see what is so depressing for you about going home to an empty house.

Thus, through careful, sensitive and perceptive questioning, the therapist can help the patient identify the mental image or thought which may have started the worsening of his mood. This then leads to the possible identification of further key cognitions.

*Moments of
strong emotion*

*Beginning of
treatment*

The use of moments of strong emotion to gain access to the patient's automatic thoughts is an extremely effective and much used tool, particularly at the beginning of treatment when the patient is unused to identifying and monitoring his automatic thoughts. Often, patients will be talking about a subject which is not necessarily emotionally laden and the therapist can detect that the patient's mood has changed. For example, they may appear suddenly tearful or their speech may become hesitant or more rapid or they may suddenly begin to fidget. The attentive therapist will observe these changes and should immediately point them out and enquire 'What went through your mind just now?' This is done sensitively as the patient's distress has increased. For example:

P: I moved here about 3 years ago for a new job and bought the house

I live in now. There have been lots of problems with the house. (*patient becomes tearful*) I've sorted these out now bit by bit.

T: Now just stop there for a minute. It seems to me that you have become really very upset about something. As you were speaking, what went through your mind just now?

P: I was just feeling sorry for myself. There has been nothing but problems since I got here. I just can't go on coping. I wish it would all stop.

T: So, as you were telling me about how well you have coped with these problems, there were a lot of thoughts going on at the back of your mind which were obviously upsetting you. 'I just can't go on coping'. 'I wish it would all stop'. These thoughts are very important as they obviously influence how you are feeling.

Although this patient was talking about how well she had coped with problems, she was experiencing a series of distressing automatic thoughts simultaneously. By noticing the patient's change in mood and behaviour, the therapist was then able to elicit the key thoughts. Had the therapist ignored the patient's tearfulness, he would only have heard that the patient had coped with the problems, not that the patient thought she could not go on coping. Similarly, had the therapist offered comfort to the patient on becoming tearful, a valuable opportunity would have been lost.

Patients can be trained to use these changes in their mood to become conscious of their automatic thoughts. Anxious patients can be trained, through relaxation exercises, to become more aware of *increases in physical tension* or the *beginnings of a panic attack*. These increases in tension can then be used as cues for the patient to monitor his automatic thoughts in the same way as changes in mood are used. As described above, the therapist can use these observed increases in tension to detect automatic thoughts within treatment sessions.

Increases in physical tension

When trying to elicit automatic thoughts related to past events or situations, if inductive questioning, as described earlier, does not help the patient to identify his automatic cognitions, it may be useful to use *mental imagery* to recreate a situation. The patient is required to recreate the situation in his mind as clearly as possible and after a few minutes the therapist asks about accompanying thoughts. For example:

Mental imagery

T: Try to recreate exactly what happened on Wednesday night. You were at home with your husband. It was after supper and you had put the children to bed. You were in the living room, watching television and your husband was reading the newspaper. Close your eyes and try to imagine the situation in as many details as possible, the sitting room where you were sitting, the time of day, etc.

T: (*2 minutes later*) OK. Have you got the picture in your mind?

P: Yes, I see it now. I had gone to sit close to John on the sofa and he was reading the paper. After a while, he got up, turned the volume of the television down a bit and sat somewhere else quite far from me.

T: Did you attach some meaning to that?

P: Yes, I thought 'He can't stand being near me. He finds me boring. He does not love me any more'.

T: Well done. We've now got hold of the *hot* cognition, as it's sometimes called. Do you now see why you *felt* so hopeless and desperate? Your husband behaved in a certain way and you put quite drastic interpretations on his behaviour. Somehow, what he did had something to do with you. You *personalized* his behaviour and somehow it all reflected badly on you. Let's look at these thoughts again, to see how realistic they are.

Role plays

Instead of mental imagery, *role plays* can be more appropriate to recreate a situation vividly so that the relevant thoughts become available. Role playing was mentioned in the previous section as a behavioural method to teach coping techniques such as self-assertion and anger control, but it can also be used to get access to underlying thoughts. For example, a patient complained that whenever she talked to her grown up step-daughter, she felt frightened. This happened whether she talked to the step-daughter on the telephone or face-to-face and whatever the topic of conversation was. She was not able to understand why she felt frightened, especially as the step-daughter was considered by all and by the patient herself to be kind and helpful. The therapist decided to role play the step-daughter in a recent example from the patient's account. This involved a telephone conversation about Christmas arrangements.

T: (*in the role of step-daughter*) Hello Mary, how are you keeping?

P: (*role playing herself*) Not too bad, thank you, and you?

T: I'm very well and busy making preparations about Christmas. For the meal, I though I might cook the turkey and you could prepare the first course . . .

At this point, the patient was looking distressed. The therapist then asked: 'What's going through your mind just now?'

P: She always makes me feel so incompetent. I get jealous feelings. Why should she be happy and competent, while I am not?

T: Is this what's frightening?

P: Yes, each time we talk I'm afraid of getting the jealous feelings. I don't like feeling jealous. Jealousy is a despicable emotion.

Thus, the role plays helped the therapist and the patient to access quickly the thoughts underlying the unexpected emotional reaction.

Patients often talk about events as if they were the cause of their bad feelings. The therapist establishes the missing link (the inter-pretation) by *ascertaining the meaning of the event*. Although it may appear evident what the interpretation is, the therapist never assumes that he knows without asking. He is then sure of eliciting the patient's idiosyncratic interpretation in his own words. The patient may say 'I feel bad when my children fight among themselves'.

T: What does it mean to you when the children are fighting over what television channel to watch, as you just described?
P: I feel that I am a bad mother.
T: Why are you a bad mother because the children are arguing?
P: Because it must mean that they are unhappy and I make them so.

Similarly, when patients described feeling depressed *because* a friend did not call or feeling anxious *because* they have a heavy work agenda, the therapist enquires about the meaning of these situations.

At the beginning of therapy when the patient is still training in monitoring his thoughts, he may find it useful to carry a *wrist counter*, for example, a golf counter, to register his negative automatic thoughts each time he begins to feel anxious or depressed. This is a simple method to increase awareness of thoughts which maintain dysphoric moods. At the beginning of such an exercise, the patient may complain that his negative thoughts have, in fact, increased. He can be reassured that this is often the case and that it only indicates that he is getting better at monitoring the thoughts. This method need only be used for a few days at the outset of therapy to sensitize the pa-tient to the cognitive therapy approach.

Getting an anxious patient to *engage in behavioural tasks* is often essential if the therapist is to help the patient identify his anxiety pro-voking automatic thoughts. Anxious patients do not generally feel anxious in the therapist's office and, therefore, access to their automatic thoughts is problematic in this setting. Also, they tend to avoid anxiety arousing thoughts outside anxiety provoking situations as these would make them feel uncomfortably anxious. It is, therefore, important to get the patient to carry out behavioural tasks so that he can become aware of the role which anxiety arousing thoughts play in both his emotions and his behaviour. By the *scheduling of activities* and the use of *graded exposure*, as described in the previous section, the patient can place himself in anxiety provoking situations he may have previously avoided and be able to detect and *record accompanying automatic thoughts* on the daily record of automatic thoughts (see Appendix 4). Initially, it can be helpful for the therapist to accompany the patient in carrying out an assignment and to use changes in physical tension and anxiety as a means of detecting thoughts *in vivo*.

Depressed patients may also find engaging in the behavioural

Ascertaining the meaning of an event

Training in monitoring thoughts

Wrist counter

Engage in behavioural tasks

tasks, as described in the previous section, useful as exercises to increase their awareness of negative automatic thoughts. These may be thoughts relating to inactivity or self-assertion for example. They would be instructed to monitor their thoughts before engaging in the task or during its execution and to write them down.

Dysfunctional thought forms

The standard technique throughout therapy is the recording of distressful emotions and thoughts on the *dysfunctional thought forms* (see Appendix 4). In the first column, the patient describes the situation involved. In the second column, he notes his emotion which he rates for intensity on a 0–100 per cent scale. Thus, emotions are used as cues for monitoring automatic thoughts which are noted in the third column and rated for degree of belief (0–100%). The fourth and fifth columns are used to examine and modify the automatic thought and to describe and rate changes in emotions if they occur, and changes in degree of belief in the original interpretation. At the beginning of therapy, the patient only fills in the first three columns and the rest is done during treatment sessions, as will be described, with examples, in the next section. It is necessary to train the patient in filling in these forms by using them in treatment sessions, before he begins to fill them in as homework assignments.

Emotions are used as cues

Modifying automatic thoughts

Modifying negative or anxiety-provoking automatic thoughts occupies the major part of the time in cognitive therapy. The aim of the therapist, which is derived from the cognitive model as described in Chapter 2, is to help the patient to adopt more *realistic* views of himself, his world and his future. Note that the aim is *not* for the patient to change his negative thoughts to positive thoughts, using superficial techniques of positive thinking. The cognitive therapist's stance is that the negative or anxious interpretation of the patient is one of many different interpretations and that some other interpretation may be more adaptive or more realistic. The therapist, therefore, uses various techniques based on socratic questioning and on behavioural tasks to enable patients to examine their thoughts and weaken their belief in them. We all tend to believe that our interpretations are correct and, therefore, we believe in them. It demands an effort to consider alternatives and to change our mind. Sometimes, of course, the negative thoughts are realistic and joint efforts are then made to change the problem situation or to increase the patient's coping skill and his sense of self-efficacy. Table 4.3 gives a list of the most commonly tried methods for modifying automatic thoughts. If the therapist can think of others which are more suitable for his individual patient, he is encouraged to use them, as long as they are stylistically and methodologically within the framework of cognitive therapy.

Adopt more realistic views

Socratic questioning

During a treatment session

Typically, during a treatment session, the therapist would choose

Table 4.3 Techniques for modifying automatic thoughts

---

1 Examine the evidence for and against
2 Substitute alternative interpretations
3 Establish the realistic probability of each interpretation
4 Collect information, for example, through experiments or polling a
   sample of people for their interpretations
5 Decentering or distancing from interpretation
6 Redefining of terms used
7 Re-attribution
8 Role plays
9 Use of the dysfunctional thought forms

---

one or two automatic thoughts and apply some of the techniques of modification described in Table 4.3. It is useful if both therapist and patient write down the thought and the answers. This is used as a training for the patient who then applies the same techniques in homework assignments. Patients often say that the questioning therapist becomes a model for them, so that they later find themselves posing the same type of questions to themselves, as if they were the therapist.

The following is an example from an interview with a primary school teacher referred for anxiety and depression. *Examining the evidence* for and against the automatic thought is probably the key technique for modifying cognitions.

Examining the evidence

T: So, you feel anxious every morning because you think you won't be able to cope, that you will collapse and have to be taken home.

P: Yes, every morning it's the same. The moment I wake up, I feel a knot in my stomach. I have to force myself to get to school.

T: What goes through your mind at these times?

P: Oh . . . 30 unruly 7 year olds, calls from an irate headmistress, the lessons not properly prepared, not interesting enough. . . .

T: OK, you imagine or even predict that a whole lot of disastrous events are going to take place and that you won't be able to cope?

P: That's it. I really can't stand it any more.

T: Has any of these events taken place in reality recently?

P: Oh yes. Ever since I was moved to a younger age group a year ago.

T: Have you ever been unable to cope and had to be sent home?

P: No, but it nearly happened a few times.

T: It nearly did, but it's important to note that it did not. So, what is it that you cannot stand, the images which come to your mind in the morning or the reality of the classroom?

P: Well, strangely, I don't get so anxious in the classroom. The images are worse than the reality.

T: Exactly. You say to yourself 'I won't be able to cope, I will collapse'. But, if I understand correctly, difficult situations have occurred and you have not collapsed and you have not been sent home. So your predictions are constantly invalidated, but you don't believe the evidence for some reason. Is that right?

P: That's right. You would not believe that I trained as a scientist, would you?

T: Well, that's what this therapy is about, to try and help you be a scientist in your own life.

Substitute alternative interpretations

The therapist would then help the patient *substitute alternative interpretations* which would be less catastrophic and cause less anxiety. In the example given above, the therapist already has a conceptualization of the patient as needing complete control of situations in order not to feel anxious and as needing her performance to be always smooth and perfect (see next section about schemata, p. 82). Questioning revealed that the patient had been a primary school teacher for 20 years, but that she had taught older children so far. The headmistress was also a new appointment and had brought in new regulations to the school.

T: So, what's happening is that you are facing a number of new situations at the moment and these make you anxious. Is that right?

P: Everything keeps changing and I don't like that.

T: OK, you don't like new situations, but you have coped with them without major disasters over the last year?

P: Yes.

T: Are situations less novel now than they were 9 months ago?

P: Yes, and it is getting easier. These 7 year olds are not so bad most of the time.

T: Good. So, if you said this to yourself in the mornings instead, would it be easier? Perhaps something like: 'This is still a relatively new situation for me, but I'm coping with it. The disasters that I fear have not occurred and are less likely to happen as I get more familiar with the new class and the new headmistress. I'm doing not too badly really.' Is that right?

Note that the therapist does not attempt to challenge the patient's basic schemata at this point of therapy, focusing instead on distressful thoughts and images only. However, the therapist takes a note of the underlying assumptions and of the examples to return to later.

Establishing the realistic probability

Asking the patient to list alternative interpretations of a situation and then *establishing the realistic probability* of each interpretation is a powerful technique, as it does not reject the original negative interpretation, unlikely as it might be, and contrasts it with more likely interpretations. This approach trains the patient to consider his thoughts as interpretations of reality rather than reality itself. Going back to the example on p. 72, the patient thought, 'He can't stand being near me. He finds me boring. He does not love me any more', when her husband moved away from her side to read his newspaper somewhere else. She believed in this interpretation 100%.

T: OK, that's one interpretation. He moved away because he can't stand being near you. He finds you boring and he does not love you any more. Are there any other possible reasons why he might have behaved like that?

P: I don't see any really. Why else would he do that?

T: Well, you said he was reading the newspaper and you were watching a film on TV?

P: Yes, he was reading the inside political page very intensely.

T: So, could he have changed places because he did not want to be distracted and needed more space for his paper?

P: Yes, I suppose so. He was a bit cramped where he was. When he moved, I noticed that he then spread out the paper. He looked more comfortable.

T: Or, could it be that he did not want to distract you from your film as he was not watching himself?

P: Could be. I must say I was pretty engrossed in it. I like these soap operas you see, and John does not.

T: All right. So, you now have three alternative interpretations of the same situation: John cannot stand being near you; he needed more space to concentrate on his paper; he did not want to distract you. Are there any others?

P: Now that we are looking at it like that, something else has just come to my mind. He did say he was developing a cold and he had a headache. Maybe the noise was getting at him, poor dear. That's why he turned the volume down a bit.

T: Here we are. You have four interpretations now. Let's see how probable each one is.

The patient then assigned probabilities of 10%, 60%, 60%, 80% to the four interpretations. The therapist concluded:

T: 'This is interesting, isn't it? Our first automatic interpretation is often the most improbable one. You put the most dire interpretation on a simple action of your husband and this made you feel very low and spoiled the rest of your evening. You could not concentrate on your film and you did not speak to your husband for the rest of the evening. I would like you to do the same sort of exercise at home in the coming week, if you find yourself feeling really bad. Check what's going through your mind. Write down the thought or describe the image and then list alternative interpretations and rate them for probability. Could you do that?'

Sometimes, to be able to change an interpretation or weaken the degree of belief in it, it is necessary for the patient to *collect*

Collect information

information or *carry out an experiment*. This empirical approach is much more powerful than the therapist providing counteracting information. It is particularly useful when the components of a problem situation have to be defined and to correct arbitrary inferences. A male student felt anxious in the classroom because he thought that everybody would laugh at him if he asked a question. His *first experiment* was to note who asked questions in the class, what the questions were and how fellow students and the teacher reacted. The information he brought back was that the most able students had asked questions, but somebody had asked a very simple question which showed how uninformed he was and nobody had laughed. The *second experiment* was that he would ask a question, having used some relaxation exercises first, and note what response he got. If this experiment had gone well, it would then be used as evidence that his prediction was wrong and that he did have the ability to ask questions in class. However, in this case, the experiment was unsuccessful. The patient was too nervous and had to repeat the question three times before the teacher could hear him or make any sense of his question. By that time, his class-mates had begun to snigger. For the *third experiment*, the patient was asked to make sure that he controlled his breathing and gave himself relaxation instruction. He rehearsed the relaxation exercises and putting a question in a loud enough voice in the session and then carried out the experiment, which was successful.

Some depressed patients, because of their low self-esteem, think that, for example, they are bad mothers because they sometimes lose patience with their children and feel less than affectionate towards them; or that they are lazy and incompetent because they put off doing a piece of work, at home or in the office. The patient can be asked to check how some people they admire as being better than themselves in these respective ways behave in the same situations.

Polling

They can *poll* a few friends and acquaintances and ask friends to carry out a poll as well. The data invariably indicate that the patient is not in a minority of one and that what they blame or denigrate themselves for is general practice.

The process which underlies all cognitive modification techniques

Decentring

is that of *decentring* or *distancing*, that is the patient is asked to stand away from his thought or interpretation and examine it in a realistic

Distancing

manner. A direct distancing technique is to ask the patient: 'If somebody else declines an invitation to go to the cinema with you because she has a previous engagement, do you reject this person and stop your friendship?', or, 'If somebody else makes some bad mistakes when you are playing bridge, do you think of him as worthless?', or, 'If somebody else loses her temper with her children and talks to them sharply or sends them up to their room, would you blame her as being a bad mother?' This technique allows the patient to see that he has two sets of rules, one which is understanding and forgiving for others, and one which is overstrict and unforgiving for himself. If he *treats himself as he treats others*, he would be kinder to himself and feel generally better.

Patients often put overgeneralized self-derogatory labels on themselves: 'I am a coward', 'I am lazy', 'I am sinful', 'I am weak'. Instead of accepting these terms at face value, the therapist asks the patient to *define the terms* he is using. Who is a coward? What does lazy really mean? What does it mean to be sinful or weak? By using examples which are generally accepted as defining these terms, the outcome is often that the patient is applying the label to himself inappropriately. Throughout therapy, it is necessary to ask the patient to define the terms he is using: 'What do you mean by . . . ?', instead of taking for granted that the therapist and the patient use what may be an ordinary word in the language in the same connotative and denotative sense.

The *re-attribution* of causes for negative outcomes to external rather than internal factors is useful to correct personalization errors, to decrease self-blame and increase self-esteem. The patient may call himself a 'coward' because he avoids taking an active role in social situations as these make him extremely anxious. Having defined the term 'coward', the next step is to reattribute the avoidance behaviour to an anxiety state. Within the framework of *learned helplessness theory* (Abramson *et al.*, 1978), attributions for negative outcomes to external, specific and unstable causes have been found to be less depressing than internal, global and stable attributions. An anxiety state is a specific and unstable attribution and partially external, whereas cowardice would be an internal, global and stable attribution. The therapist can find evidence, through questioning, that the patient has not, throughout his life, displayed the personal characteristics of a coward. Similarly, the inactivity or avoidance behaviour of the depressed patient can be re-attributed to depressive illness, rather than to laziness; loss of interest in the family or decrease in helpful behaviour towards others can be re-attributed to depressive illness, rather than to selfishness.

Role playing was discussed in the previous section as a method for bringing automatic thoughts to light. It is also necessary to role play the behavioural tests which the therapist and the patient plan as methods for collecting data or for testing out predictions. The task may, for example, involve asking questions, expressing anger or saying no to inappropriate requests. Role play and role reversals are then used for rehearsal purposes and also for learning through modelling (Bandura, 1977; Meichenbaum, 1977). It increases the patient's feeling of self-efficacy and provides counter-evidence for negative predictions.

The *dysfunctional thought forms* mentioned on p. 74 are the basic tools of cognitive therapy (see Appendix 4). They are used not only to enable the patient to learn to make the association between emotions

Table 4.4 Examples of automatic thoughts and of how to answer them

Situation	Emotion (rate degree, 0–100%)	Automatic thoughts (rate belief, 0–100%)	Answers (rate belief, 0–100%)	Outcome (re-rate belief in automatic thinking and emotion)
Waking up, thinking about sale of house	Anxious, sad (80%)	My financial affairs are in a mess. I shall not find another home in time. I should not have taken my lawyer's advice (100%)	There are some difficulties because I need to find another house to buy in two months. But I am catastrophizing when I say that my financial affairs are in a mess and I do not have a crystal ball to predict that I shall not find another home. My lawyer is experienced in these affairs and well placed to give advice. There are many houses for sale in the areas I want. It was a wise move to sell first in the current state of the housing market (100%)	Automatic thought (30%) Anxious (30%)
Getting ready to go away for the weekend	Angry (80%)	I'm just too tired to do any more. Why can't my husband help? (80%)	I am more tired than usual because of my depression. I don't need to pack tonight. John cannot read my mind. If I ask him, he will help willingly (100%)	Automatic thought (0%) Sad (20%)
Children quarrelling about a television programme	Angry (100%) depressed (100%)	The children are really angry with me—not with each other, because I'm a rotten mother to them (100%)	Children always quarrel about these things. My friends' children quarrel too. I'm personalizing something that's got nothing to do with me.	Automatic thought (0%) Depressed (50%)

Situation	Emotion	Automatic thought	Rational response	Outcome
			What's the evidence that I am a rotten mother? What is a rotten mother? I'll work out on another sheet, evidence for and against the statement that I am a rotten mother (80%)	Automatic thought (30%) Anxious (50%)
Taking kids to film	Anxious depressed (9C%)	I can't enjoy anything. I'm a useless father and a failure (100%)	Lack of enjoyment is a symptom of depression. I'm not always like this. Even now, I can enjoy some things if I stop upsetting myself by calling myself useless and a failure. I know that I'm neither useless nor a failure. I'm good at my job and the children seem to enjoy doing things with me (100%)	
Daughter tells me that bank phoned during the day. No coherent message	Anxious (80%)	Something really important concerning our finances has happened. Poverty looms on the hcrizon (80%)	Catastrophizing, jumping to conclusions, fortune telling again. I just checked our bank balance last week and there was nothing wrong with it. It is more likely that I dated a cheque incorrectly. Ring and find out what the problem is—then I can do something about it. Can't solve imaginary problems (100%)	Automatic thought (20%) Anxious (40%)

and automatic thoughts, but also to practise correcting his dysfunctional thoughts. Moreover, as the patient is asked to rate the level of his emotions and his degree of belief in the thoughts and in the alternative responses, he also learns not to see everything in black and white and to be more discriminatory. Both anxious and depressed patients have a tendency to treat different degrees of distress in the same way, using terms such as, 'I felt terribly low' or 'I felt terribly anxious'. This is not because they want to dramatize their feelings, but as they feel distressed a great deal of the time or they have often experienced low levels of dysphoria developing into major distress, their discriminatory ability is impaired.

Confusion between emotions and thoughts

Most patients find filling in the Dysfunctional Thought Forms difficult. Nobody is practised in describing his emotions and thoughts exactly. Moreover, there is usually a great deal of confusion between emotions and thoughts. The English language lends itself to this confusion. When we say, 'I *felt* that he did not like me', this is strictly incorrect. 'I *thought* that he did not like me and I *felt* bad', is really what we mean. Patients, therefore, need a lot of training within sessions in how to fill in the forms, before they can be expected to use them in a helpful fashion. The therapist should always reserve some time of the treatment session to look at least at a sample of the thoughts which are brought back from homework assignments. The examples in Table 4.4 are taken from *Coping with Depression* (Blackburn, 1987).

Basic schemata or silent assumptions

Towards the end of treatment, perhaps about three-quarters of the way through, the cognitive therapist will try to specify and modify the basic attitudes which are considered to be depressogenic or anxiogenic and which, according to the hierarchical model of the cognitive theory of the emotional disorders (see Chapter 2, Tables 2.1 and 2.3), become prepotent during illness and lead to specific dysfunctional automatic thoughts. Although the therapist is likely to have a good idea of the patient's idiosyncratic beliefs and rules early on in therapy, it is considered more appropriate to deal at the outset with behavioural problems and automatic thoughts. These can be

Idiosyncratic beliefs

conceptualized as the suprastructure of the depressive or anxious system while the basic schemata are the foundation stones. This strategy contrasts strongly with that of rational–emotive therapy (RET; Ellis, 1962) where basic beliefs are dealt with at the very beginning of therapy. In cognitive therapy, it is thought that challenging a patient's cherished beliefs too early in therapy will be counter-productive as the patient may feel threatened and resist change. Moreover, later on in therapy the patient will have developed the cognitive skills which are essential to query and modify attitudes and beliefs.

Basic schemata differ from automatic thoughts in several important ways. They are abstract and, therefore, the patient is largely unaware of them, hence the term 'silent assumptions'. They are influenced by an individual's social and cultural background and differ from more adaptive attitudes only in their form, that is they are too general, too rigid and undifferentiated. Therefore, they cannot be said to be totally erroneous, as a delusional belief would be or as automatic thoughts might be. Consequently, the therapist's aim is not to attempt to change the patient's attitudes or beliefs completely, but simply to introduce some flexibility and plasticity. This aim needs, of course, to be shared openly with the patient.

Techniques for identifying basic schemata

By using a selection of the patient's automatic thoughts, either as expressed during the treatment sessions, or as registered on the 'dysfunctional thoughts forms', the therapist and patient attempt to extract a *general rule*. The therapist either reads back from his notes or from the forms collected over the course of treatment or asks the patient to re-read some of the thoughts from his own records. He then asks 'Do these extracts appear to reflect a general rule that you apply to situations on the whole?'

If the patient does not succeed in extracting the general rule, the therapist may prompt him by asking: 'Does it seem to you that . . .?' and this suggestion is then discussed and refined and finally verbalized in the patient's own words.

A selection of thoughts from a male patient read as follows:

'I've missed the boat, I'll never get a lectureship. My boss thinks that I am too disorganized.'

'I don't want to see my friends. They all remind me what a loser I am.'

'I've messed up my life for a silly thesis. I have no house, no money, no wife. People cannot respect me.'

'I hate work, I'll never make a success of it. My parents will be ashamed of me.'

'If I mess up this job, I have no future. Nobody will want to know me.'

Table 4.5 Techniques for identifying schemata

1 Extracting general rules from specific examples
2 Looking for common themes
3 Picking out the personal rules expressed in the 'shoulds'
4 Verbalizing the implicit meaning of patient's statements
5 The use of the Dysfunctional Attitudes Scale (Weissman & Beck, 1978; see Appendix 1)
6 Developing the logical implication of automatic thoughts by the 'downwards arrow' technique

'I'm messing up the therapy, I've failed. Dr. B. will soon lose patience
with me.'

'I've messed up my relationship with my girlfriend. She sees me out
of pity.'

These thoughts were accompanied by feelings of intense depression,
despair and anxiety. When asked whether he felt these thoughts
reflected some general basic belief, the patient stated, 'Yes, I believed
I was a failure all round, but we've worked on that and I don't believe
it any more'.

T: . . . Yes, you saw yourself as a failure. But is there a general belief
here about yourself as a failure?

P: I see what you mean. People don't like failures. They don't respect
you, they don't love you.

T: Does it sound as if you believe that *nobody* will like you unless you
are successful?

P: Hum . . . Hum . . .

T: Right. So your belief seems to be: 'People respect and like
successful people. I am not successful. Therefore, nobody likes
me'. Is that right?

P: Yeah, that's it exactly.

Thus, the therapist tries to express the basic schema in the form of a
syllogism which usually follows impeccable logic, except that the
premise is erroneous. When the belief is expressed in that form, it
leads automatically to methods of change (see next section, p. 88).

Typical beliefs
*Depressed
patients*

The typical beliefs which are found in depressed patients relate to:
• *the need to be loved* by most people at all times: 'People cannot be
happy unless they are loved. X does not love me, therefore I cannot be
happy.'
• *the need for success:* as in the example given above, success in
everything is seen as prerequisite for love, respect, approval or
happiness.
• *the need for approval:* disapproval or criticism entails unhappiness
or loss of self-worth. 'If somebody disapproves of me, I am nothing.'
• *the need for omnipotence:* 'I *should* know everything, understand
everything and never make mistakes. If not, I am a nobody and
people will not respect me or love me.'
• *the need for autonomy:* 'I should be able to do things by myself
without help from others. Otherwise, I am worthless or not deserving
of respect, approval, etc.'
• *entitlement* to the consideration of others: 'If I behave decently,
others should be considerate, fair, honest and kind in return.'
• *the need for an unfailing moral code:* 'I should always do the right
thing, be nice and attentive to others. If not, I am a bad person.'
• *the need to do things perfectly:* 'I should do everything perfectly. If
not, I'm worthless'.

For the sociotropic individual (see Chapter 2, p. 29), the schemata relate to love, affection, approval and respect from others, whereas for the autonomous individual, the schemata relate to self-worth, omnipotence, success, autonomy, freedom and perfectionism.

In the anxious patient, these same schemata can also be found, although the more common and basic ones relate to the following:

- *A need for control:* 'If I am not in total control of a situation, something bad will happen.'
- *A need to be constantly on the alert:* 'If I am not always watchful and worrying, something bad will happen.'
- *A need to avoid unknown situations:* 'If it's a new situation, I shall not be able to cope.'
- *A need to be always calm:* 'If I feel nervous, I will get even more nervous and make a fool of myself or something awful will happen.'
- *A need to be as or more competent* than others in all situations. 'If I do not know as much as the others, do not contribute as much, I shall feel incompetent. When I feel incompetent, I am anxious.'

The *common themes* in the patient's communications will, very early on in therapy, alert the therapist to the main subject matter of his silent assumptions. Thus, in the example given above, the main themes relate to achievement and love/respect from others. It is helpful if the therapist underlines these recurrent themes in his notes, so that he can refer back to them when he decides to begin work on the patient's postulates. The therapist may introduce this part of therapy thus:

T: We have now spent a few weeks examining and challenging the automatic thoughts which accompany your feelings of depression and anxiety. You have become very good at this. You are also doing more of the things you want to do and enjoying yourself. Is that right?

P: Yes, a bit. I still get very low and twitchy at times.

T: Of course. It's going to take a bit longer to get quite on top of these feelings. I think it's time for us to look at some of the basic beliefs or attitudes which lead you to interpret some situations in the particular way which leads to these bad feelings. There are many ways we can do that. I suggest that we start by looking at the themes and words which recur in the forms which you have filled in over the last weeks. This would give us a clue. Does that sound OK with you?

P: I could try.

T: Good. What about starting this as your homework over the next week, if you can? I have kept a list myself in my notes here. We can put your list and mine together and see what we come up with.

Such an approach underlines the therapist's attentiveness and the collaborative relationship. Similarly, by careful listening, the therapist can note the *implicit meaning* of the patient's statements and comments and share with the patient his understanding to check that he is on the right track. The patient may comment that having to see a therapist is a sign of weakness, that asking information from a colleague is a sign of weakness, that asking one's way from a passer-by is embarrassing. The therapist may list out these comments, and state: 'These concerns seem to indicate that you should know everything and do everything by yourself, otherwise you would be weak, and also that you should never be weak. Is that right?' This can then be pursued as 'OK'. You believe that these are indications of weakness and that you should not be weak. Well, tell me why is it so bad to appear weak occasionally?' The patient can then complete his basic schema explicitly. 'I will lose my respect and others will not respect me. I will be a nothing'. The therapist then expresses the silent assumption in the patient's own logical terms:

- *Weak people need the help of other people.*
- *Weak people have no self-respect and no respect from others.*
- *I am nothing without respect. Therefore I must not show weakness.*

'Shoulds'

The patient's *personal rules* are expressed in the '*shoulds*' which he applies to his own conduct and to others. Alert attention on the part of the therapist will help in identifying these. The 'shoulds' may relate to the behaviour that an individual feels entitled to from others; they may relate to the need for perfection or to excessively high moral expectations of oneself. The therapist can gently stress these 'shoulds' in his summaries of the patient's communications, preferably with some humour. We find that patients often take this up as a game and begin to stress their '*shoulds*' wryly or even to pick out the '*shoulds*' which the therapist may inadvertently use.

Dysfunctional Attitude Scale

The *Dysfunctional Attitude Scale* (DAS) (Weissman & Beck, 1978), which is included in Appendix 1, is a self-rating questionnaire of 40 seven-point scale items which measure degrees of dysfunctional beliefs pertaining to the various areas mentioned above. Though it is primarily a research tool, it can be used in conjunction with one or several of the methods described in this section to identify basic attitudes. Items which are scored at the extreme of the scale (scores of six or seven) indicate excessively rigid attitudes which can then be discussed openly.

Downward arrow technique

Finally, developing the logical implication of automatic thoughts using the *downward arrow* technique can be very effective in revealing underlying assumptions. The two examples which follow are extracted from Blackburn (1987). When using this technique, automatic thoughts are not challenged but accepted as true until the final bottom line is reached.

Case 1. The patient was a 23 year old secretary, divorced, who lived alone with her young son aged 3. In her dysfunctional thought form, she recorded the following:

Situation: I rang up my friend and her brother said that she was not in.
Emotion: Sadness (100%).
Automatic thought: She must have told him to say she was out if I rang.

The downward arrow exercise went as follows:

T: OK, she told him to say she was out if you rang.
If she did say that, why would it be so upsetting to you?

↓

P: It would mean that she did not like me.
T: Suppose this is true, she does not like you.
What would this mean to you?

↓

P: It would mean there's something wrong with me. Otherwise she wouldn't try to avoid me.
T: Suppose this is true, what would that mean to you?

↓

P: It would mean that people will not want to have anything to do with me. They will reject me.
T: And if this were true, what would it mean to you?

↓

P: It would mean that I am unlovable, totally worthless.
T: And if that were true, what would it mean to you?

↓

P: It would mean that my life is not worth living.

The therapist then stops the exercise, by asking '*Does this indicate that you believe that unless everybody likes you, you are worthless and your life is not worth living?*' The patient may correct this statement, by saying 'well maybe not *everybody*, but most people anyway'.

Case 2. A male civil servant, aged 43, sometimes felt so acutely anxious about work situations that he just had to absent himself. He had written down the following example as part of a homework assignment.
Situation: Starting work again on Monday.
Emotion: Anxious (60%).
Automatic thought: What will I say if people ask what was wrong? They will probably think that I am not genuine, just lazy.

T: Suppose they do think that. Why is this so upsetting to you?

↓

P: People will be criticizing me or laughing at me.
T: Suppose this were true. What would it mean to you?

↓

P: They would think I'm no good, just a fake.
T: Suppose that were true. What would that mean to you?

↓

P: It would mean that I am no good and inferior.
T: Suppose that were true, what would that mean to you?

↓

P: It would mean that people will look down on me and not respect me. I would be a nobody.
T: *Does that indicate that your worth depends on the approval of various people? If somebody disapproves or thinks badly of you, it means that you are worthless?*

This conclusion happened to be right and the patient then provided a number of examples to illustrate how strongly this belief was held. He worried about what the doorman thought of him, what the various secretaries thought of him and even what the newsagent thought of him. The therapist then concluded: '*You believe that your worth is made up of the sum of various people's approval. The more approval you have, the more worthy you are. The less approval you get, the less worthy you are. Do I express this correctly?*'

Techniques for modifying basic schemata

Table 4.6 describes some of the main methods for weakening the rigidity of the basic postulates that are presented by depressed and anxious patients. As pointed out at the beginning of this section, these *Altered in degree* postulates or schemata need only be altered in degree rather than changed completely and opposite beliefs substituted. The aim of the therapist is, understandably, not to change the perfectionist into a devil-may-care individual, or the high-principled moralist into a selfish individual. It is important that the patient understands this, as he would otherwise feel that his core beliefs are being totally devalued. Similarly, the therapist has to take into consideration the individual's religious beliefs, the attitudes which are generally accepted in his subgroup and his particular personality characteristics *Gentle socratic style* and life-style. The gentle socratic style which we advocate throughout this book is particularly important when attempting to modify schemata if the patient is not to feel ridiculed or belittled. The

Table 4.6 Techniques for modifying schemata and beliefs

1 Weigh up the advantages and disadvantages of holding the belief
2 Examine the evidence for and against
3 Challenge each argument in the downward arrow exercise
4 Contrast the short- and long-term utility of the personal rule
5 Question the validity of the personal contract
6 Reality testing: test consequences of disobeying the rule (response prevention)

autonomous individual needs to feel free and in command and the sociotropic individual will react adversely to apparent disapproval or rejection.

We find that once the assumptions which had been implicit are *verbalized explicitly*, patients are often struck by their exaggerated and simplistic nature. This, in itself, begins to weaken the strength of the beliefs. However, since, by definition, these beliefs have been held unquestioned by the patient for a long time, it is necessary to work on them for two or three sessions, using one or more of the techniques described in Table 4.6.

As it can be assumed that the general rule of behaviour must have proved useful to the individual at certain times of his life, a particularly potent method is to ask him to list the *advantages and disadvantages* of the belief in two columns and to attach ratings of importance (in percentages) to each advantage and disadvantage. The ratings are then added up and a final score obtained by subtraction. Patients may find it difficult to think of many disadvantages and can be helped through questioning – never by telling. The distressful situations which the patient has discussed earlier on in therapy provides the therapist with the examples to explore which have proved disadvantageous to the individual patient. The three examples given below are derived from the work done in treatment sessions with three of our patients. The same examples were used in the self-help manual *Coping with Depression* (Blackburn, 1987).

Example 1. *Basic assumption: I must be liked by everybody. If people do not like me, this means that I am worthless.*

Advantages of this belief

1 It makes me behave nicely to everybody. (100%)

2 People will think well of me. (100%)

3 I can have many friends. (100%)

(+300%)

Disadvantages of this belief

1 It makes me vulnerable to different people's likes and dislikes. (100%)

2 Since people are different, I have to be many different things to different people, trying to please everybody at once. (70%)

3 I find myself doing things I do not really want to do in order just to please people. (80%)

4 I cannot express my own opinion in case it displeases somebody. (50%)

5 I need constant reassurance as I cannot always tell whether somebody likes me or not. (70%)

6 If somebody is in a bad mood and is not being particularly nice, I think that it's something to do with me and I feel bad.

(100%)

7 It makes me avoid social situations in case people do not like me. (100%)

8 Since it is impossible to be liked by everybody, I put myself in a no-win situation which gets me depressed.

(100%)

_____

(−670%)

Thus, though the patient derives benefits from his silent assumption, the costs are excessive, so that on balance it is to his advantage to hold a less black-and-white belief. This may be something like: 'It is nice to be liked, but I don't need to be liked by everybody. My personal worth does not depend on the love and affection of everybody I meet'.

Example II. *Basic assumption: I must do everything perfectly, if not, people will not respect me and I am worthless.*

Advantages of this belief

1 It makes me try hard to do well. (80%)

2 It makes me produce good work and be successful. (100%)

3 When something goes well, I feel really good. (100%)

_____

(+280%)

Disadvantages of this belief

1 It increases my anxiety, so that my performance suffers. (100%)

2 It stops me from doing many of the things I would like to do, because I may not succeed. (80%)

3 It makes me very critical of myself so that I cannot take pleasure in what I do. (100%)

4 I cannot afford to let my mistakes be noticed by anyone, and therefore I probably miss out on valuable constructive comments. (60%)

5 When I am criticized, I become defensive and angry. (50%)

6 My successes are undermined, because any subsequent failure wipes out their significance. (60%)

7 I become very intolerant of others. I find so many faults in others, that I cannot be warm and friendly. I will end up without any friends.   (70%)

8 I can never think well of myself because it is impossible to get it right all the the time.

(100%)

9 Because I get so upset by failures, I cannot use them as valuable experiences to learn how to do things better the next time.   (50%)

(−670%)

More flexible form

Further discussion may lead to a more flexible form of the same assumption: 'If I put less emphasis on perfection, I would be less anxious. This would, more than likely, increase the level of my performance. It certainly would make my work and leisure time activities more enjoyable. Perfection is an ideal which does not exist in reality. To pursue something which is unattainable is a loss of time and energy'.

Example III. *Basic assumption: My worth depends on the approval of others; if somebody disapproves of me or thinks badly of me, it means I am worthless.*

Advantages of this belief

1 It makes me try and do things correctly at work.

(100%)

2 It makes me considerate towards others.   (100%)

3 It makes me popular.   (100%)

(+300%)

Disadvantages of this belief

1 It makes me excessively self-conscious. I am always watching other people to assess what they think of me.   (100%)

2 It makes me less assertive than I could be in certain situations and then I feel that people are taking advantage of me.   (50%)

3 It makes me keep aloof from people, in case they get to know me better and find out about my faults.   (70%)

4 I can only be comfortable with a few people I know very well, my family and my girl-friend, as I have to be on the watch with everybody else.

(70%)

5 I cannot afford to say what I think in case it is not the right thing. (40%)

6 At work, I get very anxious in case my colleagues think that I am not doing something correctly. (100%)

7 Nearly every day, somebody says something that I interpret as criticism or disapproval and this makes me feel depressed. (80%)

8 I avoid doing something that I have not done before, in case I do not do it well. (80%)

9 If I do not know something, I cannot ask somebody in case they think I'm ignorant or ineffectual or ridiculous. (60%)

(−650%)

The conclusion, therefore, is: 'Needing the approval of everybody I meet makes me depressed and anxious a lot of the time and constrains my behaviour. It is satisfying to have the approval of others, but my standards and judgement matter as much as those of others and, therefore, my worth cannot depend on everybody's opinion'.

Such exercises will not, of course, change a life-time schema immediately. The patient is asked to keep a copy of the advantages and disadvantages listed in the session and as a homework assignment, he may add other items that come to mind in the following week. Moreover, whenever he sees himself reacting with distressful feelings in typical situations, he is to take note and make a conscious effort to rehearse his revised schema.

Rehearse Evidence

The therapist can also query the *evidence* for the patient's belief. Is it true that somebody who is disliked by some others is worthless? Can he think of somebody he dislikes? Is this person worthless? Can he think of somebody he likes a lot? Is this person liked by everybody? Does he always make himself agreeable to everybody? Does he say 'no' at times?

Can he think of somebody who is successful and generally well respected? Does this person do everything perfectly? Is his performance always at the same level? What about the way the patient thinks of others? Does he dismiss people as worthless if they make mistakes? In fact, does he know anybody who does everything perfectly?

Does he approve of everything in the people he likes and respects?

If he does not approve of certain habits or behaviour of others, does that decrease these individuals' worth? Are they liked and approved of by all others?

When the patient considers the evidence for his cherished belief in this way and finds that it is largely contradictory, he is willing to consider an altered version which is likely to make him less vulnerable to depression and/or anxiety.

The *'downward arrow'* technique illustrated in the previous section to identify schemata can be conveniently used to modify the bottom line. This time, each thought which had been left unchallenged is examined in the same way as automatic thoughts are examined (see pp. 74–82). For example, in the first illustration the thoughts can be answered as follows:

Thought: She must have told him to say she was out if I rang.

Response: I am jumping to conclusions. There is no evidence that she did that. She has never done that before. It is not like her. She could not know I was going to telephone, especially since I have not called her in a long time, as I was feeling so low.

Thought: She does not like me.

Response: She has shown a lot of attention and consideration for me recently. She has been my friend through thick and thin since we were at school. Where's the evidence that she does not like me?

Thought: There's something wrong with me, that's why she is avoiding me.

Response: First of all, there is no real evidence that she is avoiding me — she never has in the past. If she was avoiding me this time, this does not mean there is something wrong with me. She may have been unwell or very busy. Who knows? I am personalizing, relating other's behaviour to me, when there may be no connection at all.

Thought: People will not want to have anything to do with me. They will reject me.

Response: I'm overgeneralizing, making everybody the same when people differ a lot. Some people may not like me, but I know that some do. After all, some of the people I don't like appear to be very popular.

Thought: I am unlovable, worthless.

Response: If some people don't like me, this does not mean I am unlovable. They are not the arbiters of who is lovable or who is not. People have all sorts of likes and dislikes. I know that I have faults, but who hasn't. I also have many qualities. Assets, my therapist called them. I remember we made a list some weeks ago. I was surprised how good it looked when we looked at all the evidence. Therefore, I am a worthwhile person in my own right, regardless of what some people may think.

Thought: My life is not worth living.

Response: My life's worth does not depend on whether people like me. I've worked out that I am a worthwhile person in my own right. I must remember that. I have worthwhile things in my life, for example, my child, my parents, my job *and* some good friends.

Another approach is to help the patient *contrast the short- and long-term utility* of his personal rule. The self-control model (Kanfer, 1971; Rehm, 1977) has particularly emphasized a defect in self-monitoring in the emotional disorders. Depressed and anxious patients have been found to attend selectively to immediate rather than delayed outcomes of their behaviour. As shown in the examples contrasting the advantages and disadvantages of personal rules, these can sometimes be advantageous for the patient but the advantages are often only short-term. The perfectionist may feel good because work is going well and he feels in control of the situation. The love-addict can feel good, because he has made new friends and many people have been attending to him. The therapist may point out that the patient's basic schemata are helping him to strive successfully in these particular directions at the present moment but can he keep it up? Can he work at that level always and guarantee success? Can he make and keep new friends always? What other sources of pleasure and satisfaction would he have to forego? How vulnerable will he be to frustrations, disappointments, depression and anxiety? Thus, the basic rules may be useful on a short-term basis, but, on a long-term basis, would they be more useful in an altered form?

Similarly, the therapist can query the *validity of the personal contract*. Silent assumptions often present themselves as contracts: If I do *this*, *that* will follow. For example, 'If I do what others expect of me, they will love me'; 'If I do not make mistakes, people will respect me'; 'If I am nice to other people, they will be nice to me'. The therapist can help the patient renegotiate his contract in more realistic terms.

T: I have the impression that you have signed a contract for yourself which you are compelled to fulfil if you are to avoid penalties: 'If I do everything perfectly, I shall be respected and loved by all'. The penalty would be loss of respect and love and, therefore, unhappiness.

P: Yes, it sounds like that. I've always believed this since I was a child. My mother use of say: 'If you do this well, mummy will love you'.

T: OK. So you drew up the contract when you were a child. Now that you are an adult, do you think the contract is still valid? Would you draw a similar contract now?

P: It's silly, but I've never thought of it like that. Of course children don't have the experience to draw valid contracts!

T: Right. Can you imagine that a business man would allow his child to draw a business contract for him? Or that the Law Society would employ children to draw up legal contracts?
(*patient laughs*)

T: OK. Let's try a more adult contract. How would that read?

The discussions in therapy sessions should always be followed by an appropriate homework assignment, be it completing the list of advantages and disadvantages, answering automatic thoughts or checking out the evidence for and against. A powerful way of *reality testing* a basic assumption is to engage in *response prevention*, that is deliberately disobeying the personal rule in order to verify the consequences. For example, the patient who must always acquiesce to everything that is asked of him for fear of being rejected can practise saying 'no' on some occasions and test out the effect on his friends. The perfectionist, who normally spends hours on a task to try and get it perfect, can practise spending half the time on the same task; the individual who feels that he must appear competent in all situations in order not to feel anxious can actually declare his uncertainty or lack of knowledge by asking questions and check whether people look down upon him and dismiss him as a nobody. Reality testing is particularly indicated for anxious patients—for example, engaging in activities where they will not have complete control of the situation (example, social interaction) or engaging in anxiety-provoking situations (example, giving a public talk) and checking whether they can tolerate the anxiety without something awful happening. This technique has been well tried in behaviour therapy where exposure techniques are used to counteract obessional or avoidance behaviour.

Summary

In this chapter, we have described, with illustrations, the numerous therapeutic techniques which the cognitive therapist may use during the course of treatment. Some of these techniques are commonly used in the course of behaviour therapy, but most are specific to cognitive therapy. We would like to emphasize that trainees should consider the techniques defined here as illustrative of the style and method of cognitive therapy, rather than as representing a finite list which they have to learn and adhere to. Within the cognitive therapy method, the creative therapist will discover and use techniques which are appropriate to individual problems and individual cases.

References

Abramson, L. Y., Seligman, M. E. P. & Teasdale, J. D. (1978). Learned helplessness in humans: critique and reformulation. *Journal of Abnormal Psychology*, **87**, 49–74.

Bandura, A. (1977). *Social Learning Theory*. Prentice Hall, Englewood Cliffs, New Jersey.

Blackburn, I. M. (1978). *Coping with Depression*. W. & R. Chambers, Edinburgh.

Blaney, P. H. (1986). Affect and memory: a review, *Psychological Bulletin*, **99**, 229–46.

Brown, R. A. & Lewinsohn, P. M. (1984). *Participant Workbook for the Coping with Depression Course*. Castalia Publishing Co., Eugene, Oregon.

Burns, D. (1980). *Feeling Good: The New Mood Therapy*. William Morrow & Co., New York.

Clark, D., Salkovskis, P. & Chalkley, A. (1985). Respiratory control as a treatment for panic attacks. *Journal of Behaviour Therapy and Experimental Psychiatry*, **16**, 23–30.

Ellis, A. (1926). *Reason and Emotion in Psychotherapy*. Lyle Stuart, New York.

Kanfer, F. H. (1971). The maintenance of behaviour by self generated stimuli and reinforcement. In: Jacobs, A. & Sachs, L. B. (eds) *The Psychology of Private Events: Perspectives on Covert Response Systems*, pp. 39–59. Academic Press, New York.

Meichenbaum, D. H. (1977). *Cognitive Behaviour Modification. An Integrative Approach*. Plenum Press, New York.

Pignatello, M., Camp, C. & Rasar, L. (1986). Music mood induction, an alternative of the Velten technique. *Journal of Abnormal Psychology*, **95**, 295–7.

Rehm, L. P. (1977). A self-control model of depression. *Behaviour Therapy*, **8**, 787–804.

Weissman, A. N. & Beck, A. T. (1978). Development and validation of the dysfunctional attitude scale. *Paper presented at the Annual Meeting of the Association for Advancement of Behaviour Therapy, Chicago*.

Wolpe, J. (1958). *Psychotherapy by Reciprocal Inhibition*. Stanford University Press, Stanford, California.

Part 2
Application of Cognitive Therapy
Illustrated by Case Studies

Chapter 5
First Interview and Conceptualization

In this chapter, we describe the presentation of a depressed and an anxious patient, the first cognitive therapy interview and the provisional conceptualization reached at the end of this first interview. For completion's sake, the same two cases will be followed up through therapy in the next two chapters. We have chosen cases which illustrate the methodology described in the previous chapters and have changed the names and some of the details for the sake of confidentiality.

A depressed patient

Reason for referral

Jennifer, a 32 year old married woman, was referred to the hospital out-patient clinic by her general practitioner because of further threats of suicide.

History of present illness

Two weeks previously, Jennifer had taken an overdose of 40 paracetamol tablets, only mentioning it to her husband the next day after she had started vomiting. She was admitted to the self-poisoning unit of a general hospital for 2 days and subsequently she had felt increasingly suicidal and frightened.

Jennifer and her husband had been having marital therapy sessions at fortnightly intervals over the previous 9 months. These sessions had been exploring, in detail, Jennifer's very close relationship with her parents and her need to separate from them.

Shortly after the overdose, Jennifer and her husband went to see her parents to explain what was going on. This turned into a tumultuous visit, with Jennifer saying hurtful things to both her parents. Subsequently, she had felt increasingly depressed and suicidal, feeling that she had lost her parents' love and support and that she was unable to go on. She had been feeling increasingly depressed and desperate over the previous 3 months.

Mental state

Jennifer was a slim, pale, woman, impeccably dressed, who talked in a very quiet, gentle manner. She made no eye contact, wept copiously

99

and had a fine tremor of both hands. She admitted to having felt depressed for 18 months, with a worsening of her mood over the last 3 months. She described herself as a complete failure and often thought of suicide, especially in the morning. Her appetite had been poor and she had lost 1.5 stone (9.525 kg) in weight over the last year. Her concentration was poor. She had lost interest in her usual activities; she had become increasingly withdrawn, and did not want to meet people; for the last 8 months she had been unable to cope with housework. Her husband had arranged for a friend to help in the house and since this friend had been cleaning and managing the house, she had felt increasingly useless. She had lost her libido completely over the last year, felt listless and tired and could not be bothered with anything. Her sleep was very disturbed with initial, middle and late insomnia and she showed diurnal mood variation with lower mood in the morning. She had both psychic and somatic anxiety symptoms, with shaking, nausea, palpitations, butterflies in the stomach, and inability to sit down for any length of time.

Previous psychiatric history

Depression had been treated by her general practitioner with amitriptyline and diazepam 3 years previously; overdose of diazepam a year previously; overdose of amitriptyline 6 months previously; overdose of paracetamol 2 weeks previously.

Previous medical history

Nothing of note.

Family history

Both parents were still alive. The *father*, 65, was a retired civil servant. He was in good health and had a very close relationship with the patient who claimed that they idolized each other. The *mother*, 60, was in good health and described as generally anxious and nervous. Jennifer said that she was very close to her mother too. The maternal grandmother was still alive and the patient visited her regularly. The patient had had a strict and rigid upbringing, not being allowed to assert herself or show anger.

Jennifer was the eldest of the family, with two brothers who were married and lived in different parts of the country and an unmarried sister who lived with the patient from time to time. Jennifer considered her sister to be prettier and more talented than herself and she resented her monopolizing her family. There was no family history of mental illness, except that when the children were young, the patient's mother had 'suffered from her nerves', but as far as she was aware, she had received no treatment.

Personal history

After a normal birth, Jennifer had an unremarkable childhood. She went to a local school where she was an average scholar who tended to be victimized and bullied by the other children. She left school at 15 and worked as an office clerkess for 2 years before doing a 3 year course for general nursing. After having left home at 17, she visited her parents regularly twice a week. She worked full-time as a nurse until she had her first child and then part-time until 3 months ago when she was dismissed because of recurrent illness and absenteeism.

Marital history

Jennifer had never had a boyfriend before she got married. In fact, her long-term plan was to go to a divinity college and then work as a missionary abroad. She had met her husband, Jim, 10 years previously and they were married within a year. Jim was a civil servant, 5 years older than the patient, and was also interested in church activities. After they married, they did a lot of charity work in a poor area of the city, visiting parishioners, holding prayer meetings in their home and helping the needy. Their home was always open to all comers and Jennifer had to drive her husband about on their evening activities, as he suffered from weakness in one leg which prevented him from driving. All this meant that Jennifer and her husband had very little time together or time for leisure activities.

There were three children, a son aged 6 and two daughters, aged 8 and 4 years. The two older children were at school and the youngest attended a nursery for part of the day.

Diagnosis

Unipolar primary major depression, endogenous subtype.

Severity

Moderately severe, with serious risk of suicide. Hamilton Rating Scale for Depression (17 items version): 28; Beck Depression Inventory: 30.

Clinical decision

In view of her past treatment with tricyclic antidepressants in adequate doses for at least 15–18 months, the choices were mono-amine oxidase inhibitors, electroconvulsive therapy (ECT) or psychological treatment. The clinical team's decision was to try cognitive therapy on its own at first. Jennifer would be admitted to the ward and discharged for out-patient treatment as soon as possible.

First cognitive therapy interview

T: When we met yesterday, we discussed mainly how you have been feeling recently and your general life situation at the moment, such as your family and parents. I wanted to make sure that I understand exactly how bad you'd been feeling in yourself and what symptoms had been bothering you. This will allow us to monitor your progress through treatment. What I would like to do today is get an idea of what specific problems have been bothering you and make a plan for treatment. Is this all right with you?

P: Do you think you'll be able to help me? Things are too bad to do anything about them now. Nothing is going to change.

T: Well, I know that this is what you *believe.* You told me that's why you want to kill yourself. I would like to examine these problems with you to see whether, *together*, we can work out alternative solutions. Do you think that would be worth doing?

P: Maybe.

T: OK. We have 1 hour. What I plan to do is look at the different areas of your life which you are having difficulties with and then tell you a little bit about the sort of treatment we are envisaging and see what you think of it.

What sort of problems do you see in your life at the moment? . . . What do you find difficult to deal with at the moment?

The therapist has set an agenda and begun to establish a collaborative relationship by asking for the patient's reaction (see Table 3.3).

P: Everything; everything is a mess. I have failed at everything.

T: You have failed in every aspect of your life?

P: Yes, I'm no good at all.

T: What do you feel you have failed at?

P: I'm a bad mother and a bad wife.

T : You feel that you have failed in your role as a mother and as a wife. Are there other ways in which you consider that you have failed?

P: I'm a bad daughter, a bad sister, a bad friend, a bad Christian — everything.

T: Let's try and look at each of these aspects in turn. How are you a bad mother?

P: I am supposed to be a trained nurse and I can't even look after my own children. I can't play with them or cuddle them. I want to be left alone. A friend and my sister have been looking after them and after the housework.

T: How long have you been unable to look after the children?

P: It's a good 3 months now. I feel resentful and jealous when the children go to my sister, instead of coming to me when they need comforting.

T: Do they always do that?

P: More and more. They don't like me any more.

T: How does that make you *feel* when you think they don't like you any more?

P: In despair. They would be better off without me.

T: Do you mean that if you kill yourself, the children would be happier?

(*patient cries*)

T: I see that this is a very important area and we'll have to get back to it — the reasons why you have been feeling that you would be better off dead. Let's look at these other roles where you consider that you have failed. What makes you a bad wife as well?

P: Poor Jim. He works so hard and when he comes home, he gets no comfort. Our sex life is non-existent.

T: You feel that you are to blame for this?

P: Of course, who else is to blame? I told you I am a total failure. I neglect my chilren, I make my husband's life a misery; I cannot stand having my sister in the house any more, she is trying to take over everything. I shouted at my parents 2 weeks ago and made my mother cry. I won't see my friends any more, because I am jealous of them and think they are trying to steal Jim away from me. I've given up all the work I used to do for the Church, Sunday school, flower arrangement, visiting, everything. I am just bad and lazy. A friend is looking after the house now. I can't even do that any more. (*patient is sobbing*)

T: I see that you blame yourself for a number of things — in fact, you see yourself as having failed in nearly every aspect of your life, if not in every aspect, and this makes you feel very bad indeed. We will have to see later whether you are as blameworthy and bad as you consider yourself at the moment. It may be that you are being excessively harsh on yourself. We will be able to discuss this. Let's see whether there are other areas of your life causing problems.

Note that at this stage, the therapist does not attempt any modification or intervention method. Her main aim is to have a general idea of what is bothering the patient. She makes a summary of what the patient has said, thus communicating her attention and understanding and looks for other areas where intervention is needed. In particular, she lets the patient know that she is aware of her suicidal wishes.

P: Well, there is the long-standing problem that I'd been discussing with Dr T. — my relationship with my parents. I haven't cut the umbilical cord yet, he said. It's pathetic. Here I am, a married woman with three children, and I still cry when my parents leave after a visit. We had a very close relationship in the family. I think I should not have got married.

T: In what way do you feel that this 'uncut umbilical cord' is a problem to you?

P: I feel torn between my parents and my family. My mum and dad never approved of Jim. Maybe they were right. I should perhaps have gone to college and pursued my career as they wanted me to, instead of getting married. I wanted to become a missionary, help other people. I wouldn't be in such a mess now. I should have become a missionary. I think that's what God intended for me. I am being punished for not doing his will.

T: Do you really believe that? That if you had gone to college and become a missionary instead of getting married things would have been better? 100%?

P: I don't know any more. That's the problem. I am so exhausted all the time, I can't sleep, I can't make up my mind about anything. I don't know what's right and what's wrong any more. It seems disloyal to talk about my marriage like this.

T: So, another area of concern for you is your relationship with your parents, your wish to please them and your doubts about your marriage. In addition, your sleep is affected, you feel generally indecisive and tired. It sounds as if you also blame yourself for being disloyal when you have doubts about whether you did the right thing when you got married. Is that right?

(*patient nods in agreement*)

Again, the therapist makes a summary to express her understanding and to make problems more amenable to solution.

T: Is there anything else which has been causing you problems?

P: I think I'm just lazy. My husband thinks so too. No backbone, he says. I can't bear to see the state the house is in. I used to keep everything just right. And now you should see it.

T: Would you say that you were houseproud before?

P: I don't know. But I can't stand the mess. I have always liked everything to be perfect — everything in its place.

T: Did you manage to keep the house '*perfect*' with three young children and a job as well?

P: Well, in fact, it used to get on Jim's nerves. He used to say that all my cleaning and tidying restricted the children — that the house was more like a museum than a home.

T: How did that make you feel?

P: Angry. He makes me angry the way he throws his things about. The place is like a pig sty. There is just too much to do. I can forgive the children for leaving their toys about, but he could be more careful.

T: And what do you do when you are angry? Do you let him know how you feel?

P: I just withdraw into myself. I feel guilty. One should not get angry.

T: Do you get angry with other people too?

P: Yes, and it's so wrong. I get angry with my sister; the way she is always right and makes me feel inferior. I even shouted at my parents 2 weeks ago. This is what made me take the overdose. I don't think they'll ever forgive me.

T: Did they say that — that they would not forgive you?

P: No, but that's what my mother used to say when I was a child — to get angry is bad and to show it is even worse. It shows a lack of self-control and it's not Christian.

The therapist notes the possibility of a perfectionist attitude and a moralistic attitude towards the expression of anger, but again does not take up these points at this stage.

T: All right Jennifer. Let me try and summarize what you have told me so far and we'll see whether I have got it right.

You have been feeling pretty bad over a long time, but particularly so over the last 3 months.

You consider that you have failed in your various roles — as a mother, a wife, a daughter, a sister, a friend and an active Christian. And you blame yourself for that.

You feel low, you cry a lot, you feel exhausted and find it difficult to make decisions. You haven't been able to do a lot around the house and, therefore, you call yourself lazy. You blame yourself again there, because you have not been able to keep up your high standards of cleanliness.

There is a long-standing problem with your parents, in that you feel overattached to them. This makes you feel torn between them and your husband. In fact, you feel that perhaps you should not have got married and then you blame yourself for having this thought.

There is also a problem with anger — some people and some things make you angry. You then blame yourself for getting angry, because you think it's wrong and unchristian.

Things have got so bad that you took an overdose 2 weeks ago. You still think about suicide and this frightens you. Is this right? Have I got the main points? Is there anything you want to add or correct?

The therapist breaks down what the patient has communicated into discrete areas. This procedure communicates to the patient that she has been listening attentively and that she has understood the explicit and implicit meaning of what was being said. It leads to possible solutions, facilitates the prioritizing of targets for therapy and encourages hope.

(*patient is crying*)

T: What's going through your mind now? Is it something I said which is making you cry?

P: No. I was thinking that you must find me pathetic, that you won't take on somebody like me.

T: This is what flashed through your mind just now? And how did you feel?

P: Hopeless. Nobody can help.

T: So, you were reading my mind? You *knew* what I was thinking and it made you cry?

This is said with a smile which introduces some humour to relieve the patient's state.

(*patient smiles back*)

T: OK. Let me tell you what I was really thinking. As we discussed yesterday, we would like to keep you here in hospital for a few days, because of your high level of distress at home at the moment, and also, because we are stopping your medication. We think that the antidepressants haven't helped you a lot over the last few months and you also worry about the possibility of an overdose. Is that right? While you're here, we will begin a new type of treatment which does not involve taking pills. This treatment is called 'cognitive therapy'. Let me tell you what this involves.

The therapist then describes cognitive therapy as indicated in Chapter 3. First, she describes the structure of therapy. While the patient is in hospital, she and the therapist will meet for 1 hour every second or third day and after discharge they would meet twice weekly at the outset and then once weekly probably for about 12 weeks. Then she explains the basic model of cognitive therapy (that is, we feel and act according to our interpretations of situations, our thoughts or cognitions) using a vignette as a general example, as described in Chapter 3. Then the therapist uses an example provided by the patient herself.

T: You have described many instances today where your inter-pretations led to particular feelings. You remember when you were crying a little while ago and I asked you what was going through your mind? You told me that you thought that I considered you pathetic and that I wouldn't want to see you for therapy. I said that you were reading my mind and putting negative thoughts in my mind which were not, in fact, correct. You were making an *arbitrary inference*, or jumping to con-clusions, without evidence. This is often what happens when one is depressed. One tends to put the most negative interpretations on things, even sometimes when the evidence is contrary and this makes one feel even more depressed. Do you recognize what I mean?

P: You mean even my thoughts are wrong?

T: No, not your thoughts in general and I am not talking about right and wrong. As I was explaining before, interpretations are not facts. They can be more or less accurate but they cannot be right or wrong. What I mean is that some of your interpretations, in particular those relating to yourself, are biased negatively. The thoughts you attributed to me could have been accurate. But there were also many other conclusions you could have reached which might have been less depressing for you, in that they would reflect less badly on you. For example, you could have thought that since I was spending time with you, that meant that I was interested and that I wanted to try and help. If this had been your conclusion, how do you think you would have felt? Do you think you would have felt like crying?

P: Well, I guess I might have felt less depressed, more hopeful.

T: Good. That's the point I was trying to make. We feel what we think. Unfortunately, these biased interpretations tend to occur automatically. They just pop into one's head and one believes them. What you and I will do in therapy is try and catch these thoughts and examine them. *Together* we will look at the evidence and correct the biases to make the thoughts more realistic. Apart from the work that we'll do together here, we will also usually decide on some sort of homework for you to do between sessions. This will relate to what we have been discussing and ensure that you are working on the problems — not just for 1 or 2 hours when you come to see me. You may, for example, test out a different way of doing something to check what results you get or you may try to attend to some of the thoughts which make you sad, anxious or angry and note them down. You then bring the homework here and we'll look at it together. Does this sound all right with you?

P: Yes.

T: OK. We spent a great deal of time today trying to establish the various areas of concern which you may have. I'm going to read these back to you now, for us to decide on which problems to discuss first.

1 The various ways in which you feel you have failed.

2 The way your depression is affecting you, in particular the difficulty in making decisions, loss of interest, inactivity, tiredness, restlessness, and problems with your sleep.

3 There is a problem with tidiness in the house.

4 You mentioned the feelings for your parents and for your husband. You feel that maybe you should not have got married.

5 There is some problem with anger.

6 And, of course, the immediate reason for you being in hospital,

which is your preoccupation with ending your own life. Have I got all this right?

P: Hmm . . . Yes, I think that's about it.

T: Which of these different areas is the most important to you?

P: I don't know — I'm all mixed up.

T: What's causing you the most concern at the moment?

P: I guess it's how I feel about myself. The fact that I've made such a mess of everything.

T: That's right. I agree with you. You told me that's why you keep thinking of killing yourself, in particular, because of the row with your parents. That's what we will consider first. By the way, do you notice that you've been able to take a decision just now, although you said you cannot make up your mind about anything? What do you make of that?

(*patient smiles*)

T: And I don't think it was an easy decision. So, we now have some evidence that you can make decisions at times! We have also been discussing for nearly an hour; have you been able to follow it all?

P: I think so.

T: That's good. It means that we also have some evidence that you can concentrate for a while and, in spite of your restlessness, you've remained seated in this chair here.

The therapist stresses a success experience (decision taking) and other aspects of the patient's behaviour which may indicate to her that things may not be as hopeless as she paints to herself. The therapist then suggests as the first homework reading the booklet Coping with Depression (Beck & Greenberg, 1973). The rationale is to learn more about cognitive therapy. Jennifer can underline the parts which she feels applies to her most. A second task is to make a list of the reasons why she thinks she has failed as a daughter. This particular aspect is chosen first because it is likely to be related to other problem areas, the patient's role as a wife, her ambivalence towards her marriage and her inadequacy as a housewife. It is also known that the immediate precipitant for her last suicidal attempt was an argument with her parents. Suicidal wishes and behaviour were not chosen as an immediate target in this case, as the patient was temporarily admitted to hospital and the main motive for suicide, a sense of failure, was chosen as the primary target. Behavioural deficits, for example, inactivity and restlessness, would be best tackled on an out-patient basis in the patient's home environment. The sleep disturbance could be assessed objectively on the ward.

T: Do you foresee any difficulties with the two tasks we've discussed?

P: I don't know whether I'll be able to do it.

T: That's all right. The emphasis is on *trying* and not necessarily succeeding. Note what problems arise, if any, and we can discuss them next time we meet in 2 days' time. If you cannot read the booklet at one go, try to read bits at a time and take a break when your concentration flags, OK? About the list of reasons why you have failed as a daughter, don't worry if you don't manage. We'll do it together next time. If you manage to make a start, that's fine. It will save us time.

Now, is there anything you're not clear about? Is there anything I've said which rubbed you up the wrong way?

The therapist asks for general feedback, in particular for the patient's reaction to her to check for negative automatic thoughts.

P: No, nothing.
T: How are you feeling now?
P: I feel a little bit more hopeful, thank you. I'm glad not to have to take drugs any more.
T: Well, we can try and see how you get on with the cognitive therapy alone. If necessary, we can review this decision after a few weeks.

Conceptualization

It is useful for the therapist to summarize the diagnostic and first cognitive therapy interviews in a *functional analysis*, as described in Chapter 1 (p. 5). This exercise will help in formulating a strategy for treatment and in making a provisional formulation of the case. Jennifer presented with the following main dysfunctions:

Functional analysis

Affective: Sadness; anger; anxiety.
Behavioural: Inactivity; restlessness; avoidance of social situations.
Physical: Sleep difficulties; fatigue; loss of libido; loss of appetite.
Cognitive: Self-blame and guilt; hopelessness and suicidal wishes and behaviour; indecision; sense of failure; feeling of inferiority.

Emerging themes

Emerging themes

- Excessive tidness.
- Overloaded work schedule.
- Lack of assertion.
- Ambivalent relationships with parents, sister and husband.
- Moralistic attitude regarding anger and helping others.
- Jealousy towards sister and suspicion of husband's possible involvement with other women.

In terms of the schematic description presented in Figure 3.1, the following conceptualization was made.

Current stresses

Current stresses

The current stresses in Jennifer's life were mainly related to depression itself. She could no longer function in her various roles in the home and outside. Her activities as home-carer, part-time nurse and church helper were severely curtailed, giving her a sense of inadequacy and of inferiority. The quarrel with her parents was traumatic in that she had never shown anger with them before. It could mean, in her opinion, a rupture with them.

Living situation

Jennifer came from a middle-class background, her husband was in full employment and she herself in part-time employment. There were no financial problems. She had a lot of support from relatives and friends, so that the home could still run smoothly. There were no problems regarding the three young children. However, Jennifer did not appear to be able to confide in anybody. Her close relationship with her parents was not of the confiding type; she did not trust her sister and friends, and too many of the problems, from her point of view, were related to her husband to be able to confide in him.

Past traumas

There was not much of note there, except for her view that she had lost her life's ambition to become a missionary when she got married. Having had no close friends at school where she was bullied, she might have developed a view of herself as unpopular and inferior somehow.

Examples of negative cognitive triad

- *Negative view of self*
'I have failed at everything.'
'I am a bad mother, a bad wife, bad daughter, bad Christian.'
'I am lazy.'
- *Negative view of the world*
'Things are too bad to do anything about them now.'
'The house is like a pig sty.'
'There is just too much to do.'
'My sister and my friends are trying to take over.'
- *Negative view of the future*
The children 'would be better off without me.'
Feelings of hopelessness and despair.
Suicidal ideation and suicidal behaviour.
'Nothing is going to change.'

Predominant emotions

Depressed mood, anger and despair.

Examples of automatic thoughts

'Everything is a mess.' *Processing error:* overgeneralizing, catastrophizing.

'I have failed at *everything*.' *Processing error*: overgeneralization, catastrophizing.

'Who else is to blame?' *Processing error*: personalization. 'I *should* have become a missionary.' *Processing error*: arbitrary inference leading to categorical imperative.

'One *should* not get angry.' *Processing error*: overgeneralization leading to categorical imperative.

'You must find me pathetic.' *Processing error*: arbitrary inference.

Themes

Failure; being in control; tidiness; moral values.

Loss: loss of parental love (quarrel with parents); loss of achievement (career); loss of control over environment (help from others, untidiness).

Personality characteristics

Jennifer had been introverted throughout her life, tending to prefer her own company, though she could mix with people. Her social role, however, had been more in a helping capacity than for the enjoyment of the company of others. She described high standards relating to sense of duty, moral code and performance. She seemed to need to feel in total control of things, of her own emotions, as well as of her environment. Therefore, on the whole, she appeared to show more autonomy than sociotropy, valuing performance, freedom and control.

Formulation

She had been able to cope well until about 18 months ago, when possibly she could no longer hold control of her environment and of conflicting 'duties' to the same extent, because of excessive demands upon her time. The lack of control had revived regrets about her past decision to follow a career as a missionary. It had also exacerbated the conflict between her duties as a wife and her duties as a daughter. Having to rely on others had aggravated her sense of loss of control and created feelings of inferiority.

Suitability for cognitive therapy

Jennifer was a promising candidate for cognitive therapy. She expressed herself in pyschological terms and could consider alternative views when her own interpretations were queried. Her problems could be viewed in psychological terms.

An anxious patient

Reason for referral

Sheila, a 44 year old single woman, was referred by her general practitioner because of her dependency on Valium, anxiety symptoms and increasing difficulties coping with work.

History of present illness

During the previous 3 months, Sheila's general practitioner had advised her to decrease her dosage of diazepam (Valium) from 30 mg to 10 mg per day. This had resulted in frequent visits to the surgery, with complaints of a resurgence of her anxiety symptoms and particularly an increase in panic attack frequency. She was a secondary school teacher and had been given temporary promotion at work in the previous 6 months, whilst the permanent Head of Department was signed off work suffering from depression. This promotion had resulted in increasing hostility towards her from other staff in the school, especially from a younger man in her own department. She was having difficulty coping with her teaching commitments and in carrying out administrative tasks connected with her work.

Mental state

Sheila was a tall, medium built, handsome looking woman, who was dressed plainly. She had a rather loud voice and was loquacious. She described having been anxious for 6 years and having been much worse in the past 3 months. She had had occasional panic attacks which had become more frequent in the past 6 months. These attacks had occurred twice in the previous 4 weeks and were described as 'coming out of the blue'. The main symptoms were an intense feeling of being out of control, tachycardia, dizziness, choking and hot flushes. During periods of anxiety, she felt tense and shaky, with palpitations, sweating and a feeling of being choked. She had difficulty concentrating, and was short tempered. She almost always had difficulty falling off to sleep and suffered from frequent headaches. Although she described herself as always having been a 'worrier', in the past 6 years she found that she continuously worried about her work, her family and whether or not she could cope. She felt as though she had no reserves to cope with new crises.

Previous psychiatric history

Over the past 6 years generalized anxiety had been treated by her general practitioner with diazepam and sleep problems with temazepam. She had not received temazepam for over 1 year.

Previous medical history

None.

Family history

Sheila's *father* was a 78 year old retired shopkeeper. He retired around the age of 60 after having had a myocardial infarct and had had several other infarcts over the past 15 years. He was no longer very physically active and tended to worry about his health. Sheila had a reasonably close relationship with her father. She regarded him as having been a caring father who was rather indulgent towards his children at times. Her *mother* had died 4 years previously, of cancer. She described her mother as being a 'worrier'. Her relationship with her mother was not a close one. Indeed, it had been stormy during her adolescence. Her only sibling was a younger sister, aged 41. She had always been very close to this sister. The sister had emigrated to Australia with her husband and two children 2 years previously. There was no family history of psychiatric disorder.

Personal history

Personal history

Sheila was born in Edinburgh. She had a happy childhood and remembered being particularly close to her younger sister when they were both teenagers. She attended the local primary and secondary schools and was an able student who passed exams without having try too hard. She made some friends at school but tended to socialize with her sister in her teenage years. Her relationship with her mother became difficult when she began dating, as her mother always demanded that she bring young men home to meet her parents. Sheila felt that her mother criticized any boyfriend she had. On several occasions, she disobeyed her mother and this led to several serious arguments about boyfriends. Sheila left home to go to Aberdeen University to study mathematics. She obtained a good Honours degree and went on to teacher's training college there before returning to Edinburgh for her first teaching post. During her time as a student, she had one serious sexual relationship which ended after 2 years, when this man left university to work abroad. She had remained as a teacher in the same school since she began teaching. The only other serious relationship she had lasted for 8 years. This involvement was with a married man whom she had met through friends. He eventually left his wife but, at this point, she had decided to end the relationship due to feelings of guilt at the break-up of his marriage and friends' disapproval. The following year, her mother died after a lengthy period of illness. Although her mother had not approved of her affair, she became more supportive of Sheila in the final years of her life. Since her mother's death, Sheila had become more involved with her father who was now quite dependent on her. The loss of her sister, when she emigrated to Australia, had left her relatively socially isolated in the past 2 years. She had very few interests and hobbies although she claimed to like music and walking.

Diagnosis

General anxiety disorder (with panic attacks).

Severity

Spielberger State Anxiety Inventory: 50 ; Beck Depression Inventory: 12.

Clinical decision

It was considered desirable that Sheila should continue to reduce her intake of diazepam and that additional medication would not be useful. However, given the severity of her symptoms, pyschological treatment was indicated. Cognitive therapy would be attempted, along with a plan to reduce her dosage of diazepam gradually.

First cognitive therapy interview

T: Last week, we spent a lot of time going over how you have been feeling over the past 6 months. You were telling me that you have been troubled by increasing symptoms of anxiety and panic over that time, especially since your general practitioner, Dr. A., decided to try to reduce your dose of Valium. It seemed from what you said last week that you want to continue cutting down your Valium, but that it has been more troublesome than you expected. Is that right?

P: Oh yes, it's been really awful and all these horrible feelings and panics have come back.

T: Dr A. and I have talked over the phone, as I said we might, and he has agreed to cut this down very slowly. You are on 30 mg of Valium now and it will be reduced gradually, under his supervison. I hope that is OK with you?

P: I'm really glad about that. I had been worried that I was expected to come straight off it. That really terrified me, especially after all that I've read in the papers about people going 'cold turkey' after coming off Valium.

T: Well, I'm glad to hear you are pleased to be coming off it more slowly. I knew you have been on Valium for 6 years and so it must have been rather frightening to think you had to come off it immediately. We'll come back to how we can plan to reduce your dose gradually, later. Today, I would like to get a clear picture of the problems which have been bothering you recently, so that we can begin to decide what can be done to help. Would that seem a reasonable plan for today's session?

The therapist has set an agenda. By asking for feedback, the beginnings of a collaborative relationship are established (see Table 3.3).

P: Well, its all been piling in on me recently. I don't know where to start. Sometimes I just get so frightened, I can't think straight. I just don't seem to be logical about things. It just goes round and round in my head.

T: So everything seems to be piling in on you just now and it's difficult to sort it out. Maybe we can see if we can look at what is happening in your life just now that is difficult. What do you think are the main problems? We'll just take things bit by bit. We have an hour.

P: Since I cut down my Valium, I've not been coping at school. I've been acting Head of Department for 6 months and it's been nothing but trouble.

T: So, even before you cut down your Valium, there were problems at school. Tell me about that.

P: Well, my Head of Department went off sick — with depression. (*patient smiles*) It's ironic isn't it? — here I am coming to see you. I should be off sick too.

T: Is that what you think? That you should be off sick too?

P: No, I really want to keep going. It's just that I don't know if I can. It's just so difficult.

T: What are the things that you find difficult to cope with at school? Once we know what these are, we can see what might help you to cope.

P: It's the people, the other teachers, that are the problems. I really just cannot cope. They are making it really difficult for me. You see, I didn't apply for this acting Head position; I was asked to do it and the others resent it. I can't do the job without their cooperation and the more anxious I get about it, the worse the situation gets.

T: So your job is made more difficult by not getting cooperation from the other teachers. Is that *all* of them?

P: Well no, one in particular. John X is really tricky. I think he thought he should have got the job of Head. He's been really sneaky and deliberately makes things awkward. He makes me anxious.

T: What is it about him that makes you anxious?

P: Every time I have to ask him something I get anxious. I can't cope with him at all. He always gets the better of me.

T: So you think you can't cope with him and that he always get the better of you, and that makes you anxious. Does he behave in a way that you find difficult?

P: He is very clever and everyone thinks he's very good at his job. I find him very sarcastic and I'm not good at coping with that. It always puts me off my track and I get very flustered in front of him. I can't think straight and I can't get the words I want to say. I'm sure he thinks I'm a fool.

T: How do you *feel* when you think that?

P: Well, it makes me feel terrible — that I must be really stupid and awkward and not at all in control of the situation. I just get so tense about it all and I can't see how it can get any better.

T: I see. This man, because he behaves in a sarcastic manner towards you and maybe also because you believe he thinks he should be acting Head of Department rather than you, makes you feel awkward and out of control. Well, we will have to look more closely at this problem as it obviously affects how you view yourself at work. Are there other things about work which bother you?

P: It is mainly John X, but if I do get very worked up or if I haven't had a good night's sleep, I really do find it difficult to teach. I'm all behind in administration too. I'm really in a mess with that too. I keep getting worried that I'll have a panic attack in front of a class and the more I worry, the more anxious I get.

T: Have you had a panic attack in front of a class?

P: I did the other week. I had been at a staff meeting and went from there to teach fourth formers. They're not an easy group and the meeting hadn't gone well and I just got in a terrible state.

T: What happened?

P: I was trying to explain a complicated maths problem and I wasn't doing it well. I couldn't get the right words. The kids were looking bored and I knew I'd lost them. My heart started pounding and I felt really dizzy and hot and couldn't concentrate. I was really out of control. I just couldn't get my thoughts together. I just wanted to run out. It was awful. Now I'm really scared it will happen again. I'm beginning to think I'll have to give up teaching.

T: You think that you would have to give up your job if you had a panic attack again at work?

P: That's how I feel sometimes. After that panic attack, I took 2 days off school. I just couldn't face going through it again.

T: It seems to me that you are putting a lot of pressure on yourself by thinking that having another panic attack would mean giving up your job. This is obviously very important and I think we need to look at this more closely, don't you?

P: Oh, definitely. I really don't know what I'd do if it happened. I know it is putting me under a lot of pressure, even though I've only had one attack at school.

T: Well, that is an important bit of information. You've only had *one* panic attack there. We will come back to this too. But let's move on, as I want to know about other problem areas for you. So far, I have found out that you are having some difficulties with coming off Valium; that your anxiety symptoms have worsened and that you have had some panic attacks. You have also told me about how your promotion has led to problems at school, particularly with one man who is difficult to cope with. What other areas of your life concern you?

At this stage, the therapist is concerned to get an overview of the patient's problems. Summaries are used to feed back to the patient that her problems are noted. No attempt is made to modify problems.

P: I know, only too well, that I do have difficulties in relationships. I'm sure it has a lot to do with my mother, although I really cannot put the blame on her. I haven't had a relationship since she died.

T: When was that?

P: About 6 years ago. It was around the time she got ill with cancer that I decided to cool off the relationship I was in. My mother had always given me the impression that I couldn't choose suitable boyfriends. She always seemed to disapprove. She was ill and I felt really sorry for her and yet I found it very difficult to tell her that.

T: Was that around that time when you first went to your GP and got Valium?

P: I'm not sure. Yes, maybe.

T: So, tell me about this time. There were difficulties surrounding your relationship with your mother and at the same time you were thinking of breaking off the relationship you were in. Is that right?

P: I was under a lot of pressure. This man I was involved with was married. He was very unhappy in his marriage and I met him through friends. It began as a flirtation, but I was soon seeing him regularly and we got close. We saw each other over many years. We decided to get married and then it all went wrong. His wife wouldn't agree to a divorce and then she got very angry and raised an action for divorce on the grounds of adultery. It got really messy. Friends were asked to testify that we were having an affair and they took sides with her. I just felt so awful, I got really uptight then.

T: Well that sounds like an extremely difficult time for you. What effect did this have on you?

P: I got really anxious, couldn't sleep, was very worried about whether we were doing the right thing. You see, I really didn't think it was right.

T: What was it that you didn't think was right?

P: It was as if as soon as he was really serious about me, I doubted my own judgement. I just felt I couldn't go through with it, particularly with my mother being ill too. I didn't want to hurt her.

T: So what did you do?

P: I cut off from him. That scared me too. I didn't know I could be like that. I pretended it didn't matter, but I knew it did. I haven't had a relationship since then.

T: Is that something you would like us to look at too? It does seem to be important.

P: Yes. I'm 44 and sometimes I feel very lonely since my sister left for Australia. I have felt more in need of an intimate relationship. I know men and me haven't exactly been a great success. I need to sort it out. Do you think that it's possible? I keep thinking it's just me and there's nothing I can do about it now.

T: Well, there are important issues here for you. Just because there have been problems in the past doesn't mean that you cannot have a relationship now. The relationship you talk about seems to have been complicated to start with. Your mother's attitude to the men you chose may have also had an influence on how you feel about relationships. We can look at this together in another session — would you agree?

P: Yes.

T: Tell me a bit about your family. You say that your sister's leaving left a gap in your life.

P: I have always been close to her. She was my best friend. I really miss her a lot. (*patient looks tearful*)

T: I cannot help noticing that you are looking sad when you are talking about your sister.

P: (*breaks into tears*) I really miss her. I feel that my closest ally has left me. There's just me and my father now and I find him really difficult to cope with since my mother died. He's become so frail and dependent on me. I just have to do so much for him and I'm often very short tempered with him, especially if I'm uptight or if my day at school has been bad, which it usually has been.

T: Is your father quite difficult to cope with?

P: Yes. He's had all those strokes and he keeps thinking he's going to have another one. He oftens phones me late at night to tell me he has pains. I can never tell if they are really serious or whether I should get up and drive round to see him. If I don't go, I lie there worrying, feeling guilty. What if he died in the middle of the night? I just can't sleep.

T: Has he been more dependent on you since your mother died?

P: There was a big change in him then. He's become very niggly about things, really fussy about his food. He hardly ever goes out unless I take him. I really think he would like me to move in with him.

T: Has he said this?

P: Well no, it's just an impression I get. I just feel he's such a burden and I'm his mean-hearted, neurotic daughter.

T: What makes you think you are mean and neurotic?

P: I *should* be more patient. I should be nicer to him. He's old and I really do care for him a lot.

T: You really do feel you are not a good daughter to him?

P: Mm.

T: How much do you believe that?

P: Quite a lot.

T: Maybe you are being overcritical of yourself. I know that ageing parents can be a considerable problem and as your sister is no longer here, the whole burden of looking after your father does seem to lie with you. This is another problem area we'll be able to discuss at more length another time.
(patient nods)

T: Are there any other areas of your life which upset you that we haven't covered?

P: No, not really. These are the main problems. I feel that these are enough for me. If there were any more I just wouldn't cope at all. As it is, I barely cope.

T: That's why you are here isn't it, to see if together we can help you to cope better. Let me just see if I have a reasonable idea of what problems you have just now, so that we can go on from here to make a treatment plan. Would that be OK?

P: Yes.

T: **1** You have been feeling that you have not been coping well in several important areas in your life.
2 As a result of this, you have been troubled by anxiety and panic attacks, both of which have got worse in the past few months. Difficulties sleeping, feeling tense, sweating, feelings of choking and palpitations particularly bother you. These are worse in a panic attack when you also feel hot and dizzy and out of control.
3 You want to come off Valium but you want to do this slowly.
4 There are problems at school, particularly with asserting yourself with one male teacher in your department. Also, there are problems with keeping up with administrative tasks.
5 You have told me about difficulties in deciding about relationships with men and how you believe your mother's attitude towards your past boyfriends may have been a factor in this.
6 Since your mother died, your sister left for Australia. Your father is worried about his own health and you find being the only one looking after him difficult.
7 You miss your sister a lot and have no other close friend. Have I got that right?

The therapist describes cognitive therapy using the vignette described in Chapter 3 as a general example along with some examples from the patient herself. She again summarizes the main problems the patient has discussed. Feedback is designed to ensure that a reasonably accurate understanding of the main problem areas has been reached. Targets for therapy and possible strategies for change are selected.

P: (*pause*) It sounds very strange to have the problems said back to me like that. I didn't think I'd made myself very clear at all.

T: You seem surprised by that.

P: I am. I didn't think I could be that clear about things, as I had been feeling very overwhelmed and confused and felt that things were out of perspective.

T: Do you still feel confused and overwhelmed?

P: No, I don't. But it does seem like a lot of problems.

T: There are some problems but you managed to be very coherent about telling me about them. So, it's good that you can do this, as it will help us to tackle these problems.

The therapist emphasizes to the patient that she has managed to break down the problem areas and by doing this, the patient no longer feels so overwhelmed by her difficulties. An outline of the structure of therapy is given. The therapist suggests that she and the patient will meet weekly for about 6 weeks and then have another two or three sessions thereafter with several weeks in between them.

T: Which of these problems do you want to start off with?

P: Well, really the worst thing is feeling anxious. It's so frightening. I know if I could do something about that I'd feel more able to cope.

T: OK. That seem a very good starting point.

The therapist suggests that the patient reads Coping with Anxiety (Beck & Emery, 1985). She explains that this booklet will help in understanding how cognitive therapy works. She is asked to note which parts of the booklet make more sense to her. She is asked not to decrease her Valium at all over the next week, but to keep an hourly record of how anxious she feels on a scale from 0 to 10, using the Weekly Activity Schedule (see Appendix 3). This task is chosen so that a more detailed account of fluctuations in anxiety can be made and to find out if degree of anxiety may be related to specific situations. From her account, high anxiety levels are associated with several of the problem areas outlined: her difficulties coping with her colleagues at work, some classroom situations and the problems associated with her father.

The difficulties surrounding relationships were not chosen as an immediate target for treatment as she has no current relationship. No immediate change in the dosage of Valium was made so that a baseline assessment of anxiety symptoms could be made. Any change in dosage may also have been perceived as too threatening at this stage in treatment, particularly since altering the dose appeared to have increased the likelihood of panic attacks.

T: Do these tasks seem relevant to you?

P: Yes, they do, they shouldn't be difficult to do. It's really just helping to get a picture of what's happening to me.

T: That's right. Do you envisage any difficulties in the next week with this?

P: Just one. What if I have a panic attack at school?

T: OK. Let's look at that briefly. How many attacks have you had at school?

P: Well, only one.

T: So, only *one*. And from what you told me, that day had been a difficult one for you. You had had a difficult staff meeting just before teaching that class. Do you think that had made you particularly vulnerable to having an attack?

P: Yes, I suppose so.

T: Is this week likely to be as stressful as then?

P: No, that week was really bad.

T: So, let me put a theory to you. If you are under a lot of stress and are feeling anxious, you may be more likely to have a panic attack. What do you think?

P: Hmm.

T: This week is not that likely to be stressful so that decreases the likelihood of a panic attack — though it may be possible that one occurs.

P: Yes, I can see that. But I'm really scared of having one.

T: Yes. So part of the problem is that you are getting anxious about becoming very anxious and having a panic attack. Is it a bit of a vicious circle?

P: Oh yes.

T: Shall we go into this next week? We will make it a priority on our agenda. Would that be all right?

P: Yes.

T: OK, let's do that. Now is there anything that I have said that you didn't like or that you would want me to make clearer.

P: No, I don't think so.

T: How are you feeling about what we have discussed?

P: Much better, thanks.

T: So, we'll meet again next week and begin to try to tackle some of these problems you have been having. We must also remember to have a review of how the treatment is going in about 3 to 4 weeks' time.

Conceptualization

Following this first treatment interview it is useful to make a provisional formulation of the case to aid in generating a treatment plan. (See Chapter 1, p. 8: Functional analysis)

Sheila presented with the following main dysfunctions:

Affective: Anxiety, sadness, anger.

Behavioural: Inhibition; avoidance of anxiety provoking situations; disruption of speech.

Physical: Physical symptoms of anxiety and panic: tension, shakiness, sweating, choking, tachycardia, dizziness, hot flushes.

Cognitive: Fear of losing control; fear of not being able to cope; worry about the future; indecision; difficulties concentrating; self-blame and guilt; sense of being overwhelmed and overburdened.

Emerging themes

- Impaired work performance.
- Disorganization at work.
- Lack of assertion.
- Loss of confidante (sister) and consequent social isolation.
- Ambivalent attitude towards father whom she regards as being dependent on her.
- Ambivalence towards forming relationships with men, possibly due to mother's critical stance towards boyfriends.

Using the schematic description presented in Figure 3.1, the following conceptualization was made.

Current stresses

Sheila's current stresses are related to anxiety and to the convergence of situations which have highlighted more long-standing problems. Her temporary promotion at work, with its additional responsibilities, has emphasized her difficulties asserting herself and increased her sense of being unable to cope. Her general practitioner's instruction to decrease her dosage of Valium has led to an increase in anxiety symptoms and several panic attacks. The loss of her sister, who was also her confidante, has left her bearing sole family responsibility for her father and socially isolated.

Living situation

Sheila is from a middle-class background. She is a full-time teacher in a secondary school, has never been married, and lives alone in her own home. She has no financial problems. Since the break-up of her last relationship about 6 years ago, and her sister's emigration to Australia, she has no one to confide in and her social life is very restricted. Her father is suffering from ill health and worries about having another myocardial infarct. He lives in the same neighbourhood as Sheila and she has taken on the responsibility of looking after him, doing his shopping with him, helping him with housework and so on.

Past traumas

Her relationship with her mother appears to have been a particularly problematic one. Her mother was critical of her choice of boyfriends and this led to many arguments throughout her adolescence and adulthood. Sheila is aware that her mother's attitude towards her having relationships with men may have strongly influenced her own stance in such relationships. She may, therefore, have difficulties in relying on her own judgement in choosing men and in deciding on the nature of and degree of commitment to the relationship. The timing of the break-up of her previous relationship and her mother's illness also suggests this is an important area of concern.

Examples of anxiogenic cognitive triad

- *View of self as vulnerable*
  'I can't cope.'
  'I must be really stupid and awkward.'
  'I should be nicer.'
  'I should be more patient.'
  Feelings of being out of control.

- *View of the world as threatening*
  'My father . . . is such a burden.'
  'The other teachers are the problem — they make it difficult for me.'
  Feelings of being overwhelmed.

- *View of the future as unpredictable*
  'I'll have to give up teaching.'
  'If there were any more problems, I just couldn't cope at all.'

Predominant emotions

Anxiety, anger.

Examples of automatic thoughts

'I must be really stupid.' *Processing error*: arbitrary inference
'I can't think straight.' *Processing error*: overgeneralization
'I really just cannot cope.' *Processing error*: overgeneralization, catastrophizing.

● *Themes*

Inability to cope, losing control.

Being vulnerable and overwhelmed by difficulties at school and with father.

Loss of confidante (sister).

Loss of self efficacy in relationships with men.

Threat: Assertiveness situations at work and with father.

Personality characteristics

Sheila shows herself to be a rather introverted, autonomous woman who has some difficulties in making close relationships. She has difficulties in situations where she has to assert herself and is lacking in self-confidence. She sets herself high standards in relation to work performance and in her role as a dutiful daughter. She has a need to feel in control of social and work situations. She values control and has difficulty in situations which are not clear cut.

Formulation

The onset of Sheila's anxiety state began around the time her mother became ill. Her mother was critical of her, particularly regarding her choice of male friends and Sheila had difficulties asserting herself with her mother. Rather than following her own judgement, she 'resolved' the guilt she felt in her relationship with her fiance by ending the relationship. In the past 6 months, her promotion at work to a managerial position has highlighted her difficulties in asserting herself and the extra burden of duties has increased her sense of being out of control. Her previously close relationship with her father has been threatened by his becoming more physically and emotionally dependent on her. This has led to her feeling vulnerable and unable to cope.

Suitability for cognitive therapy

Sheila would appear to be a good candidate for cognitive therapy. She views many of her problems psychologically and can make some links between her attitudes towards herself and her current problems.

References

Beck, A.T. & Emery, G. (1985). Coping with anxiety, Appendix I. In: Beck, A. T. & Emery, G. *Anxiety Disorders and Phobias.* Basic Books, New York.

Beck, A.T. & Greenberg. R. (1973). *Coping with Depression.* Institute of Rational Living, New York.

Chapter 6
Progress in Therapy:
a Depressed Patient

In this chapter, we discuss the progress in therapy of the depressed patient described in Chapter 5. Our intention is to illustrate the structure, style and content of cognitive therapy as described in Part 1 of this book, so that the reader can familiarize himself with the practical application of cognitive strategies and techniques. Parts of each session will be transcribed verbatim and the progress from session to session described.

Course of treatment

Jennifer was in treatment for 12 weeks, receiving 20 cognitive therapy sessions in all. She remained in hospital for 2 weeks during which time she was seen three times a week. After discharge from hospital, the sessions were reduced to twice weekly for 4 weeks and then once weekly for 6 weeks. Over the 6 months following discharge from treatment, she was seen for follow-up at 6 weekly intervals on four occasions.

Session 2

This session took place 2 days later. The ward nurses had noted that Jennifer looked depressed most of the time, but she was able to socialize with the other patients, being particularly attentive and helpful to an old lady suffering from senile dementia. Her behaviour changed when she had visits from her husband and from a friend, when she became agitated and tearful. Her sleep at night was disturbed and she had spent part of the nights sitting up and talking to the night nurses.

At interview, in response to the general question 'How have you been since we last talked?', she said that she was feeling a bit better.

T: Do you have any comments to make on our last session? Has anything come to mind since?
P: No, I don't think so.
T: Is there anything special you would like to put on the agenda today?
P: Well, my sister rang up yesterday and said she wanted to come and visit me in hospital. I refused to see her. Do you think I was being selfish and mean?

T: We can set some time to discuss this. I would also like to look at the homework you were going to try. Is that all right with you?

The patient acquiesces and the therapist first enquires how the patient got on with reading the booklet Coping with Depression. She says that she had found it interesting—it seems to describe her (this is typical of most depressed patients' reaction to the booklet).

T: You recognized some of your thoughts in it? Can you show me which, in particular?

P: Well, it was reassuring somehow to see that other people must react the way I do. I thought I was the worst possible case. This bit here, the 'checklist of negative thoughts' is just me — especially the 'negative opinion of yourself', the 'self-criticism and self-blame' and the 'negative expectations of the future'.

T: Good, you are beginning to recognize the negative bias in your thinking. The next task will be to correct the bias. This brings us to your second home assignment. One of the negative assessments of yourself was that you have failed as a daughter. Did you manage to begin to itemize the reasons why you think so?

The patient produces a sheet of paper with two items on it:
1 I do not visit as much as I should.
2 I got angry with them and told them to stop interfering in my marriage.

T: Are there other ways in which you think that you have failed as a daughter?

P: Well, it's what I told you last time — they did not really approve of me marrying Jim.

T: So, you feel that you have failed because you disobeyed them?

P: Not exactly disobeyed, but went against their wishes.

T: I see; are there other ways in which you have failed them?

P: It's the way I feel. Sometimes I feel that I never want to see them again. I get so angry. At other times, I feel that I don't really want to be cut off from them. They don't deserve to be treated like that. They've never done me any harm. It's normal that they should want to see more of me and their grandchildren.

T: All right. We have four reasons here: You don't visit often enough; you got angry with them and told them to stop interfering; you went against their wishes in marrying your husband and then, you feel that you are being unfair to them, somehow, both in your feelings and your behaviour? Is that right? Is there anything else?

P: That's it really.

T: How much does all this bother you? How does it make you *feel*?

P: It's on my mind a lot of the time.

T: And what do you *feel* when these thoughts come to your mind?

P: Low, angry, guilty, disgusted with myself.

T: That's a whole lot of distressing feelings, isn't it? Let's look at each of these thoughts in turn and see what you mean exactly and whether there is any misinterpretation or whether there is anything you can do to change the situation.

It is important for the therapist to elicit the feelings related to what the patient is communicating, first to underline the relationship between thoughts and feelings and secondly to verify that there is an improvement in the patient's feeling state at the end of the treatment session.

T: OK, take this sheet of paper so that you can record some of the points which come up. We will both write down the main points as they come up. Take the first thing that you wrote down: 'I do not visit as much as I used to'. What does that mean to you?

P: It means that I'm failing in my duty and my love. They must feel hurt.

T: So, let's write this down and see whether there's any evidence for what you say. How often did you visit in the past?

P: At least twice a week and they would come round twice a week.

T: Was this right then? Was this often enough?

P: I thought so — but Jim used to complain.

T: He didn't think it was right?

P: He thought it was too much, that I spent too much time with my parents.

T: Do you think that he was wrong?

P: I suppose he had a point. My schedule used to be very busy — a continuous rush every day of the week.

T: Does it look as if there isn't an absolute correct frequency of contacts with your parents? That different people can have different views about it?

P: Yes, I suppose it depends on your point of view.

T: Exactly. When you said 'I don't visit often enough', it sounded as if you were failing a set, universal standard. How often were you visiting before you came into hospital?

The therapist began to make a point about standards of right and wrong to introduce some flexibility in what appeared overstrict standards, and to alleviate guilty feelings. This was going to be a recurring theme with Jennifer, supporting the original formulation of overstrict moral standards.

P: About once a fortnight, I suppose, sometimes once a week. They were coming once a week for a little while. Except that since I fell out with them a fortnight ago, I haven't been to see them at all and Jim has told them not to come for a while.

T: So, there's been a 2 week break. Now, what is the reason for this, is it because you are an unloving and undutiful daughter or is it because of some other reason?

P: Well, I still love them and I do not want them hurt. The real reason why it happened was that I had this row with them.

T: Yes, this was the other reason why you blamed yourself. You got angry and told them to stop interfering. What was making you angry?

P: They kept saying that Jim was not looking after me well enough, that he was making me ill, and that the children and I should go and stay with them for a while. Jim was very angry too; I'd never seen him like this.

T: Let's say you had a friend who confided in you that she had fallen out with her parents because they kept blaming and criticizing her husband. Would you feel that she was failing as a daughter?

P: It would depend on what the husband was being blamed for. Whether he deserved it or not. I wouldn't think she was in the wrong, if the criticisms were unjustified.

T: Right. Did Jim deserve the criticism that he was making you ill?

P: No, I don't think it's right. He is doing all he can, even taking time off work to be with me and help in the house. He would miss the children terribly if we all upped and went to stay with my parents.

T: Here we are then. If your friend would not be in the wrong in the same circumstances, how come you blame yourself?

P: Yes, maybe I was right. But I still feel guilty.

T: I can understand that. It may have something to do with your attitude to anger which, as you said last time, is morally wrong. We'll have to come back to that another time. We'll put it on the agenda. Let's see where we've got to then. What can you write on your sheet in answer to the first item. I don't visit as much as I should.

P: I think, maybe, it's not easy to say what is the right frequency of visits. Different people will have different views, for example my husband, my parents and myself.

T: That's right. You can write this down and the real reasons why your visits had decreased. Can you summarize what these were?

P: Mainly the row we had.

T: Is there anything else that might explain the decreased frequency of your visits?

P: I don't know . . .

T: Well, are you your usual self at the moment? Have you been doing everything as you used to?

P: No, of course not.

T: So, maybe one of the reasons is just that you are ill at the moment. You are trying to get over a depression and this has affected many areas of your life. Is that right?

P: Yes, that's true.

T: So you can write this down as well. Now, about the row you had with them, it seems that we agree that there were reasonable causes for that; you had a row because they were making unfair criticisms of Jim, not because of some flaws in your character. Is that right? So, you can take a note of this as well.

Thus the therapist helps the patient in summarizing the discussion and by encouraging her to write down the main points, she trains her for future homework and ensures that a record is kept that can be referred back to. The strategy has been to decrease self-blame and challenge overstrict moral rules expressed in 'shoulds'. The techniques have involved 'distancing', that's asking the patient to view the situation from somebody else's point of view (her husband and a friend), re-attribution (to depression and not to inner weakness or fault) and correction of a personalization error (the change in pattern of visits is due not to her 'badness' but to a reasonable reaction to unfair criticism).

T: How are you feeling at the moment?
P: A bit less confused. Maybe I also feel less bad about myself.
T: Good. This leaves us with two more points: you went against your parents' wishes when you got married and you are treating them unfairly. Since time is passing I suggest we leave this for next time, because I would like to begin to talk about the special item you put on the agenda for today, namely your refusal to see your sister. Is that right?

As homework, the therapist suggested that Jennifer should write down what it meant to her to have gone against her parents' wishes when she married. This ensured that the topic chosen for this session was followed through. Questioning regarding her sister revealed that they had been quite close as children, but the sister, who was 2 years younger, was considered by all to be brighter, more gifted and more beautiful. The sister, however, had made 'a mess' of her life, not finishing her course in languages at university and going from job to job. She was currently unemployed, and had been, over long periods of time, lodged and fed by the patient. Jennifer felt that she had been used by her sister who had not shown enough gratitude. Recently, as stated in the case description, the sister had helped in looking after the family, because Jennifer was unable to do so. This area of concern appeared too vast and important to reach closure in this session. The therapist, therefore, expressed her understanding by summarizing the main issues — these related to feelings of inferiority, jealousy and anger and a general attitude of entitlement, that is her sister should treat Jennifer well because she had been kind to her. Partial help at this point was provided in the following way:

T: If your sister wanted to visit you, do you think that she had you in mind or herself? I mean was she trying to be helpful to you?

P: I suppose so.

T: OK, would it have made you feel better if she had come?

P: No, it would have made me feel worse! I might have been rude to her.

T: So, you would have felt worse and maybe she would have felt worse if you had been rude to her. So, do you think you did the right thing by telling her not to come?

(patient smiles broadly))

T: Maybe you were being considerate for her feelings, instead of 'selfish and mean'. It's nice to see you smile! We're going to stop here. We'll meet in 2 days' time. You're clear about the homework? . . . Is there anything that has rubbed you up the wrong way or that you're not clear about? . . .. OK, we'll meet on Friday.

The strategy at this point was not to pursue the problems in Jennifer's relationship with her sister. The therapist's reasoning was that Jennifer needed to 'ventilate' her feelings on this topic at this particular time, and that it would be more fruitful to pursue the subject of her relationship with her parents at this point. The real problems relating to her sister, sense of duty, difficulty in setting limits, anger and sense of inferiority would probably arise again and were common to the other problem areas.

Session 3

This session took place on the Friday and the decision of the ward staff was that Jennifer could go home for the weekend. She had been on the ward for a week and the nursing staff reported that she appeared less depressed on the whole, that she took part in ward activities and appeared generally calmer and less distressed. She still became tearful and agitated when she had visitors, however, and it usually took 2 to 3 hours for her to regain her composure after the visitors left. She no longer expressed suicidal thoughts and wishes. These observations confirmed that her depression was reactive to problems in her home environment and that the current treatment approach was likely to be the right one.

After the usual short review of the patient's mental state since the last session and asking again for feedback about the last session, an *agenda* was set up. This consisted of: (a) completing the homework regarding her parents' attitude to her marriage and challenging associated automatic thoughts, and (b) eliciting foreseen problems related to the weekend at home and planning for time there. The latter item was put on the agenda by Jennifer who said that she looked forward to the weekend but also felt apprehensive about it.

Jennifer had written down that 'going against her parent's wishes when she married her husband' was wrong because.

1   It showed lack of obedience and respect.
2   They must have known that it was a wrong match for her.
3   She was being punished for not doing God's will.

Thus, ascertaining the meaning of an event had elicited key areas of conflict for the patient: a strict concept of duty, ambivalence towards her husband and a view of her duty as a Christian which was as yet very unclear to the therapist.

T: Let's see why these three points that you've made are so upsetting to you, why they may indicate that you have failed as a daughter. First, by marrying Jim, you showed lack of obedience and respect. Did your parents actually say 'We forbid you to marry him'?

P: No, they would not say something like that. But my mother made a number of discouraging remarks.

T: What sort of remarks did she make?

P: Oh, I can't remember them all — but she made it very clear. I remember she said I was still very young. I was 22 mind you. That I would regret not pursuing my original plans of going to Bible College. That Jim was much older — 10 years older. And so on. You know, on my wedding day, she never came into my room to help me get dressed or talk to me or anything.

T: Did your father also say discouraging things about your marriage?

P: Well, he didn't actually. But he never disagrees with my mother openly. Privately, he told me not to mind my mother, that she was just upset at losing her older daughter, that I should do what I thought was best.

T: So, he at least did not think that you were disobedient and disrespectful.

P: No, he said he was proud of me.

T: It sounds as if neither of them actually said you were disobedient and disrespectful. It's a label that *you* put on yourself. You were 22 years old at the time, an adult, a qualified nurse, in full control of her mental faculties. Do you think you had the right to make your own decisions, your own mistakes even?

P: I suppose so.

T: Well, in so doing, you would inevitably sometimes go against one or other of your parents' ideas, wouldn't you? Is this really disrespectful?

P: I suppose not.

T: Can adults have different opinions about a subject and still respect each other?

P: Yes, of course. And I respect my parents and their opinions even if I don't agree with them always.

T: Right. What about obedience? Where is it written that a 22 year old adult should obey her parents?

P: The Bible?

T: Well, I don't know. Maybe you can check that out. If my memory serves me right, what's written in the New Testament is 'Honour thy father and thy mother'. But I may be wrong. Can you verify this for us?

Note that the therapist works within the patient's own sphere of reference. In Jennifer's case, we often had to have recourse to Christian teachings and the Bible. If the therapist is not familiar with the patient's sphere of reference, it is a useful strategy to set as homework 'data gathering' in the form of polling individuals of his own group or checking a reference book.

T: How much do you believe now that you were disobedient and disrespectful after this discussion?

P: I guess I wasn't, but it looks as if they were right. They must have known better.

T: Yes, that was your second point, that they must have known it was the wrong match for you. Is this true though? What makes you say that it is the wrong match?

P: I feel so hurt when Jim is unkind to me. I immediately withdraw and become depressed. I don't think I love him any more. I can't give him anything, emotionally or physically.

T: In what way is he unkind to you?

P: Verbally — when he criticizes me for sitting about crying doing nothing or when he gets impatient with my nagging him about tidiness.

T: Do you mean that, recently, he has been criticizing your 'depressed' behaviour?

P: I suppose you could call it that.

T: What I mean is, what about before? You have been married for 10 years and you have been depressed for the last 18 months only. Was he unkind to you before? Did he criticize you then?

P: No, not really. He has always been very attentive and kind to me.

T: Was it a right match for 8½ years then?

P: I see what you mean. Maybe he can't cope with my depression.

T: Exactly, it often happens when one spouse is depressed. The other spouse may feel frustrated because he cannot help and may get impatient. Also, when people are depressed, they find it difficult to give out love and affection. They don't like themselves and, therefore, they have no love to give and they feel others can't love them either. Do you recognize what I'm talking about?
(*patient acquiesces, crying*)

T: What I'm saying is that the problems which you describe are recent and coincide with your depressed state. It would be misleading to *generalize* from them. It may be difficult at the moment, but it is necessary for you to look back — to the pre-depression era — and make judgements on that basis. Do you agree with this?

P: Yes, but you see, I've always wondered whether I took the right decision when I married Jim instead of going to Bible College, whether I did not follow God's will.

T: How does one know whether one is following God's will or not?

P: I don't know, but maybe I am being punished for not doing what he wanted of me.

T: You mean that your depression is a punishment?

P: Mmm . . .

T: God is punishing you for taking the wrong decision? Is this the concept you have of God?

P: I don't know. God is also loving and forgiving.

T: You know, Jennifer, I am no theologian, but I know something about depression. There are many causes of depression and, in your case, you have given me a good idea of what's been distressing you. You have just given me a very good example. You blame yourself for a hypothetical situation — not a real failing. You *think* you may have offended God, you don't really know that — you then *think* that you are a bad Christian, which is very important to you, and you naturally feel bad. Anybody who feels that he has failed in an important moral concept would feel guilty and bad about himself, wouldn't he?

P: Of course.

T: OK, what we can do is look back on your decision to get married instead of becoming a missionary. Was it an impulsive decision?

P: No. Of course not.

T: So you weighed up all the pros and the cons and you decided marriage was the better option. Was it the best decision you could take *at the time*?

P: That's what I thought at the time.

T: OK, let's see what the advantages and disadvantages of getting married have been.

Jennifer wrote down in answer to inductive questions, that the *advantages* of marrying Jim were:

1   She has had a lot of happiness in her marriage.
2   Three lovely children.
3   Because of Jim's similar interests, she had been able to be very involved with her local church and help the pastor in his parish work. So, she has been some sort of missionary after all.
4 She had made Jim happy.
5 She had a nice house and a secure future.
6 She had been able to carry on with what she was trained in, namely nursing.

The only *disadvantage* was that she had not been able to go to Bible College and become a missionary abroad.

T: Do you know what the advantages of Bible College would have been?

P: No, I can't say really.

T: Exactly. You know what the disadvantages would have been — you wouldn't have had any of the advantages you've just written down here. This is the nature of decisions isn't it. They are *not inherently* right or wrong. They are just alternatives with their own positive and negative aspects. Moreover, it is fortunate that most decisions are not irrevocable. You try them out and if they do not work, you change course. For example, if the evidence was very much in favour that getting married was disadvantageous for you, you could get out of the marriage and go to Bible College, couldn't you?

P: That's true, I suppose I could do that.

T: When you took the decision you did 10 years ago, you thought it was right. You used your judgement and you even ignored your mother's strong hints — which must have been difficult for you. You've derived a number of benefits from that decision. Is it at all useful to agonize now about whether it was the *right* decision, especially since you can't tell what the alternative decision would have brought you?

P: Well no, It can't be undone, can it? In any case, as you say, I've gained a lot by it.

T: No, it cannot be undone. But you can think about now and the future. I think that there is a lot more we need to discuss regarding your view of your marriage and how you and your husband interact; but, would you agree that decisions about your marriage would be better left for later, when you are back to your normal self?

P: Yes, that's right.

T: And how are you feeling now?

The rest of this session was devoted to the weekend at home. Jennifer worried that she would not be able to cope and that she might get back to square one. It was jointly decided that since we did not know how the weekend would go, she could approach it with an open mind and use it as an experiment to check what difficulties arose. She could write down the problems as they occurred and the automatic thoughts that went through her mind and bring them to our next session on Monday for discussion. Particular attention was paid to preparing for activities.

Because one of Jennifer's concerns was her standard of housework, it was decided to begin a schedule of graded activities. The rationale

*was to relieve the process of decision-making, ensure that not too
much was attempted and hence gain a certain degree of success. This
would decrease the likelihood of self-blame if a great amount of
housework was not attempted. A weekly activity schedule was used
to plan for Saturday — change bedclothes in the children's room and
go shopping with her husband; and for Sunday — help prepare lunch
and go to Church service.*

Homework assignments: Attempt the graded tasks and begin to fill in
the first three columns of the dysfunctional thoughts form.

Feedback: Jennifer said that the discussion about her relationship
with her parents had been helpful. She had never discussed her
ambivalence about her marriage before and she now saw it in a
different way. However, she needed to think about it further.

Session 4

On Monday, Jennifer reported that the weekend had been awful. On
questioning, it transpired that Saturday had been pleasant and she
had managed the two tasks we had scheduled. Sunday did not work
out well. Jennifer got very upset by the untidiness of the house and
she felt she just could not stand it. She had a recurrence of suicidal
thoughts, panicked and decided to come back to the hospital early on
Sunday afternoon. She had not managed to go to Church because she
worried about what people would say to her and what she would
answer.

The In general, she felt a bit better; her sleep was a little improved and
she felt less tired.

The *agenda* consisted of examination of problems arising on
Sunday, with reference to recorded thoughts on dysfunctional
thoughts form:
1   Tidiness in the house.
2   What to say to people who enquire after her health.

T: All right Jennifer, let's look at the weekend in more detail. First,
you told me that it had been awful. Then, it seemed that Saturday
had gone well, but Sunday had not. Do you recognize the bias in
your interpretation there in terms of the list that you looked at in
the booklet *Coping with Depression*?
P: I guess I was overgeneralizing? Not the whole weekend was bad,
but Sunday was pretty bad.
T: That's right. You interpreted the 2 day weekend on the basis of
one day only. What really happened on Sunday?
P: I wrote it down on the form you gave me. I stayed in bed late on
Sunday morning. It was rather nice. Jim brought me breakfast in
bed. When I got up, the bathroom was in a shambles. There were

clothes littered about. Jim had just dropped his clothes on the floor and the bath was filthy.

T: OK, so you wrote down here: 'Jim always gets somebody to do things for him. I can't stand the mess' and you were angry 100%. What did you do then?

P: I tidied up and then I started tidying up the living room.

T: How were you feeling then?

P: I began shouting at Jim and the children and I was crying.

T: What was going through your mind?

P: That I'll never be able to cope with all this mess.

T: OK Jennifer, I see that the plans we had made for Sunday broke down. You got caught up with the housework, you felt angry and then sad. What does it mean to you when the house is untidy?

Tidiness was one of the themes which had emerged from Session I and was one of the goals of therapy. The therapist had formulated that tidiness probably played an important role in Jennifer's sense of control of her environment. At this stage of therapy, the therapist decides not to deal with the topic as a basic assumption or rule, but instead to concentrate on related automatic thoughts and behavioural components.

P: It means being less well organized.

T: Is this bad if you are less well organized?

P: Well, I need things to be well organized, because I normally lead a very busy life. Without organization it would be chaos.

T: OK, would it have been chaos on Sunday if you had not cleaned the bathroom and tidied up the living room?

P: I guess not; everybody else seemed happy enough.

T: What else could you have done?

P: I could have ignored it.

T: Yes. What would have happened if you had asked Jim to do it?

P: Well, that's what he said — that he was planning to do it later.

T: So, he was not expecting you to do it, as you wrote down?

P: Apparently not.

T: How would you have felt, if you had kept to your schedule and waited to see how things developed?

P: I would have felt better very likely. My friend Margaret was going to come round later to help in any case.

T: OK, you can write this down in the fourth column: 'Jim is busy just now and will tidy up later. If not, I can ask him, or Margaret will do it when she comes in. I could try and ignore the mess for a while'.

Jennifer writes down the comments on her thought form. This in-session practice in answering thoughts is essential in training the patient to complete the forms on her own.

T: What I'm also wondering, Jennifer, is how tidy must things be to be well organized? Do you have friends of your own age, with young children?

P: Yes, my friends Anne and Susan. They are not really friends, but I have babysat for them sometimes.

T: Are they normally as busy as yourself?

P: Yes, they do a fantastic amount and they work full time.

T: Are they very tidy always?

P: Susan is quite tidy, but Anne isn't.

T: Would you call Anne disorganized and living in chaos?

P: No, not at all. On the contrary, I admire her very much.

T: Does it look as if you have two sets of rules there, one for others and one for yourself? If your house is not completely tidy, you're disorganized, verging on the chaotic. If somebody else, in the same circumstances as yourself, is not very tidy, that's admirable.

P: I never thought of it that way.

T: What we could do, if that's all right with you, is make a list of the activities you used to have before you became ill. You could write down how you used to pass each day, so that we could decide whether any changes are desirable. Could you do that this week and bring the list for our session on Wednesday or Friday. This would be useful as you are being discharged on Friday and we will have to pay special attention to how you spend your time.

The therapist's strategy is to prepare the way for discharge from hospital. As Jennifer appears generally not depressed when in hospital, but has obvious difficulties at home, it seems that progress would be quicker if she was in her own environment, as the problems could be tackled in reality. The problems at home, apart from that of her relationships, appear to relate to an overloaded schedule and unrealistic expectations of herself.

Finally, the problem of meeting friends and acquaintances is discussed before the end of the session. This is a situation which is often encountered in psychiatric patients as they feel ashamed of their illness and think that people will look down upon them if the truth were known.

T: What did you *think* would happen if you'd gone to church?

P: Lots of people know me there because of the work I do for the church. They would have wanted to talk to me after the service.

T: Why would that be a problem?

P: They would have wanted to know whether I was feeling better and what the problem was. I couldn't stand that. I would have felt ashamed.

T: What would have made you feel ashamed? Have you done anything wrong?

P: Not really. But they would have looked down upon me as somebody pathetic.

T: Is this what you would do if you knew that somebody was being treated for depression, look down upon them as pathetic?

P: Of course not.

T: So, you wouldn't, but they would? Are they different from you?

P: Well, I suppose here I go again, with two sets of rules — one for others and one for me. But, I'm supposed to be strong, always helping others and now I can't help myself.

T: Does this mean that you are weak? Is everybody who comes to see psychiatrists and psychologists weak and pathetic?

P: No, I don't think that. But I've heard people make comments like that.

T: Yes, maybe some do think that. I guess that such people lack experience. They may be completely ignorant about psychological problems. If this is the case, who's problem is it, yours or theirs? If some people are ignorant, who should be ashamed, you or they?

P: That's true. Maybe I should just tell them and not care about it.

T: Well, it may be that you are making inaccurate predictions. Most people know about depression. They've experienced it either in themselves or in friends and relatives. With anxiety, it's the most common emotional disorder. In any case, do you need to go into great details when you talk about your illness?

P: Well, what if they ask what's really wrong?

The therapist and the patient then engaged in a role play, the patient playing the role of an inquisitive acquaintance and the therapist playing the role of the patient. The roles were then reversed. This was done as a game, in a light-hearted way, which Jennifer found amusing. At this point she was smiling broadly.

T: OK, Jennifer. We're going to stop for today. Could you summarize what you think are the main points of today's session?

Feedback: Her double standards had struck her. She was more severe towards herself than others. Perhaps tidiness was not a black and white entity. There were degrees of tidiness and some untidiness did not mean disorganization and chaos. Similarly, it could be that she was not the only person who did understand depression. If some people were ignorant, they needed to be informed.

Homework assignments

1   Continue to monitor automatic thoughts and answer them.

2   Begin to prepare an account of her weekly activities before she became ill.

The ward nurses confirmed their original impression that Jennifer looked well and relatively calm on the ward. She was pleasant to everybody, but tended to keep to herself. Her sleep was still disturbed.

At the next session, she brought back samples of automatic thoughts which she had started to challenge and she had completed a programme of her premorbid activities. The *agenda* was (a) to spend some time on the homework, in particular, to examine her activity level, and (b) to begin to learn techniques which might improve her sleeping pattern.

All the automatic thoughts she had recorded related to her husband and her marriage:

Situation: On the ward, thinking about Jim.

Emotion: Sad (100%).

Automatic thought: I am frightened of being hurt by him (100%).

Her rational response was: I must learn to accept hurt and take it for what it is (100%).

The outcome was: Belief in automatic thought (50%). Sad (35%).

It did not seem to the therapist that the rational response was adequate. Jennifer was giving herself an injunction instead of looking at what the automatic thought really meant and correcting any bias it may contain. On questioning, she revealed that 'being hurt' by her husband meant that he sometimes appeared impatient or ignored her or ordered her to do something.

T: So, you feel hurt when he is impatient or does not pay much attention, or orders you to do something.

P: Yes, I remember a little while back, before coming into hospital, he ordered me to go and get the newspaper for him. I had put it away because I thought he had finished with it. I said that I wouldn't go for it, that he could go himself and he said I'd tidied it away, so I could go and get it.

T: What happened then?

P: I went and got it and then withdrew to the bedroom. I felt so hurt.

T: What did you find hurtful?

P: His anger.

T: And you felt frightened? Did you think that he might physically harm you?

P: No, he would never do that. I'm frightened of the hurt itself — of not being able to stand it and not being able to cope with it.

T: I see. But why is his anger so hurtful? What does it mean to you?

P: I don't know. Maybe it means that he does not love me any more, that he does not want me about.

T: Do you really believe that? What about when you get angry? We have talked about this before. When you get angry with the children or with your parents, does it mean that you don't love them any more?

P: Oh, I just get frustrated and it passes quickly.

T: What about Jim's anger, does it last a long time?

P: No, it does not. It's the hurt which lasts. I can withdraw for days afterwards.

T: And this is what you are frightened of? What you do with the hurt? First of all, would you be as hurt if you did not put such a catastrophic interpretation on his behaviour? He is angry or irritated — anger is a normal emotion, isn't it? Everybody feels it, children, adults, even animals. Jim gets angry because he is frustrated about something. He does not shout, he does not hit you.

P: Well, that would be less hurtful.

T: Right. Secondly, maybe there is a problem about the way you react. You have said before that anger is a problem for you. In a way, you have no model because your parents would not tolerate the expression of anger. We will have to spend more time discussing this, how to deal with anger. Do you see that there is a problem there?

P: I think that one should not show anger.

T: This is a strong rule of behaviour which we must assess another time. It explains why you react in such a hurt way to your husband's anger, controlled as it is. However, people do get angry. Have you ever talked to Jim about your reaction to his anger?

P: No, never. I can't talk about it.

T: That's maybe something that you could do. You could try and tell him how you feel and discuss what's really making him angry. We will be able to practise this in a moment. Let's see whether you can summarize in the rational column on the thought form what we have just discussed.

Anger is a recurring theme and the therapist withholds from dealing at this point with the 'should' which reflects a basic rule. Instead, she elicits the hidden meaning in the situation which triggers the patient's strong emotion. The hurt feeling is caused by the interpretation put on the anger and the frightened feeling is caused by the patient's perceived lack of skill for dealing with the situation.

Jennifer recorded on the dysfunctional thought form that her husband's anger was a normal reaction to frustration, not an indication of loss of love. Loss of love would be a persistent state, whereas his anger blew away quickly. She recorded 10% for hurt feelings in the last column. She recorded that she was frightened because of her lack of skill in dealing with anger and that she needed to practise alternative methods to withdrawing and sulking for days. Fright had now decreased to 25%. A role play was then engaged in where the therapist played the role of the patient. It consisted of explaining why the papers had been put away, apologizing, and asking why this small incident was causing such strong emotions in Jim. The outcome was that Jim's anger was related to Jennifer's excessive tidiness. Jennifer agreed that her tidiness was excessive, as we had discussed before.

Other recorded thoughts related to her feelings for her husband. The patient and therapist agreed to leave these for a later session as they pertained to a particular goal of therapy, namely her role as a wife.

The next stage of the session involved examining Jennifer's daily pattern of activites when she was well. It was a horrendously heavy schedule which the patient agreed was excessive. She said that, once she had written it down, she was surprised at how much she had been trying to do. In summary, she got up at 6.30 every morning, including weekends. She prepared breakfast and got the children ready for school during week days. While the children were accompanied to the bus stop by her husband on his way to work, she started on meticulous housework. This included cleaning all work surfaces, dusting, polishing, washing floors and using the vacuum cleaner all round the house. She then went to the nursery at midday to collect her youngest child and leave her with a child minder on her way to her part-time nursing job, which ran from 12.00 to 5.30 p.m. She got home and prepared supper (her husband and children would already be at home). She then started cleaning and tidying the kitchen and living-room again. In the evening, she was often out, either attending a ladies' group which she ran, or visiting old parishioners. The only free evening of the week was Saturday night, when she enjoyed a quiet time with her husband.

It was agreed that she did not leave herself enough time for leisure activities and that it would be to her advantage and beneficial for her marriage and her children to try an amended schedule in the future. Meantime, when she went home the following week, we would start on graded activities with the aims of resuming her role as housewife and developing a more relaxed schedule.

Finally, as there was no time left to practise relaxation in the session, Jennifer was given a relaxation tape which she would use before going to bed. The rationale for relaxation as an aid to better sleep was explained.

After a final summary of the session and feedback, *homework assignments* consisted of (a) continuing to fill in automatic thought forms, and practising relaxation exercises.

Session 6

A re-assessment of mental state using the BDI and the HRSD revealed a marked improvement: BDI = 18; HRSD = 13. Jennifer said that she no longer had suicidal thoughts. She was pleased with her progress and was hopeful for the future.

The *agenda* consisted of (a) reviewing homework and (b) preparing for discharge and rehearsing possible problems.

Homework review: The relaxation exercises had worked well. She had been able to follow the exercises on the tape and had fallen asleep before the end of the tape. When she woke up at 4.00 a.m. she did the exercises again and managed another 2 hours' sleep. Listening to the tape and following the instructions had not only helped her to relax, but had acted as a distraction from her distressful thoughts and emotions.

The two recorded automatic thoughts related to going home for good.

Situation: Thinking about going home tomorrow.
Emotion: Apprehensive (80%).
Automatic thought: I shall be disrupting a happy home (100%).
Response: None.
Situation: Same as above.
Automatic thought: Jim does not want me home. He does not love me any more.
Emotion: Very sad (100%).
Response: I'm jumping to conclusions without evidence. He does say that he loves me and that he misses me. As I discussed with Dr. B., he may get frustrated, but that does not mean he does not love me. When I am home, I can try and work things out by talking to him more (100%).
Outcome: Belief in automatic thought (10%), Sadness (20%).

The way Jennifer had challenged her second automatic thought indicated that she was becoming more skilful at checking the bias in her thinking and in modifying her negative interpretations. However, at this stage, she was still learning and did not always manage to answer the thoughts.

T: In what way will you be disrupting a happy home?
P: Everything is running smoothly at home. The children have got used to Margaret, my friend, looking after them. Jim is back at work, not having to worry about me.
T: It's good that the home is running smoothly. Does that make you worry less?
P: That's true, but it makes me feel redundant.
T: Redundant and also disruptive, you wrote. Will Margaret continue to help when you go back?
P: I guess so.
T: Will you be able to take back some of the responsibility from her?
P: Yes, that's what I plan to do.
T: Do you think she will like that, having more time to herself, getting back to her own responsibilities?
P: Yes, I'm sure she would.

T: Good. At least one person will be glad to have you back. What about the children? They are being well looked after by Margaret and your husband, but do they miss you nonetheless?

P: Well, they were glad to see me last weekend and on Sunday, when I left to come back here, the little one started crying and Karen, my eldest daughter, said: 'Do you have to go back Mummy?', and she was fighting back tears.

T: OK, does that indicate that they will be happy to have you back, that at least for them you are not redundant and disruptive?

P: I guess so. You always make me see things differently. It's all right while I'm here, but when I'm on my own, all the dark thoughts come back again.

T: I understand that. It's going to take a while for you to begin to see things, including yourself and your environment, in a more realistic light. That's what the therapy is about. OK, the children will be happy to have you back; your friend will be happy to have more time to herself and your husband misses you, as you wrote down here in relation to the second automatic thought that you registered. How does that make you feel? Do you feel as apprehensive about going home?

P: No, I feel better about it now.

A detailed plan of activities for the next few days was then drawn up. The rationale was to *try* only a few activities, as it would be unreasonable for her to expect to be able to function at her previous level — which was excessive in any case.

Homework assignments: (1) Fill in activity schedule and begin to rate for mastery and pleasure. (2) Continue with relaxation exercises before going to bed. (3) Fill in dysfunctional thought forms.

Sessions 7–14

Jennifer was now an out-patient and she was seen twice weekly over the next 4 weeks. She was compliant with homework assignments at all times and never missed appointments. Her progress was slow, but steady.

The recurrent topics of discussion related to the original goals of therapy and tended to be prompted by her records of automatic thoughts and the problems relating to housework and tidiness. One additional topic, which had not been elicited at the first interview but which emerged through the sessions, was Jennifer's compulsion to respond to people's needs and her inability to say 'no' to people. This resulted in unwelcome and excessive demands being made upon her, with ensuing anger and low mood.

In the weeks following immediately after discharge, she brought back a number of thoughts relating to her insecurity in her marriage.

She worried that she might lose her husband either because of his chronic bad health (he had been asthmatic since childhood and, as mentioned earlier on, had a deformity of one foot which prevented him from driving) or because of his involvement with other people, in particular women. She also worried about not being able to share her feelings with him. *Typical recorded automatic thoughts were*:

I can't tell Jim how I feel about him, because I don't know.
I wonder whether I have always resented his disability.
When other women get too close to Jim, I feel insecure.
He treats me the same as Margaret or Helen, I'm nothing special to him.
He is so scruffy, not clean enough. I can't stand it. He should shower more often.
I can't show him any affection.

The *accompanying emotions* were primarily sadness and/or anger.

These thoughts were examined in detail with the aims of helping the patient to clarify her feelings and her thoughts about her husband and of improving their marital relationship. The cognitive bias, which is a common one in depressed patients, was that she was allowing her current mood to distort her view of her husband and then to assume that this current view was reality. It seemed to the therapist that there were also real problems which needed to be worked on.

One of the techniques used was to redress the balance in the patient's appraisal of her husband by asking her to list what she used to admire in him. What are/were the qualities which made her choose him as a husband? She provided a long list, with supporting evidence, of his qualities — he is considerate, generous, intelligent, has a sense of humour, works hard, is nice with the children and has boundless energy. His health was not as bad as she had made out. In fact, since their marriage, she did not remember him taking a single day off work. The only thing she had to do for him was drive him about occasionally. Usually, he was quite happy to walk or use public transport. However, it was true that he spent a great deal of time away from home as he was deeply involved, as she was, in various church and charity activities.

Role plays were used to practise ways of improving her communication of thoughts and feelings to him. The problem of his 'scruffiness' recurred often and Jennifer decided that she would try to talk to him about it. She had never been able to do this in the past, except in a nagging or angry way. Again, role plays were used both to elicit associated automatic thoughts and to practise methods of communication.

It was agreed that they needed to plan to spend more time together, at the expense of dropping some of their charity work; when

Jennifer managed her housework better, this would also give her more time to spend with her husband.

The problem of her insecurity regarding other women was partly based on reality. Jennifer particularly resented the amount of time her husband spent trying to help her friend Margaret and her sister Helen with their continuous problems. Both these women had become very dependent on Jim for advice and moral support. *It seemed that both the patient and her husband shared the compulsive need to help others.*

Having vaguely referred to the problem on several occasions, in the second week after discharge (fourth week of treatment), she described a crisis with her friend Margaret who had continued to spend a lot of time at Jennifer's house, to help with the household.

P: I just could not stand having her about any more. It came to a head with Jim. He would not do anything, so I told her to go because I could not tolerate her presence any more. Jim is very angry about it.

T: And how do you feel about it?

P: I feel incredibly guilty.

T: Guilt is about doing something wrong, isn't it? What wrong have you done in this context?

P: I feel that I was ungrateful and that I haven't been able to cope with a situation my husband wanted me to cope with.

T: Did you tell Margaret why you wanted her to go?

P: Well . . . not entirely. I said that I was extremely grateful for what she had done for us for the last few months, but that now it was important that I learn to cope on my own.

T: This was not the reason?

P: It was, but I also thought that she was getting emotionally involved with Jim and he with her.

T: Is that right? Have other people also noticed that and corroborated your impression?

P: Yes, at least in the case of Margaret. My mother had commented on this and Jim's parents have also made allusions, and I know that they have talked to him about it. She has dropped all her own activities and just panders to his every need.

T: OK, was this situation doing anybody any good then?

P: Not to me anyway.

T: To your husband?

P: No. In fact, he had said to me months ago that he wanted her out of his life. He felt oppressed by her and all her problems, but did not know how to get rid of her.

T: What about Margaret, was it a good situation for her?

P: I don't think so really. It wasn't going to do her any good in the long term. It would be to her advantage to have a life of her own, get a job and make other relationships. She was also seeing a doctor at some point for depression and that's what he advised her to do, I remember Margaret saying.

T: So, Jennifer, altogether it seems that you have done something good, instead of something wrong.

P: Maybe. But why couldn't Jim have done it himself? He is so angry now.

T: Yes, he is angry at the moment. People sometimes feel angry when they are told that they have not behaved correctly. But, perhaps he is thankful to you as well?

P: Yes, maybe. He did say he had made a mistake by getting so involved with Margaret, but could not get out of the situation.

T: Here you are. Are you feeling as guilty now?

P: No, just a bit unhappy.

T: Of course, I see that. It must have been a delicate situation for you to handle. Maybe you can get in touch with Margaret from time to time. It may not be necessary to drop her completely.

P: Oh yes! That's what I said. We've invited her round for supper next week. And since she is very attached to the children and they to her, she could babysit for us from time to time.

T: Good. There may be other advantages too in what you've done.

P: What are they? I can't think of anything.

T: Well, we have talked about your problems with assertiveness before. Do you think that this was appropriate assertive behaviour?

P: Yes. I've been able to do it without making a big scene.

T: That's right. Now you might experiment with other situations which demand *appropriate* assertive behaviour — for example, setting limits with your parents and your sister? I can think of yet another advantage in what you did.

P: You can? (*smiles*)

T: I was thinking that perhaps you have shown to your husband and to yourself that you can take decisions, that you're back in the house as wife and mother and that you intend to be back at the helm.

P: Maybe. Jim is angry with me, but taking a long-term view, it might help.

T: I'm glad to hear you contrast the long-term with the short-term view. How are you feeling right now?

P: Fine.

T: Good. We must remember to put on our agenda soon, how you may apply what you have learned on this occasion to your relationships with your parents and your sister. Many of the thoughts that you have recorded since your discharge from hospital have related to them — again with mixed feelings of guilt and anger.

The therapist used this example of a crisis at home to deal with several key problems—self-blame, self-assertiveness, role in the household and relationship with the husband.

In addition to dealing with automatic thoughts relating to Jennifer's negative view of herself in her various roles, the eight sessions in this part of treatment dealt with a number of behavioural tasks and the thoughts related to them. It took the whole of 4 weeks to reach a satisfactory level of activity. In spite of a weekly programme of activities which she set in collaboration with the therapist, Jennifer found it difficult to alter her previous pattern of continuous cleaning and tidying. The obsessive cleaning was invariably accompanied by thoughts such as 'I can't cope' and 'Why can't they clean up after themselves?' and feelings of anger, resentment and depression.

The *strategies* used were to rehearse the advantages of more controlled tidying, test out new ways of organizing her time and check the effect on herself and her family. On *questioning*, the advantages elicited were:

1   She would have more time to engage in pleasant activities — for example, reading and listening to music which she used to enjoy and found relaxing.
2   She would have more time to spend with the children and hence feel better about her role as mother.
3   She would feel less tired and hence probably less irritable.
4   Her husband would feel less irritated, as he had complained about her dusting and cleaning around him, when he was trying to relax after he came back from work.
5   With a more realistic standard of tidiness, she would probably succeed, feel in control and hence, feel more contented.

These advantages were set as *hypotheses* which she could test in reality.

At the end of the fourth week, that is, after ten sessions of treatment, her BDI score was 12 and the HRSD score was 9. Both scales, therefore, reflected progress and only a minimal level of depression.

At that time, the therapist and the patient began to rehearse ways of getting in touch with her parents and her sister and resuming her relationships with them. Her fear was that she would be taken over by her parents again. They would visit too often and look after the home for her. Or, they would expect her to visit more often than she could. The problem with her sister was that she was not coping well with her own life and would expect Jennifer to help her, put her up in her home and do things for her.

Resolving these problems entailed *training in new patterns of behaviour:* self-assertion, control of anger and saying 'no' to excessive demands from others. The *therapeutic strategies* involved eliciting associated thoughts and predictions, explaining the long-term advantages of new behaviour patterns, and engaging in reality testing. The following is an extract from a discussion relating to saying 'no' to people at times.

T: Let me just summarize what I understand from what you have just been saying: You often find yourself agreeing to do things for people, even when it is very inconvenient for you. This may involve letting people stay in your house for long periods of time, doing a number of things for them and responding to their various needs. This has happened in the case of your sister and Margaret, for example. With regard to your parents, you haven't been able to tell them to visit less often or that you could only visit them now and then. When your mother has stepped in and told you that you should bring up your children in a certain way, you haven't been able to say 'No thank you. I prefer to do it some other way'. Consequently, you have often felt frustrated and angry in these situations and then depressed because you blame yourself for being angry. Have I got it right?

P: That's it exactly.

T: OK, I'm wondering what makes you do these things, if they cause you so much distress. What would happen if you just said 'no' occasionally?

P: I guess I would feel bad as well. I would feel selfish and inconsiderate.

T: So, it sounds as if you can't win either way. Let's see whether your interpretation is right. It sounds a bit black and white to me. It seems as if you're saying: Not to do what other people want, not to respond to their needs is selfish and inconsiderate. One *should not* be selfish and inconsiderate. Therefore, you should *never* say no and *always* do what others want. Does that reflect what you believe?

P: I suppose so. It sounds a bit extreme when you put it that way. (*patient is smiling*)

T: That's right, it does sound quite extreme. You appear to have made up a rule for yourself. A very strict one and it's not helping you. It may be that you learned this rule when you were a child and you still apply it now, although you are an adult. Let's see whether we can alter the rule a bit, so that nobody suffers — neither you, nor the people you want to help. Why is it selfish not to respond to other people's needs at all times, and to say 'no' occasionally?

P: I suppose I believe one should always put others before oneself.

T: Should? Is this written down somewhere, in the Bible, or somewhere else?

P: I don't know really.

T: Well, take the examples which you discussed about your parents and your sister. We know that your strict rule makes you feel bad a great deal of the time. What about the others, does it help them really?

P: I guess not. You know what happened with my parents, with my sister and with Margaret. There seems to be a last straw. Then I explode and everything gets messed up.

T: I'm not sure whether *everything* gets messed up, but certainly these particular relationships got disturbed and then you've had to put a lot of effort into damage repair. If you had set limits at the beginning, limits which were convenient for you, do you think these problems would have arisen?

P: Probably not.

T: Would everybody be happier as a result?

P: Probably.

T: How probable do you think? 100%?

P: Um . . . Um . . .

T: Well, it's something that you can test in the future. See how it works. Let's see how your new code of behaviour would sound if you rewrote it now. What would be the balance between your wishes and that of others?

P: Perhaps equal.

T: Wouldn't that be selfish?

The therapist tests whether the patient's belief has been altered by feeding back what her original reaction would have been, in question form.

P: No, it wouldn't because it would be more helpful for everybody involved.

T: Bravo. So in deciding what to do for other people, when to say 'no' and when to say 'yes', it would be advantageous to take into consideration your needs and your opinion *as well as* theirs?

P: That's right. I see that now.

T: It would be helpful if you wrote down, as your homework for next week, some of the reasonings we went through today. Write the original rule at the top of the sheet — I should never say 'no' and always do what others want, otherwise I would be selfish and inconsiderate. Draw a line in the middle of the sheet, head one column advantages and the other disadvantages and see what you come up with. It may be that you can think of other arguments than those we've discussed today. We can then have a look at what you've got next time you come round. Is this OK? Are you clear about what you have to do?

This illustrates how it may be necessary to deal with a basic rule even fairly early on in therapy, to facilitate behavioural changes and changes at the level of automatic thoughts. This particular intervention took place in the fifth week of treatment (the twelfth treatment session).

At the end of week six (fourteenth treatment session), the assessment scores were BDI = 8, HRSD = 5.

The patient was now seen at weekly intervals. *The goals of therapy were to consolidate on previous gains and modify basic assumptions (rules or schemata).*

The *agenda* for Session 15 consisted of a review of homework and, at the suggestion of the therapist, a review of what had been achieved in therapy so far. *It is important, at about this point in treatment, to refer back to the original goals set out in the first session and to review progresss.* This is useful not only for the patient, who can be helped to assess his progress realistically and hence derive a sense of achivement, but also for the therapist, to ensure that he remains on track and has a general view of the terrain.

The therapist also has enough information by then to go back to her original formulation. This may need to be refined or altered.

The review, in relation to treatment goals (see Chapter 5, p. 107) suggested that:

1 The depression was much improved. Most of the symptoms and signs of depression had disappeared. Jennifer was no longer preoccupied with suicide, she was active, enjoyed a number of things and could take decisions. Her sleep was back to normal, as was her appetite. Her interest in sex was normal, but *her sex life was still impaired because of the unsatisfactory relationship with her husband.*

2 She no longer saw herself as a failure in her roles as daughter, friend and sister.

3 *There were still occasional problems with her husband and children.* These related principally to the issue of tidiness and not being able to be in *complete control of her environment.*

4 She was no longer ambivalent about her marriage. She was confident that the marriage was right for her and that pursuing a career as a missionary would not necessarily have been perfect, nor right for her.

5 Anger was reported far less often and when present, Jennifer was able to be assertive and express her feelings in an appropriate way.

The therapist summarized the *remaining issue* as: marital relationships and problems ensuing from a need for control, for tidiness and perfection. She then commented that they were now three-quarters of the way through therapy and that she envisaged that they would meet another four to five times. She then asked for feedback and comments about therapy so far.

T: How do you feel about the way your therapy has progressed so far? Do you think that we have been on the right track, that we have been dealing with what's important for you?

This allows the patient to make general comments about her treatment and air any misgivings she may have. The therapist is also

beginning to prepare the patient for discharge to facilitate a smooth
termination of treatment.

151

*Progress in
therapy: a
depressed patient*

Reformulation

The original formulation stressed a need for control and this was
partly an accurate hypothesis. Further discussions and records of
automatic thoughts revealed a particular aspect of this need for
control — namely that Jennifer felt that her needs and values were of
paramount importance and that she must have what she wanted.
This, in conjunction with a rigid moral code, created inevitable
problems regarding her role within the family. The problems were
compounded by her lack of assertion, and her belief that anger was
morally wrong. Her coping behaviour consisted of withdrawal from
conflict situations with ensuing self-blame and depression.

Sessions 16–19

The next *four* sessions were directed primarily by this formulation.
*The focus was on improving the marital relationship and on eliciting
and modifying basic assumptions.* Concurrent efforts continued to be
made, through planning and discussions, to keep the patient's daily
schedule of activities within reasonable bounds.

Thoughts sampled from Jennifer's records relating to her marriage were:

I have failed to convey my feelings towards Jim, physically, verbally
and emotionally.
He is distant with me; he is not as affectionate as he used to be.
He has no idea how I feel about anything.

A *joint interview* with Jennifer and Jim was revealing. Jim said that
he tried to keep out of Jennifer's way, because everything he did
seemed to annoy her. He had tried to help, but thought that he had
probably not done enough. He blamed himself for being less than
understanding at times. He described, with intense feeling, how
Jennifer kept fussing about, cleaning all the time. He said that, at supper time, he had scarcely put his fork down on the plate than the plate
was whisked off and washed. This produced some laughs from both of
them — which was a positive sign in that they could share humour.
Some discussion ensued about the effects of depression and we talked
about the progress that Jennifer had already made. It was decided
that the self-blame that each felt and the implicit resentment were not
helping them. The decision was to let the other partner know more
about how they felt, about what was irritating in the other's
behaviour, and to put time aside to be able to be together and do things
together. Jim was glad to have had this opportunity to air his feelings,

as he was afraid that Jennifer might be painting a very black picture of him behind his back. In fact, Jennifer was surprised to see him cry at the thought of losing her, and he was in his turn, surprised to hear that she thought she was losing him, if she had not lost him already.

The therapist decided on a joint interview because the marital problems involved, by definition, both partners and a joint interview might help to 'unblock' the communication problems between them. Dealing only with the wife's automatic thoughts and rehearsing different behavioural strategies which she might engage in had not proved sufficient, and the therapist suspected that many of the problems predated the onset of her depression.

The *basic rules and assumptions*, in the case of this patient, were not difficult to elicit, as the patient herself had often explicitly described them and noted them in her records of automatic thoughts. The following are examples from the record sheets:

I can't cope because everything is so disorganized.
I can't stand the mess.
I'm frightened of being out of control.
I've never had a feeling of control in my home since I married. Mother came and took control; then my sister came and took control and then my friend did the same.
I can't stand things in the house that don't work.
If things aren't physically and emotionally perfect, I can't cope.
Things must be exactly the way I want them or I can't cope.
I have to be perfect. Things under my control have to be perfect.

T: We have spent a lot of time over the last 2 months examining the negative interpretations that you had about yourself, your life and the future. We have also rehearsed different ways of dealing with situations which were difficult for you, for example expressing anger, being more assertive with people and keeping your housework under control rather than letting it control you. We have also talked about one of the beliefs or rules that you had been following. You remember? Your moral code about how not to be selfish? You did some work on that. What I would like to do now is discuss some other attitudes which may be causing problems. I want to read you some examples from your record sheets that I have jotted down here and we will try and extract a general attitude from them. OK?

The therapist then reads the list given above and asks for a general rule.

P: Yes, I see what you mean. It seems that I want things to be perfect. Then, I feel in control. If not, I can't cope.

T: That's right. Does it also sound as if things have to be perfect on your terms, according to your definition of what's perfect?

P: Hmm . . . it's very selfish isn't it?

T: No. I don't think it will be useful to make a derogatory moral judgement on it. It is a general basic assumption that you have had for a long time probably. I guess that it was not a *conscious moral decision* on your part. Was it?

P: No, I never thought about why I was reacting the way I've been doing all these years.

T: That's why we call these basic attitudes 'silent assumptions' — they are rules of behaviour and belief systems which influence our interpretations of certain types of situations and make us react in certain ways — without us being quite aware of them.

P: But what can I do about it? It must be my personality. I can't change now.

T: Well, you don't need to change *completely*. You don't need to change your personality. We're only talking about one or two attitudes, not every aspect of your personality. And, you don't even have to change these completely, just perhaps make them less strict. Everybody likes things to be right and to feel in control, I think. We also generally prefer things to be the way we like them. However, as you know, life is not like that, especially when four or five people are living in the same household. As you have found out, *everything* cannot always be perfect and under control, on our terms, at *all times*. So let's see how you can make a few changes.

The techniques used to modify the attitude 'I need to feel in control. To feel in control, I need things to be perfect around me—people's emotions, my emotions and everything in its place and shining. If not, I can't cope' have been described in detail in Chapter 4. The techniques used were: a list of weighted advantages and disadvantages, probabilities of succeeding to satisfy the need and response prevention.

The last two assessments over this period showed consecutively BDI = 8, HRSD = 3; BDI = 5, HRSD = 1 .

Jennifer went for job interviews and after her third attempt, obtained a part-time nursing job in a private nursing home for 2 nights a week.

Session 20

This last session was focused on rehearsal of coping behaviour if problems arose. These included reinstating what she had found most useful during therapy: plan of activities, scheduling rest periods and pleasant activities, noting and correcting negative automatic thoughts, discussing problems with her husband, refraining from taking on too much in response to others' demands and re-reading her written work on need for control and perfection.

Six weekly follow-up sessions indicated no recurrence of depression. Some of the previous problems recurred in a milder form, in particular self-assertivness with her parents, anger at untidiness and taking on too much. However, Jennifer was able to put in practice techniques which she had mastered during therapy and her dysphoric episodes were only transient.

Summary

Not all depressed patients require 20 sessions of cognitive therapy. In the case of this patient, as she was admitted to hospital at the beginning of treatment, she was seen more often than would normally be the case. We find that in-patients treated with cognitive therapy need to be seen at least three times a week for the continuity of treatment and for both the patient and the ward staff to feel that active treatment is taking place. In practice, the other patients on the ward are on medication, so that treatment is seen as being implemented. In addition, the therapist must ensure that feedback is given to the nursing staff about issues discussed in therapy and that he obtains feedback about the patient's behaviour on the ward.

The issues dealt with in therapy were representative of problems discussed with depressed patients in general: depressive *symptoms* themselves, for example disturbed sleep, activity level, loss of enjoyment and indecision; cognitive components, for example negative view of self, world and future and typical information processing errors; coping style, for example anger management and self-assertiveness; and finally, basic schemata, for example need for control, need for perfection and excessively high moral standards.

The course of therapy indicated that behavioural and cognitive techniques were used in conjunction to modify automatic thoughts, behaviour and mood. Basic schemata were modified towards the end of treatment, although it was neccessary to elicit and modify a schema half-way through treatment.

Chapter 7
Progress in Therapy:
an Anxious Patient

This chapter, like Chapter 6, will describe progress in therapy, but this time with the anxious patient introduced in Chapter 5.

Course of treatment

There were eight treatment sessions which lasted over a period of 3 months and one follow-up session 4 months later. The patient's general practitioner was involved in a programme to reduce the patient's intake of Valium over a period of 2 months.

Session 2

One week after the first cognitive therapy interview.

T: Well Sheila, it is a week since our first treatment session and I would like to ask you about how you have been getting on since then. We have about 50 minutes.

The therapist begins the session by suggesting an agenda arising out of how the patient had been and the homework. This includes an indication of how much time is allocated to emphasize that this should be used judiciously.

P: Yes, that's OK.
T: So how have you been?
P: Well, much the same really. Most of the time I've been very uptight and I haven't been sleeping at all, so I've been very tired.
T: Have you had more difficulty than usual sleeping?
P: Yes, it's been really bad.
T: Maybe we should look at that then. What other problems have you had this week?
P: Well, I've been anxious of course. I really don't know what to do with myself when I get like that. It's been pretty bad at school this week.
T: Did you keep a record of your anxiety?
P: Yes, I did. It's here. (*gives therapist the record sheet*)
T: Good. We can look at this and see how anxious you have been.
P: I actually found it quite difficult to fill in at school, because I couldn't always do it hour by hour, as I was teaching.

T: That's OK. The main thing is to know how your anxiety has fluctuated and what situations, if any, make you more anxious than others. It looks as though you have some variation in how anxious you have felt, so we can have a close look at that. Do you think that would be helpful?

P: Well yes. (*looks perplexed*)

T: You look a bit puzzled just now. What is going through your mind?

The therapist notices a change in Sheila's mood and uses this to access automatic thoughts.

P: It's just that I feel I've been bad all week. I know I have rated things differently at times but it seems all bad really.

T: So your overall impression of the week is that it's been a bad one. When you looked at the form yourself, did that impression hold true?

P: Well no, I don't suppose it did. It's just how I feel the week's gone.

T: OK. Let me have a brief look at your ratings in a moment, as there seems to be a discrepancy between how the week has felt to you — 'it's all bad' — and how it may actually have been. Have I picked you up right?

P: Yes, I see what you mean.

T: But, before we do this, can I also suggest that we discuss the booklet *Coping with Anxiety*. Did you read it?

P: Yes I did. It made a lot of sense to me.

T: I'd like to know which bits you related to most and if there were things in it that you found less striking. What else would you like to discuss?

P: I suppose cutting down the Valium. I really feel I'm dependent on it and I'm worried about that.

T: OK, anything else?

P: Not really. Well, things at school, I suppose.

T: School in general, or have there been particular incidents this week?

P: Well, I have been anxious at school this week and I'm just so scared about panicking there.

T: Right, so we must discuss these things too. I think we agreed to discuss your panic attacks this week, didn't we? (*patient nods*) So let's see. We want to look at cutting down your Valium, sleeping problems, your anxiety levels over the week from your ratings and what has been happening at school, your panic attacks and also how you found the booklet. That is quite a lot. I don't know if we will have time for all of that. Maybe we could concentrate on just a few things. Which do you think are the most important?

P: I'm not sure, it all seems to be so much part of the same thing.

T: These problems are all related to each other. How would it be if we started with what you have done for homework? That might cover

many of these things. I also want to ask you about how you found
our last session.

*The therapist has now set the agenda. Homework has been selected as
a main target for the session, as this will provide information about
how the week has been and should highlight some specific problems
for intervention.*

P: OK. The last session was fine. I think it really helped to talk about
everything. I hadn't told someone everything before. There's
really no one I can talk to about it.

T: Yes, telling someone how you feel can be helpful, can't it. Was it a
relief to talk?

P: Yes, it was.

T: That's good. I'm glad you found it helpful. Was there anything you
weren't sure of from our last session or anything that upset you
afterwards?

P: Well, I did realize how lonely I was and how I missed my sister. If
she was here, I could have talked to her.

T: Yes, she is important to you and from what you have said about
her, you find her easy to talk to. At another time, it might be helpful to look at who there is around you now, whom you could talk
to.

P: I can't think who there is, but I know I do need more contact with
people. I've become very isolated.

T: So let's talk more about that in another session. Right now, we
want to concentrate on your anxiety. How did you find the
booklet?

*The therapist keeps the patient directed towards the agenda as he
believes that discussing Sheila's lack of confidence is not going to be
fruitful at this point in therapy.*

P: It made a lot of sense to me.

T: Which particular bits did you find helpful?

P: The first parts. The ones (*looking at booklet*) about the nature of
anxiety. I'm like that. I'm so aware of how awful it feels to be
anxious that I dread it and that just makes it worse. Do you know
what I mean?

T: Yes, I can understand that. That vicious circle is a problem, isn't
it?

P: Oh yes, it affects all sorts of things. I just can't do as much and I
hate feeling this way. It just goes on and on.

T: Shall we have a look at how this week has been then, from your record sheet. We may then understand a lot about how your anxiety
affects you from that. Would that be OK? (*patient agrees*)

Therapist and patient together looked at the weekly activity schedule.

Each hour had been completed by rating degree of anxiety on a score from 0–10 and the specific situation in which this was experienced. This revealed that Sheila's anxiety level had certainly been quite high during school hours, but that there had been considerable fluctuations in anxiety (ratings 4 to 7). Ratings of 6 and 7 were associated with being in the staff room with colleagues and with teaching some classes. Lower ratings were associated with being alone marking papers and with preparing classwork. High levels of anxiety were also reported on several evenings during the week and on Sunday afternoon. The therapist decided to challenge the patient's interpretation that the whole week has been a bad one, and to help the patient relate thoughts and feelings.

T: At the beginning of the session, you said that the whole week had been bad. How did you feel when you thought that?

P: Well, it made me feel pretty low.

T: Now that you've looked at what you recorded, do you still think it was all bad?

P: No, it did vary. Sometimes I was quite anxious, but not all the time.

T: So there is evidence that you did not feel continuously anxious? How do you feel now?

P: Not so bad, I suppose. The ratings are actually quite accurate.

T: Can you see from this example what we were talking about last week — the way in which our thoughts influence our feelings?

P: Yes, I can.

The therapist has emphasized the link between thoughts and emotions by using an example from the patient's experience. They go on to discuss specific situations where the patient experienced high levels of anxiety. On Sunday afternoon, the patient had experienced high levels of anxiety and this was focused on, as it appeared to relate to worrying about going to school the following day and the events of the previous week.

T: Sunday afternoon was fairly typical of how you were at your worst?

P: It was awful. I was really bad that day.

T: You were at home that afternoon, tidying your flat and watching television. What happened?

P: I wasn't really doing anything properly. I wasn't concentrating on the film I was watching and I don't think I really tidied the flat properly either.

T: How were you feeling?

P: Uptight. It started after I began tidying. My thoughts were just going round and round in my head. I thought I was going to have a panic attack. I couldn't really sit still, yet I was completely exhausted physically by 5 o'clock. The phone rang, my father, to ask me when I was coming round and I just about burst into tears with him over the 'phone. I just didn't know how to cope with myself.

T: Can you remember what was going through your mind during that afternoon?

P: It was mostly about school, but other things too.

T: What went through your mind about school?

P: I kept thinking that I had to go to school the next day. That it would be awful, that I wouldn't cope. I keep doing this.

T: So you were thinking 'I have to go to school tomorrow'. It will be awful'. 'I won't cope'. Is that right? (*patient agrees*) Can you think of what else went through your mind? There you were, tidying the house, trying to watch a film, what else went through your mind?

Therapist tries to build up a clear picture in the patient's mind of that afternoon to increase her ability to recall thoughts and emotions.

P: I think I was just wishing I could escape from going. I had an image of myself in the staff room last Thursday. I was sitting there sweating, really anxious. John X was on the other side of the room and he was talking to Marion, another teacher, and they kept looking over. I was trying not to look at them but I couldn't help it. I was so exposed there on my own. I kept thinking they knew I was anxious.

T: So you were thinking about being in the staff room last Thurday. You were replaying this in your mind and becoming anxious. Did you think of anything else?

P: I felt so stuck. You see, I couldn't get out of the staff room. I was sort of frozen there with them looking at me. On Sunday, I kept thinking it would happen again.

T: How did these thoughts make you feel?

P: Terrified. I couldn't see a way out. I kept thinking I'll feel trapped again this week.

T: So mainly you felt very anxious. The thoughts were to do with last Thursday's incident in the staff room where you thought that Marion and John were looking at you. You thought they knew you were anxious and you felt very exposed. You also felt very trapped. On Sunday, you were going over this incident and were anxious because you were thinking this could happen again. Have I got that clear now?

The therapist summarizes the main thoughts and emotions relating to Sunday's high levels of anxiety. She goes on to write these thoughts down on a dysfunctional thought form, explaining what each column is for. She then considers which strategy she should select to help the patient cope with this typical situation of worrying about the future.

The options open to the therapist are as follows:

1 *Modify the automatic thoughts.*

2 *Behavioural techniques to cope with the anxiety symptoms.*

3 *Behavioural strategies to help the patient cope in similar situations. The therapist decides to try modifying the automatic thoughts first, as it was these thoughts which distressed the patient on Sunday.*

T: (*showing the patient the thought form where the situation, emotions and automatic thoughts are written*) So these are the thoughts and images you were having on Sunday when you became anxious. In fact, you were thinking mostly about Thursday's incident in the staff room and wondering about whether this might be repeated in the next week. Is that right?

P: Yes. it was going through my mind all afternoon.

T: Let us examine first what happened on Thursday, as this influenced how you were on Sunday. The thought relating to this was 'Marion and John were talking about me'. What made you think that?

P: Well, they were looking at me.

T: What did that mean to you? (*uses guided discovery to obtain further automatic thoughts*)

P: That they were talking about me maliciously.

T: Could you hear what they were saying?

P: Well no, I couldn't.

T: So did you just assume, or jump to the conclusion that they were talking about you?

P: Yes, I did.

T: So on Thursday you couldn't hear what they were saying, but jumped to the conclusion that they were talking about you. That made you anxious. Were they staring at you or doing something else which made you think it was you they were talking about?

P: Well no. They were only looking at me now and then.

T: Can you think of another explanation as to why they were looking at you?

P: Well, maybe it was just that they were looking around as they talked.

T: So it could have been looking around, as all of us do when we talk to people. Would that have explained their behaviour equally as well?

P: Well yes, it would have.

T: So can you see that you jumped to the conclusion that they were talking about you when there was not enough evidence for this.

P: Yes, I can see that.

The therapist then modifies the other thoughts in a similar way. The patient concludes that although she was anxious in this situation, Marion and John may not have been paying her any more attention

T: So on Sunday you were assuming that your interpretation of Thursday's events was correct. That made you feel anxious and you thought you would not cope with this week. How have you coped this week?

P: Well, a bit better really — so far.

T: So you were making a prediction on Sunday that you wouldn't cope which has not been proven. Is that right?

P: Yes. I was assuming the same thing would happen. It hasn't.

T: So are your predictions always accurate?

P: No, they are not.

T: If you had been able to examine those thoughts like this on Sunday, do you think you would have felt differently?

P: It wouldn't have gone round and round in my head. I would have been less anxious. It is the way I feel about situations that's the problem. I'm just not sure I would be able to tackle these thoughts on my own.

T: Well, I wouldn't really expect you to be able to do this perfectly just now. The important point is to become *aware* of your automatic thinking in the situations in which you feel anxious and to practise trying to challenge these thoughts so that you can cope without becoming too anxious. Maybe you would want to practise this as homework for next week, by writing down the situations, emotions and what your automatic thoughts are? If you only use these first three columns, we can go over how you might challenge the thoughts next time. What do you think?

P: OK, I think I could manage to do that.

T: One of the things that you have to be clear about is the difference between thoughts and emotions. Sometimes we say feel, when we actually mean think. For example, I think you just said it's the way you feel about situations that is the problem. It can help you deal with these if you remember that it's the way you are *thinking* about situations which make you *feel* bad. It's easier to change the way we think than the way we feel and, as you have seen, changing interpretations *also* changes feelings. So it's a helpful idea to separate these two things out and I think you'll find the homework task easier if you do that. Does that make sense to you?

P: Yes, it does. I see what you mean.

The therapist has suggested a homework assignment which follows on from the contents of this session. She has underlined the difference between feelings and thoughts to help the patient understand their relationship as well as to aid the homework task.

T: So what we have spent most time on today are the situations and thoughts which relate to school, which make you anxious. I also think it might be helpful for us to summarize what we have found out. Would you like to have a go at that?

P: It seems that it is mostly the way I think about things which makes me anxious. That isn't to deny that John X is difficult but I make things worse by thinking that I can't cope with him. Then I get anxious and can't cope with that.

T: That is a good summary. Now I would like to show you, in the next fifteen minutes, some relaxation techniques which might help you to manage the anxiety symptoms themselves. These would have to be practised at home too. Would that be all right? (*patient acquiesces*)

The therapist then instructs the patient in a simple relaxation procedure (see Chapter 4). After a few minutes of silence,

T: OK, how was that for you?

P: It was fine. I actually felt quite sleepy.

T: Do you feel less tense than before?

P: Yes, I do a bit. I was aware of finding it difficult to let go of the tension at first.

The therapist gives the patient a tape of the relaxation instructions to practise daily at home to help her feel less anxious and to help her to sleep. Feedback on the session is then elicited and the rationale for the homework emphasized. Homework consists of recording situations, emotions and thoughts on the record of dysfunctional thoughts, and practising relaxation exercises. An hourly record of anxiety level is to be kept using the weekly activity schedule. At the end of the session, patient and therapist agree to contact the GP again about reducing her dose of Valium.

The therapist then asks for feedback on the session. Sheila has found the session useful and although she has not had a panic attack recently, she wishes to know how to deal with these. Coping with panic attacks are put on next week's agenda.

Session 3

This session took place 1 week after the previous one. The therapist began the session by asking Sheila how she had been over the last week. She replied that the week had been mixed, with times of high anxiety, but also some relatively tranquil times. The therapist asked how she had found the last session and Sheila said that she had found it 'all right'. She added that she was rather depressed about feeling anxious so much of the time and was still finding difficulty coping with many things. The therapist asked how she had got on with the homework assignments. She had managed to carry these out. It was agreed to look at the homework and to discuss ways of coping with panic attacks in this session. Sheila had specifically requested the latter in the last session. This formed the agenda.

T: *(after studying the weekly activity schedule and record of dysfunction thoughts)* It looks as if you have been anxious mostly at school again, particularly in the staffroom at lunch times and also when marking papers in the classroom during free periods. This past weekend seems to have been better than the last weekend you had though. Would you agree with that?

P: Yes, the weekend was better. I actually managed to do quite a lot. My father was in good form too, which helped a lot, as I didn't get so irritated by him.

T: How did you get on with the relaxation tape?

P: Fine. I actually liked the time out that it gave me.

T: Could you use it to help you to relax then, Sheila?

P: Yes, at home. It also helped me get off to sleep on a few nights. I'm not sure about how to go about doing that at other times.

T: OK, we'll come back to that in another session as we have other things to do today. But maybe you'd like to practise that at home again this week to get more skilled at relaxion. *(patient agrees)*

T: Your scores of high anxiety levels of 7 on the Weekly Activity Schedule relate to some of the thoughts you have recorded on the thought sheets — is that right?

P: Most of them are there. I found that it was often the same thoughts over and over again, so I didn't bother to put them down.

The same thoughts often recur in anxious, as in depressed, patients. The therapist underlines this and says that the patient need only note a sample of her thoughts.

T: That is often the case. The same thoughts are repeated. So, it's OK not to put every single one down. The situations that relate to the thoughts are mostly 'at school' — often in the staff room. The thoughts which made you anxious were:

'I'm not going to get better.'

'I can't stand this.'

'I won't be able to tackle John.'

'I can't think straight.'

These thoughts are mostly to do with predicting the future and thinking that in some way, you won't be able to cope. Is that how you see them too?

P: Yes. I just get so worked up that I can't cope.

T: Is it that you cannot cope, or is it that you believe you will not be able to cope in future?

P: That I will not be able to cope.

T: So the thoughts mostly relate to the future and you seeing yourself as not coping. Shall we look at just one of these thoughts right now, as we must also find a way of helping you with panic attacks. Which of these thoughts then, Sheila, do you want to tackle?

P: 'I'm not going to get better'. Every time I get anxious, I think that. At night, that one goes round and round in my head. It makes me feel so fed up.

T: So you wrote that thought on the sheet yesterday. For example, when you were at school, marking papers alone in a classroom?

P: Yes, I wasn't concentrating on what I was doing. I was on automatic pilot, marking homework.

T: What was going through your mind?

P: I was anxious. I had just finished teaching for the day and was feeling tired and under a lot of pressure to get that homework out of the way before I went home. I could feel myself becoming more tense. I was thinking 'I can't stand this school. I'm trapped here. I'm not going to get any better. This will never go away'.

T: How did these thoughts make you feel?

P: Well, anxious, but also quite low and hopeless.

T: So there was more than one thought and together these made you feel anxious and low.

The therapist has elicited a fuller description of the patient's mood and related thoughts so that a clearer understanding of these can be reached before beginning to modify the thoughts.

T: Let us look at the thoughts 'I'm never going to get any better. This will never go away'.

The therapist challenges this thought by trying to establish the realistic probability of this thought.

How likely do you think it is that you will remain anxious forever?

P: When I feel like that, I think it is likely.

T: How likely? What would you estimate the probability of being anxious forever as being?

P: Well, maybe 90% when I feel like that. That's what makes me feel so hopeless.

T: So when you are very anxious, you think it may have a 90% chance of lasting. Are you always that anxious or does it come and go even within a day?

P: Well, it does change.

T: How long did your high anxiety level last yesterday?

P: Maybe 20 minutes.

T: So what is the evidence that you remain very anxious all the time and that it doesn't change?

P: OK, I see what you mean. It does change.

T: Do you think that these thoughts reflect reality, or do they reflect how you feel at the time?

P: It's how I feel at the time.

T: So what is another way of thinking about these feelings and thoughts?

P: That I won't always feel this bad. In fact, it does vary throughout the day. Actually, I suppose I do only get very anxious for about 20 minutes.

T: So you confuse feelings with facts when you get very anxious. Is that right?

P: That seems to be the case.

T: So what about this thought 'I'm not going to get better'. What evidence do you have for that?

P: Well, I have felt bad for a long time now, but I don't feel bad all the time. I'm not sure if I can get better.

T: Well, at least we have evidence that you don't feel bad all the time. That is a good sign. There is no evidence that you won't get better because that would be predicting the future, wouldn't it? I don't know about you, but I've never been very good at that. (*patient laughs*)

The therapist attempts to bring humour into the interaction, which the patient accepts.

T: So maybe all that we can say is that getting better is an empirical question. We have to wait and see. This treatment should help you as there is some evidence from research that these techniques help people to cope better with anxiety and to recover. I do not see any reason why it shouldn't help you.

The therapist encourages hope by using humour and by referring to the research evidence to counter the patient's negativism about getting better. A summary is then made of the methods used to modify the automatic thoughts.

T: So, Sheila, we have summarized how to tackle these thoughts. It seems that asking yourself questions such as:
1   what is the evidence for that thought?
2   am I confusing a feeling for a fact?
3   what is the probability of a particular thing happening?
4   am I jumping to conclusions?
5   am I predicting the future?
may be helpful in challenging your thinking. Maybe you would like to try asking yourself some of these questions in response to your automatic thoughts and write these down for next time.

The patient agrees to this homework assignment. The therapist then moves on to the next item on the agenda which is Sheila's concerns about coping with panic attacks, and asks Sheila to recall her last panic attack.

P: Well, it was a few weeks ago. It just came out of the blue.

The therapist attempts to challenge the idea that the panic attack came 'out of the blue'.

T: What were you doing at the time, and where were you?

P: It was at home. I had just come back in from school and had been to my doctor's that day at lunchtime, so I had really been rushing about. I was quite tired and tense. I had just sat down at the kitchen table and I began to panic.

T: Can you remember what was going through your mind just before the panic attack began?

P: I know I was feeling rather low, because my doctor had said to cut down my Valium. I was wondering how I would cope with that. I couldn't really see how I could, especially since I had been on it for so long. I was also feeling very worried about a staff meeting I was to hold the next day with the staff in the department. There are only three of us, but I knew John would make it awkward for me and I was going to have to ask them all to prepare a new style of test. I just knew I would be faced with opposition and that I'd get flustered.

T: So all these thoughts were going through your mind and you were already feeling a bit low and anxious. Do you think that these thoughts and the anxiety you were already experiencing contributed to your panic attack?

The occurrence of Sheila's panic attack is re-attributed to her having been very busy that day and having been in anxiety provoking sitiuations.

P: I did think that the attacks came out of the blue, but maybe that one didn't. I really was already quite upset that day.

T: Another thought I have is related to your cutting down your dosage of Valium. Have you had more panic attacks since you tried to come off Valium?

P: Yes, they began again around that time. Why?

T: It could be that you were experiencing panic attacks as a result of withdrawal from Valium.

P: I hadn't thought of that. Certainly, I haven't had that many attacks since I have been on the same dose of Valium.

The therapist asks Sheila to describe in detail the sensations she experienced during her last panic attack, which occurred before cognitive therapy began.

P: Well, my heart was beating very fast, I got very sweaty and hot. I felt dizzy and I had difficulty breathing, in that I felt as though I couldn't get enough air and as if I was choking.

The therapist then enquires about thoughts during that panic attack.

P: I felt totally out of control, utterly terrified. I thought I was going to faint or collapse. I thought something terrible was going to happen to me. It was awful.

T: What was the worst thing that you think could have happened?

P: I suppose I thought I might die, that I wouldn't get enough air or that my heart would give out.

T: How much do you believe in those thoughts when you are having a panic attack?

P: Well, quite a lot.

T: In percentage terms from 0–100%?

P: About 80%.

T: And now, when you are not so anxious?

P: Maybe 20%.

The therapist then discusses the discrepancy in the patient's belief in the thoughts when she is having a panic attack and now.

T: So do you think that your interpretation of these sensations and how realistic these thoughts were to you made it more likely you might panic once you got a bit anxious?

P: Yes, I think that is very likely.

T: What exactly makes you think that you would faint during an attack?

P: Well, I just feel so dizzy and as if I'm losing control.

T: What makes you think you will die because your heart might give out?

P: Well, when I feel my heart beat so fast and I get so hot and sweaty, I just think I'll collapse and die of a heart attack.

T: And what do you think would happen if you couldn't get enough air?

P: The same really. I wouldn't be able to breathe and I'd die.

T: Have any of these things actually happened to you during a panic attack?

P: Well, no they haven't. It's just that, at the time, I believe they might.

T: It seems to me that you misinterpret these sensations in a catastrophic way during a panic attack and that this makes the panic attacks very terrifying for you. Does that make sense to you, Sheila?

P: Yes, I think it makes good sense to me. But how do I cope with them? Because at the time I really do believe it and it's so awful, I'm terrified of having another panic attack.

Although the patient comprehends that her catastrophic interpreta-
tions of her symptoms during a panic attack do not reflect what
actually happens, she continues to be overcome by her fear of another
attack occurring. As a result, the therapist continues the process of
finding alternative interpretations to her symptoms by designing a
behavioural experiment. The therapist decides to test out whether the
sensations in a panic attack may be due to hyperventilation (see
section of Chapter 4 on respiratory control, p. 66).

T: So, let's try an experiment. I'm going to ask you to overbreathe for
a couple of minutes through your nose and mouth. Fill and empty
your lungs as much as possible. Do it quite quickly and deeply.
(*therapist demonstrates how to breathe for a few seconds*). Now,
don't do this just yet because I want to show you how you can get
rid of any unpleasant sensations you may have by using a paper
bag. I'll show you. I'm going to put this bag round my nose and
mouth so that all the air I breathe comes from the bag. I will also
just breath normally. (*therapist demonstrates this and asks*
patient to try it too)

T: So, let us both start breathing quickly and deeply together so that
you can get the idea of the right rate. It's about one breath every 2
seconds. I'll then stop and you carry on for about another 80
seconds or so. Is that OK?

P: Yes, OK.

Therapist and patient begin to breathe rapidly and deeply. The
therapist then stops and encourages the patient to continue. After
about 1 minute, the patient looks very uncomfortable and the
therapist tells the patient to stop overbreathing.

T: Well done! Now stop there and I want you to close your eyes and
notice how you are feeling.

The patient continues to have difficulty returning to a normal rate of
breathing and is gasping for air initially.

T: Now Sheila, I think you should use the paper bag. Try to just
breathe normally. (*patient uses the bag*) That's good. You're OK.
Just keep breathing into the bag for now (after about 1 minute)
That's fine. I'd now like you to fill in this checklist of symptoms,
some of which are experienced by individuals during a panic
attack.

Patient fills in the checklist and then discusses with the therapist the
similarity between the symptoms produced by voluntary hyperventi-
lation and those produced by an actual panic attack. On the whole,
the symptoms produced by voluntary hyperventilation were present

*during a panic attack. However, the patient rated all the symptoms
produced by the experiment as being less severe than during a panic
attack, except for the sensation of choking which was more severe in
the experiment. Given the similarity in symptoms, the therapist
decided to focus on hyperventilation as a non-catastrophic alternative explanation of panic.*

T: So the point of that experiment was to find out if there were any
similarities between your panic attacks and overbreathing. It
seems that you think there were a lot of similarities. The
difference was that most of the symptoms were not so severe
except for the sensation of choking. Is that right?

P: Mm . . . that's right. I felt more difficulty getting air.

T: Now the sensations were similar, but less severe except for the
sensation of feeling choked — were you as anxious as you would
be in a panic attack?

P: No, I wasn't anxious initially, but when I had difficulty breathing
in enough air, I did feel more scared then. I knew it would
probably be all right though.

T: Why did you think it would be all right?

P: Because I was here.

T: What would have happened if you had been on your own?

P: Well, I just panic and think I'll die.

T: So, do you think that the thought 'I'll die' makes it even worse?

P: Yes, I suppose so.

T: Do you think that when you are a bit anxious, you may increase
your breathing, even though you don't notice it?

P: Well actually, I think I do breathe differently. I often feel I'm hot
and just gasping for air. I really feel quite breathless in a way.

*The therapist gives the patient more information about panic attack
symptoms.*

T: Some people do feel breathless, even though they are, in fact,
overbreathing. This is really quite normal. I noticed that you were
gasping for air just after you had been overbreathing a few
minutes ago. Let me explain what I think may happen to you
during a panic attack. When you are already a bit anxious you
may, like many people, increase the rate and depth of your
breathing. This means you are overbreathing; in other words,
simply breathing in more than you need at that time. This is very
common when people are under stress. Now anyone who over-
breathes will experience sensations in their bodies similar to
those experienced in a panic attack. These are due to an excess of
oxygen in your lungs and blood and a corresponding decrease in
carbon dioxide. That is why breathing into the paper bag quickly
redresses the balance and gets rid of the sensations. These

sensations are harmless. Your experience of feeling breathless is paradoxical as, in fact, you are getting too much air. Now Sheila, it could also be possible that the more anxious you get, the more you overbreathe and the more likely you are to experience the sensations of a panic attack. Some of the sensations you experience when anxious are quite similar to those you get in a panic attack, aren't they?

P: Yes, but I don't feel so terrified of them because I'm not caught up with not thinking straight.

T: Do you think that your panic attacks may be the result of a vicious circle? The more anxious you get, the more you overbreathe. You may interpret the sensations you experience as being catastrophic, which further increase your anxiety and leads to panic. Does that make sense to you?

P: I do think that's right. I know that I am so terrified about dying during an attack, or at least passing out because I can't breathe, that I get more anxious. One thing I don't understand though is that I had the idea that these attacks came out of the blue and that has made me more anxious. Why don't they occur more often than they do, because I am often really very anxious?

T: Well, I think that there could be lots of reasons. For example, they may occur at times when you are very tired, when your blood sugar level is very low. That might increase the chance of having a panic attack as small changes in breathing may produce symptoms which you then interpret as being the beginnings of a panic attack. You then think the worst and this increases anxiety even further, which then leads to an attack. Do you think that is possible? Maybe the panic attack you described earlier was due to some of these factors — you were tired, had been to your doctor at lunchtime, maybe not had lunch and you were already worried about what was to happen the next day.

The therapist has given more direct information on panic attacks to help the patient have a rational explanation of her panic attacks.

P: I see what you are getting at. I may have had all of those things I think.

T: Do you think that the thoughts that you have about the sensations you experience are important in terms of them being catastrophic types of thoughts. I'm going to lose control, I'm going to die, and so on?

P: Well yes. I didn't think about these thoughts when I was overbreathing earlier on and I didn't feel terrified.

T: Could you just go over what we have been saying to make sure that we both understand what may be happening during a panic attack?

*The patient summarizes what has been gone over in the second part of
the session. She emphasizes that she is glad to have an explanation for
her panic attacks that is less threatening than the one she held
previously. She accepts the idea that a vicious circle may be
occurring which increases the likelihood of her having a full blown
panic attack. The therapist then begins to suggest ways in which she
might control her panic attacks. This is done by questioning.*

T: So it seems that you think a vicious circle may be occurring when
you panic. Do you think you could do anything to help you gain
control over these attacks when they occur?

P: Well, if it's because I overbreathe, I might be able to stop doing
that.

T: Yes, that's right. That would stop the vicious circle. There is some
evidence for this procedure working. If you learnt to breathe in a
way which is incompatible with overbreathing, then you could
use that to stop you getting so anxious that you panic. It seems that
the best way of doing this is to breathe in for 2 seconds then out for
2 seconds like this. (the therapist demonstrates the rate of
breathing by saying 'in' and 'out' at the suggested pace). It's really
quite gentle breaths you should take, not quick gasps in and out. I
can give you a tape of this to listen to at home, which will help you.
Shall we listen to it now?

*The therapist plays a tape of herself saying 'in' for 2 seconds and 'out'
for 2 seconds.*

T: (*after several minutes*) The tape is just an aid for you. You may
need to practise this as it takes some time to master the skill. Let's
try again, sit back, we'll both close our eyes and concentrate on the
tape so that we can get into the rhythm.

*The therapist also makes some additional suggestions after this is
practised. She suggests placing a hand on the chest to monitor
breathing. She also suggests that the patient reduces the depth of
breathing as she has tended to take quite deep, audible intakes of
breath. The rate proves to be quite difficult for the patient to master
within the session and as time is running out, the therapist suggests
that this is practised daily at home when the patient is not too tired
and in a warm, quiet room. The general aim of the procedure is
emphasized: that is, to control breathing so that it is shallow, slow
and smooth, all of which are incompatible with overbreathing. The
patient is then asked for feedback on the day's session. Some
difficulties are expressed about being able to master the tape. The
therapist reassures the patient that this is a difficult learning task but
urges the patient to try it to see if it is helpful. The patient agrees to try
and then homework is summarized.*

T: So for next time, you are going to practise breathing at the tape's pace as this will give you a coping technique to deal with panic attacks. What else have we agreed on for homework?

P: I am to continue with the relaxation exercises and I'm going to monitor my anxiety and my thoughts and see if I can challenge them myself.

T: OK. Can you see any difficulties with that?

P: No, that's OK I think.

T: Well, let's meet again in a week's time and see how you are then.

Session 4

The session began with the therapist asking Sheila 'How have you been since we last met?'

Sheila said that her week had been much better than the past few weeks. She had not had any panic attacks. She had, however, had some difficulties at school which had made her upset and anxious. These difficulties were described in the assignments she had completed as part of her homework. She had also visited her general practitioner and they had agreed to reduce her Valium by a further 10 mg. She was to try to take the remaining dose of 20 mg at night but could take 10 mg during the day if she thought she needed it. The therapist then asked how she had found the last session. Sheila said that it had been all right but that a lot of new techniques had been introduced and that she was not sure if she had fully understood these. She particularly wanted to review controlling panic attacks by breathing slowly as this had been difficult to practise. The therapist put this item on the day's agenda along with the rest of the past week's homework. She then asked if there was anything else she particularly wanted to discuss. Sheila requested that her relationship with her colleague, John X, be discussed. This was agreed. The therapist then suggested that they begin the main part of the session by discussing homework which would include her progress with controlled breathing experiments.

T: So, how did you get on with the tape to help you pace your breathing?

P: It was OK, but I found it difficult to keep to the pace set by the tape.

T: That can be a problem. What do you think you were doing which made it difficult?

P: I'm not sure, but I kept feeling out of breath.

T: Was that how you felt when we practised the tape in our last session?

P: Yes, but the longer I went on for, the worse it became.

T: During the last session I remember that we wondered whether you were taking too deep breaths. Has this been a problem?

P: Yes. It's difficult to correct that.

T: What about practising this again? This time putting your hand on your stomach as well as a hand on your chest to see if you can get this pattern of breathing mastered. Remember to take quite shallow breaths.

The tape was then played again with the patient placing one hand on her stomach and one on her chest. The patient continued to feel uncomfortable and so a slower rate of breathing was suggested (3 seconds instead of 2 for both 'in' and 'out' breaths). The patient was more comfortable with this pace and no longer felt breathless. At the faster rate of breathing, she tended to breath too deeply 'in case she couldn't get enough air'. At the slower pace, no difficulty was experienced. The therapist also discussed the fact that not taking in enough air to breathe is not possible as the body will automatically produce an increase in respiration. Again the strategy used here was to reduce her worry about panic attacks by giving information. An experiment was then designed to test out the usefulness of paced breathing. She coped well with this slower rate of breathing.

T: Now that you are quite comfortable with that pace, would you like to see if you can use this way of coping with panic symptoms? What I would like you to do is to overbreathe for, let's say, 1.5 minutes and then use the paced breathing to see if you can relieve the symptoms.

The patient then overbreathed for this period of time and then the therapist asked her to stop and switch to paced breathing. Within 20 seconds, the patient felt more comfortable.

P: That's OK now. I'm amazed. I didn't think I could do that.

T: So, by using the paced breathing you can, in fact, reduce the symptoms produced by overbreathing. It actually took you only 20 seconds to feel a lot better. Maybe you would like to try that again?

The patient once again overbreathed, this time for 2 minutes and then used paced breathing to ameliorate the symptoms.

T: Well done! Do you think you could practise that at home?

P: Yes, I think so. I've got the idea of it now.

T: Do you think you could use that technique when you feel yourself becoming panicky?

P: I could try.

T: Absolutely; you could try it out next time you become panicky. Of course, you also need to remember that the symptoms you experience when panicking are not dangerous. Do you remember us discussing that too last week?

P: Yes, I do, but I need to remind myself.

The therapist repeated the automatic thoughts the patient mentioned in connection with panic attacks in the previous week and asked the patient to counter these. She did this easily and was obviously much more confident about her ability to modify these convincingly. She now did not believe that she would lose control, choke or die during a panic attack. The therapist then asked if she continued to worry about having another panic attack.

P: Well, I'm not so worried really. I think I may have broken the vicious circle — a bit anyway.

T: That's good, Sheila. Now, we have half an hour left today. Shall we move on to the record you kept of your thoughts? You were going to try to work at the validity of some of the automatic thoughts which make you anxious. Is that right?

P: Yes. You'll see that most of them concern school again. John X is again the main problem. (*sighs*) (*the therapist notices that the patient's mood has changed*)

T: You sighed just now. I'm wondering what went through your mind right then.

P: Oh it's just that I don't know how to cope with John. I don't know if I can tackle him. I really am beginning to dread any contact I have with him.

T: What is it about him that makes you dread contact with him?

P: He just makes me feel so incompetent, so stupid.

T: How does he do that?

P: I always feel he's trying to get the better of me. It's as though he's always one step ahead of me. I think he always wants to show me up in front of other people.

T: How does that make you feel?

P: Stupid. Ridiculous. An idiot — a jibbering one at that.

T: So he makes you think of yourself as being stupid and ridiculous. Tell me Sheila, have you put these thoughts down here?

P: Yes, they're mostly about him.

T: OK, let's look at the situations in which you end up feeling like this.

Note that the therapist, up until now, has not challenged these thoughts. Rather she has let Sheila ventilate her thoughts about herself in relation to John X. The therapist decides to look at the situations which bring about these thoughts and feelings. By doing this, she hopes to clarify where Sheila's problems lie. One hypothesis is that this man may, in fact, be behaving unreasonably and the patient is not skilled to deal with him appropriately due to her lowered self-

*efficacy. The therapist enquires about an incident with John X which
the patient has described on the dysfunctional thought form.*

P: I was just about to leave the school. I was walking down the
corridor. There were quite a few pupils and other teachers around
and I saw him coming towards me. He called my name — I was
trying to look away from him — and I could feel myself tensing
up. I thought 'What does he want? I wish he'd leave me alone'.
Anyway, he came over to me and asked me if I had been at the
Head of Department's meeting and what had been said there. I
told him 'nothing much from our point of view' and he started
smiling. That really confused me.

T: Why was that confusing?

P: Well, I thought he knew something I didn't. It made me feel
stupid.

T: So what happened then?

P: Well I know it sounds stupid but I just said 'Look John, I have to go
now. I'm late' or something like that and I left. I just didn't know
how to respond to him.

T: Do you often think and react to him like that?

P: Yes. I just don't know how to respond to him.

T: So what happened then?

P: Well, nothing. I left. Got home quickly and was still feeling
anxious and thinking I was stupid.

T: From your form, that incident looks like quite a typical one.

*From Sheila's description of what happened in the incident, it
appears that John's behaviour may not be particularly unreasonable.
Her behaviour, on the other hand, seems inappropriate in the
situation she described. As a result, the therapist decides to explore
this possibility by first of all getting Sheila to examine John's
behaviour more thoroughly using the technique of guided discovery
and re-attribution.*

T: Let's look at this incident more closely, Sheila. John came up to
you in the corridor, having called out your name. He then asked
you a question about how the meeting had gone. Can you think of
any other explanation for John's behaviour?

P: I suppose he wanted to know what had happened at the meeting.

T: OK, that is true. What about him smiling? Are there any other
explanations for that? Your thought was 'He knows something I
don't'.

P: Well, I suppose he could have been laughing because he was
genuinely amused by the fact there was nothing relevant for our
department.

T: Why would that amuse him?

P: Well, our department has never been one that has caused a lot of problems really. It did when the Head was ill, but not now, and the other bigger departments are always raising problems that seem trivial, so I suppose it is just typical of the meeting that there was nothing relevant for us.

T: So why would he have smiled then?

P: Because he was pleased, because he was amused by it.

T: You now have a different interpretation of his behaviour. If you believed that, would you still feel stupid?

P: No.

T: Do you think you misinterpreted his behaviour then? Jumped to the conclusion that he was deriding you when there was not enough evidence, if any, to support that conclusion?

P: I think that is probably true.

T: I agree with you. However, I'm wondering whether you have other evidence which makes you feel on your guard with John and jump to conclusions about his behaviour.

P: Well, since he came to the department, I've always thought he was very ambitious and one of those people who would walk over others to get to the top. He talked quite openly about not wanting to hang around at the level he's at and how he wanted to become a department head before he was 40.

T: So what did you think about that?

P: It made me think he could be ruthless.

T: What would that mean to you personally?

P: It makes me feel threatened I think. He might walk all over me to get what *he* wants.

T: If he did do that, what would that mean to you?

P: I couldn't cope with it. I'd feel completely powerless. I wouldn't be strong enough to stop him.

The therapist decides to check out whether this is a general assumption or specific to John.

T: Have you felt vulnerable in this way with other people who you see as being ambitious or powerful?

P: I don't know. I've not really thought about it. (*pauses*) I've certainly had this kind of reaction before.

T: Maybe you'd like to think who, other than John, has made you react like this, that is feeling threatened and unable to cope.

The therapist does not proceed with this further at this moment but makes a note to return to this in a future session. It is possible that Sheila has an assumption about her own vulnerability with people whom she perceives as being powerful.

T: Going back to John's behaviour, has he behaved in a way which could be described as walking all over you?

P: He is sometimes very sarcastic to me and I know he was very insulted when I became acting Head of the Department. I think that had made me feel he's dangerous.

T: In what way is he dangerous?

P: Well, threatening. He wants to get at me, put me down.

T: How do you know he was insulted about your promotion?

P: Well, another teacher, who is a friend, told me he was saying how disappointed he was about not being thought of when they asked me to take on the new position.

T: Is there any other evidence he took this badly or was insulted?

P: Well, he didn't congratulate me, if that's the right word, nor did he speak to me for several weeks.

T: Apart from not speaking to you, did his behaviour change in any other way towards you?

P: Well no, he's always been sarcastic I suppose. No, not really. I think I've always found him rather unapproachable.

T: Do you think that he was very disappointed (rather than insulted) at not being thought of for promotion?

P: Hmm, maybe.

T: So he may have been upset rather than insulted. If you thought he had been insulted, how would you expect him to behave and feel?

P: Well, angrily really and wanting to get back at me.

T: If he had been upset, might he have avoided you for a bit?

P: Well, I suppose so.

T: Do you *really* know how he felt?

P: Not really. I just assumed he'd been insulted and angry with me for getting promotion.

T: So now you have an alternative explanation for his behaviour. He avoided you because he was upset. He was very disappointed at not getting the job. Does that make him 'dangerous'?

P: Well, no it doesn't. I just saw things like that. He is the sort of person I find difficult to cope with anyway. I suppose I thought this would make it even more difficult.

T: Well, it seems that John may have always been the sort of person you find difficult to cope with and you expected him to behave in an even more difficult way when you were promoted. This doesn't seem to have happened but there are aspects of his behaviour you find difficult to handle. Is that a fair summary?

P: Yes.

T: Let's look at which aspects of his behaviour you find difficult and see if there are ways you could cope better with it. Is that a good idea?

P: Yes. I would like to be able to stand up to him and feel OK about doing so.

The therapist then asked in detail about John's behaviour and Sheila's reactions to it. It was evident that John was often sarcastic, particularly when Sheila was making a request or stating her opinion. She tended to say nothing when he did this and often ended the meeting quickly to escape. She did not have this difficulty with other teachers whom she regarded as being friendly and cooperative. When asked if other people found John difficult to cope with, she replied she didn't really know. It seemed appropriate to find out if other people found John difficult. She agreed to ask the teacher whom she had mentioned earlier. She said she would feel comfortable doing this as she thought of this woman as a friend. This task was then given as homework. The rationale for this was that Sheila might not be alone in finding John's behaviour difficult. If this was true, then it would mean that he had a problem getting on with some people and that she was not alone in finding him sarcastic. Also, the patient suggested she discuss with her friend, the teacher, how she coped with John. This might help her to develop new behaviours to cope with him. She also suggested that she could watch how others coped with him. The therapist agreed this was an excellent idea and praised her for taking an experimental approach to the problem in gathering this information.

The therapist then asked Sheila how she was progressing with the relaxation exercises. She said she was doing well with these and that she often did them before bedtime which helped her to get off to sleep. The therapist suggested she continue to practise these and that she might like to try relaxing without the tape to see how she got on. It was agreed to keep recording and modifying automatic thoughts over the next week as this had proved helpful. The paced breathing technique was also to be practised in conjunction with overbreathing. Feedback on the session was then elicited and the session ended.

Sessions 5 and 6

The sessions will be described together. Session 5 took place 1 week following Session 4. At the beginning of Session 5, *Sheila's scores on the STAI-S and BDI were 41 and 8 respectively.* Session 6 took place 2 weeks after Session 5.

The therapist scheduled into Session 5's agenda *a review of progress in treatment.* Ratings of anxiety over the time period of these sessions revealed that she was now generally less anxious than before. Indeed on several days, her anxiety levels were very low, or zero. When asked by the therapist 'What do you think has helped?' Sheila said that she had found examining her thoughts particularly helpful. She was now more aware of her automatic thoughts and realized that she often jumped to conclusions about situations when there was little evidence to support them. She was also greatly relieved to have discovered that her panic attacks were not life-threatening and said that the simple knowledge that this was true had helped her break the vicious circle of fear that she had experienced. She had not had a full blown panic attack since treatment began, but was more confident in her ability to control the beginnings of a panic attack by controlling her breathing. Sheila and the therapist concluded that considerable progress had been made in terms of symptom control and that more work needed to be done on the remaining problems: these were restated as being her difficulties in coping with her colleague John; keeping up with administrative tasks at school; her relationships with men; coping with her father on her own; having no confidante.

Session 5 concentrated on her relationship with her colleague John and keeping up with administrative tasks at school. In the previous session, it had been agreed that Sheila would ask another colleague at school how she found John.

T: As part of your homework, you were to ask your colleague how she found John.

P: Yes, I did ask Miriam. She didn't seem at all surprised at my asking her and immediately said that *everyone* found him a bit odd. We talked for a long time about him and it seems that he is regarded as being a very cynical person. Miriam said that she couldn't take him seriously when he's cynical and that she just jokes with him. He can't be that cynical though because he obviously gets on well with her. She said that he was really upset around the time I got promoted, but it was to do with his own problems. He has two children and one of them had been in hospital with pneumonia and had been really ill. I felt so guilty, as I had known nothing about that. He must have thought I was really awful not asking him how his child was.

The therapist decides that, at this point, a strategy is indicated to reduce Sheila's guilt and unrealistic demands on herself. The technique used is to question how she could have known.

T: If no one had told you that his child was in hospital, how could you have known?

P: I know, but I thought he wasn't speaking to me because I had got promotion. That was really nasty of me and so self-centered.

T: If you had known about his child, what would you have done?

P: I'd have gone up to him and asked about how his child was. I'd have tried to give him some support, maybe even tried to rearrange his classes so that he could visit his child in hospital.

T: So, if you had known, you would have been very kind and helpful. But you did not know. In fact, you thought he was ignoring you because he was envious of you getting promoted. You may have jumped to the wrong conclusion there, but is there any reason to feel guilty about that? Did you actually do anything wrong?

P: Well no, I didn't do anything wrong. I just didn't see the situation for what it was. I made an assumption about why he was behaving the way he was.

T: So the only thing you did wrong was to make the wrong assumption. Can you blame yourself for that?

P: No, not really.

T: It was just a misunderstanding then.

P: Actually, when I heard about what had happened to him from Miriam, I talked to John about his children. I said I hadn't known his child had been so ill. He said he'd been very worried about him, but that he was all right now.

T: So you talked to John. You don't often do that. How did that make you feel?

P: I felt really good about it. He was really quite nice and I think surprised at me chatting to him.

T: Has this changed things between you then?

P: A bit, but he is still very sarcastic. I'm not thinking of him as being so threatening though.

The therapist decides that Sheila requires a strategy to change her behaviour towards John.

T: What would help you to cope with him better then?

P: Finding a way of saying something to him when he's sarcastic.

T: Rather than saying nothing or leaving the situation?

P: Yes. Exactly. I've been blowing this all out of proportion, haven't I?

T: Well, maybe. You certainly seem to have decided that he was a threat of some sort to you and it's possible that you behaved in a way which was consistent with that. Do you think you could change how you behave towards him?

P: With difficulty, but I could try.

T: Good, you could try. Can you give me an example of what you refer to as John's sarcasm?

The patient describes an incident which occurred the previous day. She had been in the staff room during the morning break. It was very crowded and John was sitting next to the fridge where milk was stored. She had asked John to get her some milk for her coffee from the fridge and he had said 'You're too fat Sheila. You should take it black'. She had pretended to laugh and repeated her request. She had by now begun to feel quite anxious and thought she must have looked flushed. He had then said in a very loud and dramatic voice to other people 'So now she wants me to wait hand and foot on her. I am to be a servant as well as being servile to the Head of the Department'. She had just stood there, saying nothing until he passed her the milk from the fridge. Other people were sniggering.

T: So how did this make you feel?

P: I was very embarassed. I was hot, flushed and really quite anxious. I couldn't do anything but stand there.

T: What would you like to have done?

P: Well, I suppose he was being quite funny. I would like to have made an appropriate reply but I think I couldn't quite speak; my voice would have been shaky.

The therapist and patient discuss what an appropriate retort to John's sarcasm would be. Sheila decides that, at least initially, she might manage to acknowledge the fact he is being sarcastic by saying something like 'Well John, you are being cheeky today' or 'Did you get out of bed on the wrong side this morning?' When this was rehearsed in the session, Sheila was still uncomfortable with this, saying that she didn't feel it was natural.

T: Well, I wouldn't expect you to feel natural with it right now. Can you think of anything else you might try with him?

P: No, not really.

T: If you could say something to him, in a joking way, do you think you might feel less anxious, even if it didn't feel natural.

P: Well, I'd feel more in control of the situation, not so stupid.

T: Are there any advantages in trying out this strategy or any disadvantages?

P: Well, I might make a real mess of it.

T: What do you think would happen if you did that?

P: Well, nothing really. I'd just feel stupid as usual.

T: So at the worst, you'd feel the same. At the best, you might learn a new way of coping with John or have more experience so that we could think of a new strategy which might work. Is it worth giving it a try — experimenting?

T: Well, I don't have anything to lose.

It was agreed that Sheila would try out replying to John's sarcasm should the opportunity arise over the next week. The therapist also wanted to capitalize on the fact that Sheila had spoken to John about his children and had been surprised at how well this had gone.

T: Now, given that you *did* speak to John this past week and he was not sarcastic to you, do you think it might be helpful to try to initiate more conversation with him this week?

P: I hadn't thought of doing that. I'm so used to not speaking to him.

T: Any disadvantages?

P: Only that he might be sarcastic.

T: OK, but now you have a strategy to try to cope with that, you could try it out if that happened.

The therapist has encouraged Sheila to view the situation with John as being an opportunity to put into practice what they had discussed. She has also encouraged Sheila to talk to John. The therapist emphasizes that if she got to know John better, she might not find him so threatening as she would understand him better.

The remainder of session 5 was spent reviewing the record of dysfunctional thoughts form. Most thoughts recorded concerned John but several were to do with Sheila's worry that she would not be able to accomplish administrative tasks at school.

T: So let's take some typical thoughts about administration, Sheila. 'I won't be able to get all this done by tomorrow. I shall get in a mess — fall behind with everything. I just can't keep up with all this'. These thoughts made you feel 60% anxious and at the time you believed them 80%. I notice that you tend to counter these thoughts by thinking 'You can get through it, just don't panic about it'. You then felt 50% anxious and you only believed this 50%. Shall we look at this more closely as these thoughts occur quite frequently.

The therapist has noted that even though Sheila attempts to modify these thoughts, her degree of belief in the thoughts and her anxiety level has not altered significantly. She therefore attempts to modify these thoughts more convincingly by questioning.

T: So the situation was that you were at home working on administration. It was late in the evening. You were anxious and thinking 'I won't be able to get all this done by tomorrow. I shall get in a mess — fall behind with everything. I just can't keep up with all this'. What effect did this kind of thinking have on you?

P: I just got more anxious. It put a lot of pressure on me.

T: Thinking like this made you feel under even more pressure and you felt more anxious as a result. So the way you were thinking actually didn't help you to get on with the task you had to do. Is that right?

P: Yes, that is exactly right.

T: If you had instead asked yourself, 'What can I realistically complete tonight?', would that have helped?

P: Yes, it would have. I would have been able to do something rather than getting anxious.

T: If you had made a plan, taking into account that you were not going to do everything that evening, what would you have decided?

P: Well, I would have probably just done the more mechanical bits of the task and not even attempted to do some real thinking. That way, I would have felt better because I'd done something. It would have felt more under control.

In collaboration with Sheila, the therapist then planned ahead the foreseeable administrative tasks which Sheila was expected to accomplish as Head of Department. Advantages and disadvantages of planning ahead were discussed. Sheila saw a clear advantage in planning in that she felt more in control. The only disadvantage was that occasionally she might have to change her plan if something unexpected happened. This disadvantage was then discussed and Sheila decided she could be flexible *and* in control and that this was a useful skill to acquire. Session 5 ended with a review of homework and feedback.

Session 6 followed a similar pattern to the previous session. By this stage, Sheila was very able to modify her automatic thoughts, was considerably less anxious and using relaxation techniques effectively. A review of homework revealed that she had, in fact, spoken to John, her colleague, with surprising results.

T: So, how did you get on with John?

P: I took up your suggestion and spoke to him. I didn't know what I was going to talk to him about but I think that it helped that Miriam had said she couldn't take him seriously when he was sarcastic or cynical. Anyway, I wasn't so afraid of him. We talked for ages one evening when we were both leaving school. I was surprised to see him working late and said so. I discovered that he is really trying to get promotion and is thinking of moving to another school. Being a maths teacher means that his choices of a promoted move are quite good. He told me that his wife gave up work after their child was ill and so they are really short of money. Evidently, their little boy is much better, but they both realized how important their children were to them and his wife wants to spend more time at home with them whilst they are young.

T: You found out a lot about John then. Are you still so afraid of him?

P: Well no, I'm not. When you get him on his own, he's really quite different. I actually thought he was quite nice really.

T: So that must have helped. People can sometimes be very different in a crowd. What do you think makes him so sarcastic when there are other people around?

P: I'm not sure, but I think in many ways he puts up a front.

T: Does that help you to cope with his sarcasm?

P: Yes. I can see it for what it is. I won't take it so personally now and I think I could joke with him now that I know him a little better.

T: So now that you have more information about John, you can understand his behaviour a bit better and you don't see him as so threatening. Also, having found out how other people see him has helped you in not personalizing his behaviour, so that you don't automatically conclude his sarcasm is designed to get at you in some way. Is that a reasonable thing for me to say?

P: In think so. I really was quite fixed in my view of him and this has changed now, so that as a result, I'm not so afraid of him and can cope with him better.

The therapist then discussed how Sheila was getting on with her schedule of administrative tasks. She had managed to cope with these easily and was, in fact, using the technique of scheduling for other things too. In general, she was feeling much calmer about everything.

At this point, the therapist decided to introduce more underlying issues, such as Sheila's lack of a confidante and her consequent isolation, her relationships with men and her father's dependency on her. There had been very little discussed about her father in the previous five sessions and her father seldom figured in her homework assignments. As a result, the therapist decided not to discuss her father at this stage on the assumption that Sheila had been coping with him better than previously. The assumption was checked out with Sheila and they agreed to discuss her father briefly in a future session. The therapist then brought up the issue of relationships with men.

T: So, Sheila, over the past few weeks we have not really discussed your relationships with men, but at the beginning of treatment you did think this was an important issue for you. I know we have talked about your relationship with your colleague but I'm not clear if there are elements in that relationship which echo your more intimate relationships with men. Maybe we could discuss this issue together. What do you think about that?

P: I'd like to discuss this. As you know, I am 44 and I really feel I've made a mess of the relationships I've had. You see, I would like to get married, but it has never seemed right.

T: You have told me a little about being engaged once and breaking it off. You also had another relationship when you were at University, didn't you? What happened with that relationship?

P: That was Alan. He went to work in Africa. I was quite young then and I don't think I really could have seen us together in the long term. He was quite nice really but I always felt that he relied on me too much. At University, he always made sure I was around him — he would like us to go to the library together in the evening to study and he'd spend all weekend with me. I found it very claustrophobic.

T: I am curious about why he went off to Africa then if he was so reliant on you. I would have predicted he would have wanted you to stay together.

P: That was my doing. I more or less planned that he go away. It was me who saw a job in Africa advertised and thought he should apply. I more or less wrote his application.

T: Why did you do that?

P: I think to get rid of him. It was my way of finishing the relationship. You see, I wasn't really too upset when he left. I felt quite relieved.

T: Why did you want out of the relationship?

P: I could see that I would feel too hemmed in by it. I wouldn't have had enough freedom. He was too dependent on me.

T: So you did not like the idea of Alan being dependent on you? What about the other relationship you had? What was the problem there, if you can say?

P: Well, it was more complex. Andrew was married. My mother didn't approve, because we were having an affair, so I didn't tell her much about him. That made it awkward. It always felt as though there was a big secret there. Anyway, he and I were to get married after his divorce came through but then his wife got angry and was going to divorce him on the grounds of adultery. I lost my confidence then. I couldn't cope with the disapproval from everyone. Our friends knew both him and his wife and they sided with her. I just felt it wasn't right.

T: Why wasn't it right?

P: Well, because people didn't approve.

T: Were there other reasons why it didn't seem right to go through with marrying him?

P: Yes, there were. I've spent a lot of time thinking about things. I really found myself being very unsure of how much I actually wanted to be in the relationship. I had enjoyed it for years when we didn't see each other too much — that was when he was still with his wife. Then, when he left her, I think the magic went out of the relationship. It just wasn't so good. I got rather bored with him being around. I really rather resented him encroaching on my own time and physical space.

The therapist hypothesizes that Sheila is ambivalent about intimate relationships. She had only enjoyed her relationship with Andrew when he was unavailable, i.e. still married and living with his wife. Also, she had found Alan's dependency on her stifling and, in fact, had got out of this relationship by 'sending him off' to Africa.

T: From what you have told me, Sheila, I am wondering whether you think about your relationships in a way which may be particular to you. For example, I am wondering whether you believe that being in a relationship means someone being overly dependent on you?

P: I'm not sure, but I think there is something to that. I always felt very stifled by both these relationships in the end — sort of out of control. They stopped me from being me.

T: In what way did you feel out of control?

P: Well, I couldn't just be myself. I always had to bow to someone else's needs.

The therapist searches for an underlying assumption.

T: What did that mean to you?

P: It meant that I could never get what *I* wanted. I would always have to look after them. They wouldn't be strong enough for me.

T: So, do you think that you have an underlying belief about relationships that goes something like this: If I am involved with someone, I won't be able to get what I want.

P: Well, something like that maybe.

T: What do you think the belief or, if you like, personal rule might be?

P: Something like if I am involved with someone, I will not be able to have my own needs met. I will always end up dissatisfied.

T: OK, maybe we now have an assumption that you make when in relationships. If this assumption is true, does it fit in with what happened with both Alan and Andrew?

P: I'd have to think about that, but I think it does explain some of what I felt in those relationships.

T: Would you like to think about this a bit more for the next time we meet? It could be that this assumption is unrealistic and has not always worked in your favour in the past. Or it might be that it is an assumption that has been helpful to you in the past, but may no longer be so. Maybe it stops you getting involved in other relationships? What do you think about looking at this more thoroughly next time and you working on it by yourself before them?

P: I think it would be a good idea but I'm not sure how to go about doing it.

T: OK, let's break it down. Maybe you would like to define what you think are your needs in a relationship. Make a list and we can go over this. Would that be a reasonable start?

P: Yes, I can do that.

The patient and therapist then reviewed the session. Sheila had found this session very helpful. Homework for Session 7 was discussed. As well as the task based on defining what Sheila meant by her needs, she also wished to continue modifying her automatic thoughts and practising relaxation. The therapist enquired about how she was progressing with cutting down her Valium and was told that Sheila was now on 10 mg daily and had been advised by her GP to remain on that dosage for 1 or 2 more weeks. She was more confident about stopping it altogether.

Reformulation

The original formulation emphasized the importance of Sheila's mother's critical attitude towards her. It is now apparent that the relationship with her mother had been instrumental in creating a dysfunctional belief that closeness with another individual invari-

ably meant that her personal needs would be frustrated. Her auto-nomous style had been deliberately adopted as a protection and was not entirely natural to her. Close relationships were seen as threatening because they would make demands upon her and she had difficulty with asserting and setting limits.

Sessions 7 and 8

Session 7 took place 2 weeks after the previous session, Session 8 one month after that. Sheila and continued to make progress and was now only occasionally a little anxious. She was getting on well at school and she was coping better with her colleague John. The agenda for Session 7 included her relationships with men and how she was getting on with her father. Session 8 was a general review of therapy and included future plans.

Regarding Sheila's relationships with men, she had set about looking at what she meant by her 'needs' in relationships. She had found this exercise quite illuminating.

P: So I made this list of what I needed in a relationship. It sounded rather over the top really, but it helped me to see why I felt so unsure about Alan and Andrew. Neither of these men could have offered me what I wanted.

T: Can I have a look at your list, Sheila? (*patient gives the therapist her list*) So you have written a list here of needs?
Love (affection and sex)
Time on my own
My own room in a house
My own friends
Holidays together
Someone to talk to about anything
Trust and honesty
When you wrote this list out, did anything strike you, Sheila?

P: Yes (*laughs*) I'd be better off on my own.

T: (*therapist laughs*) I see what you mean. You want your own room, friends and time on your own. You *also*, however, do want affection, sex and in many ways a good friend. Someone you can be honest with, talk to about anything, share holidays. Do you see what I mean?

P: Yes, I do. I miss having a good friend.

The therapist then discussed why Sheila thinks that it might be difficult to combine a sexual relationship with friendship. Sheila thinks that sexual relationships are more likely to overpower her or 'consume' her as the boundaries in these relationships are less clear cut. The therapist agrees in so far as the boundaries in a sexual relationship allow for more intimacy and asks Sheila why she might feel 'consumed' in a relationship.

P: Well, I think that my experience has been like that. I've always felt uncomfortable when people have got very close to me. Sort of closed in, suffocated.

T: Who are you thinking of when you say that? Your mother as well as Alan and Andrew?

P: Obviously Alan and Andrew but also I think my mother made me feel like this.

T: What did she do which gave you that feeling?

P: She was so demanding. If you gave her an inch, she'd take a mile.

T: Can you give me an example?

P: When I was a teenager, she would always ask what I was doing. If I told her a bit, she always wanted to know more and more. She really interfered with my life. She wouldn't leave me alone. And she was so critical of me. She always made me feel I was doing things wrong, that I wasn't good enough and didn't come up to her high standards.

T: That must have been difficult for you Sheila. How did you cope with that?

The therapist does not ask Sheila what evidence she has to confirm that her mother actually behaved in this way. Rather, she concentrates on Sheila's feelings and attitudes towards her mother and how she had coped with her mother's negativism. The therapist chooses to take this route because now Sheila can only come to terms with her mother's attitude towards her as a teenager and cannot change her mother's behaviour towards her. Also, Sheila may still be functioning as an adult with these same attitudes which may be inappropriate today. This is discussed explicitly.

P: I coped badly really. I just got on with my life — closed off emotionally, so I didn't get hurt by her.

T: Well that may have been an appropriate and healthy response to the situation. What do you think might have happened if you had *not* cut off from your mother emotionally.

P: Well, I would not have had my *own* life. She would have controlled me even more. I think I would have had some sort of breakdown and I certainly would never have had any relationships with men.

T: So your response to her was actually helpful to you.

The therapist then discussed with Sheila how her assumption affects her life now. Sheila is aware that she values her independence: it has given her the freedom to pursue her career and enjoy being reliant on herself. However, she is also aware of a desire to have a close relationship. The therapist asks whether this has to be with a male or a female or if it matters. This introduces another issue, that is, Sheila's isolation and lack of friends and confidantes. The therapist asks Sheila if she thinks it might be possible to meet her needs within a relationship with a man.

P: Well, it would have to be a man who was special! I know that sounds rather obvious but I would like a man who was quite independent too. One who had his emotions sorted out and who wasn't relying on me for everything.

T: Do you mean someone who has matured and benefited from the experience life gives one? (*jokingly*) Someone around your age, or older, Sheila?

P: Yes, it is an ideal isn't it.

T: Yes, but maybe if you had the opportunity to meet men, you might meet someone like that. However, in relationships people do sometimes lean on each other emotionally. Could you cope with that?

P: Well, I don't know, but if it wasn't all the time, I might be able to cope without feeling resentful.

T: Would someone leaning on you make you feel resentful? I'm not exactly sure why that should be.

P: It would just be my automatic reaction I think. It would scare me as I'd think it would go on and on and I'm selfish enough to want my needs met too.

T: I don't think that having your own needs met is selfish. Any relationship would be unsatisfactory to some extent if your needs weren't met. But do all your needs need to be met at *all* times?

P: No, I don't suppose they do. After all, they are *not* being met now and I'm beginning to feel all right about myself.

The therapist and Sheila then discussed if Sheila would be able to risk getting involved in a relationship. Sheila thought she would be able to try at least. They agreed that she may not get it right the first time but the idea was to experiment. This then brought them on to the issue of Sheila's isolation and lack of friends. She missed her sister and had not socialized much over the past few years, mostly because she had been so anxious and because she had coped with her father when he lost his wife. She realized that she did have many acquaintances but had not really had much contact with them in the recent past. The therapist suggested that she may like to have more contact with these people and Sheila agreed to this, saying that she would welcome getting to know them again. Regarding meeting men, Sheila had little idea of how to go about this. The therapist suggested that Sheila may feel more comfortable with increasing her social circle and may, in fact, meet men through that. Dating agencies were also discussed, but Sheila resisted using these as she thought that this would be very time consuming. Towards the end of this session, the therapist asked Sheila how she was coping with her father.

P: Much better, somehow. I have been less irritable with him and actually he's not as demanding as he was. I think my attitude towards him has changed a bit. He does get scared of being seriously ill, and I can understand that. Sometimes he does phone in the middle of the night and I'm not sure how to react.

T: What does he want when he phones in the night?

P: Well, reassurance mostly, but I'm never very sure if I can reassure him as he might be ill.

T: What could *he* do to help himself with this?

P: I don't know.

T: I'm wondering if you might suggest to him he talks to his doctor so that he knows when his symptoms are really bad and when they are just minor.

P: Yes. I could ask him to do that. I could go with him to the doctor, then I'll know what he says too.

T: Is there anything else you could do?

P: I could phone him last thing before going to bed. That might help him to feel more secure and he might then not phone me during the night. I think he gets very worried on his own at night.

The session ended with a review of Sheila's progress. She was confident about her ability to maintain her progress by herself and asked that she have another appointment in a month. The therapist agreed to this (recognizing Sheila's need for independence and autonomy), but pointed out that over this period of time she would have come off Valium completely. Sheila argued that she would like to try to cope on her own with this now that she was more confident. The advantages and disadvantages of doing this were discussed and there were clearly more advantages. Sheila suggested herself that she 'phone the therapist if problems she found difficult to cope with arose.

Final session

This session took place 1 month after Session 7, that is, 9 weeks after the initial interview. Sheila was now no longer taking Valium and had experienced very few anxiety symptoms for a month. The session concentrated on rehearsing coping strategies to help her in the future. These included continuing to practise relaxation techniques and to apply these in situations which she might find anxiety provoking, being aware of the difference between normal and inappropriate anxiety. Her main technique for discriminating between these states was to monitor and challenge her anxiety provoking thoughts. Over the intervening month, Sheila had increased her level of social contact by inviting people to dinner. This had gone well and she had received two invitations out as a result. She had also gone to the cinema with Miriam, her colleague.

It was agreed to finish treatment. At the end of treatment, her score on the STAI-S was 34 and on the BDI 6.

At follow up, 4 months later, Sheila had maintained her progress. Her anxiety symptoms were minimal and she had continued to use the behavioural and cognitive techniques learnt during treatment. The difficulties at school with her colleague John were no longer there as he had left to go to another post. She was still acting Head of Department and now coped with this well. Her social life had improved. She had become quite close to Miriam and the two of them had planned a summer holiday visiting Sheila's sister in Australia. The father's health was deteriorating and he had been hospitalized. She was concerned about him, but not anxious. She expected him to die in the near future, but believed she would cope with this.

Summary

This patient had eight sessions of cognitive therapy. This is not unusual for anxious patients, in contrast to depressed patients who generally need a more lengthy course of treatment. This patient's dependence on, and withdrawal from, benzodiazepines was managed with the cooperation of her general practitioner; this was helpful in that cognitive therapy sessions could be focused on other problems.

As with the depressed patient in Chapter 6, the issues dealt with in therapy were representative of anxious patients' problems: anxiety symptoms, cognitive components and coping strategies. In this case, the patient's autonomous personality was an important factor in treatment.

Both behavioural and cognitive techniques were used during the course of treatment to modify automatic thoughts, mood and behaviour. Basic schemata were dealt with towards the end of treatment and were shown to be directly related to the patient's autonomous style.

Chapter 8
Specific Problems and Difficulties Encountered During Therapy

In this final chapter, we deal with specific complicating psychopathological features which may accompany depressive and anxiety disorders and we end by giving some tips about how to surmount difficulties which may impede the progress of cognitive therapy.

Patients presenting with multiple problems

Mixed anxiety and depression

Mixed anxiety and depression

For the sake of simplicity, the two patients described in the previous chapters represented relatively uncomplicated cases of depression and of anxiety. Patients, however, often present with *multiple problems*, the most common being *mixed anxiety and depression*. In such cases, the therapist would establish a hierarchy of problems for goals of therapy, on the basis of both degree of importance for the individual patient and of his own understanding and formulation of the patient's problems. If the genesis of the disorder clearly indicates that the depressive symptoms followed a pre-existing anxiety state, treating the anxiety symptoms first would, as a consequence, often have an effect on the depressive symptoms and vice versa. A detailed history of the onset of symptoms and their duration will guide the therapist in his formulation and in his choice of treatment goals.

Obsessive-compulsive symptoms

Obsessive–compulsive symptoms

Both anxious and depressed patients often have concurrent *obsessive–compulsive* symptoms. These can be very disabling and increase dysphoric mood further, as well as decrease self-esteem and self-confidence.

A patient with a 12 month history of depression described increasingly severe obsessive–compulsive symptoms. The initial problem was 'obsessions with thinking and doing things'. She started examining her breasts four times daily to check that she was developing no breast lumps. This would include an examination during the night. She then started to examine herself generally, looking for enlarged lymph nodes, signs of vascular insufficiency and other signs of illness, particularly cancer. She had become totally preoccupied with the thought that she might be developing an illness and was unable to

192

resist the compulsion of examining herself. Being a medical practitioner, she realized that such examination was illogical. As her obsessional symptoms worsened, she became troubled by obsessional thoughts which she could not remove from her mind. These involved the repetition of phrases from conversations or from something that she had read. She had become afraid of listening to conversations, watching television or reading newspapers and books, for fear of picking up phrases that she would ruminate about. Praying had become difficult and she had to go through a 2 hour sequence of prayers at night and in the morning which had to be repeated if she mismanaged it. Over the past 4 months, she had been concerned with personal cleanliness, going through a variety of obsessional compulsive rituals involving frequent hand washing, cleaning of taps and washbasins. She also had to check several things: for example, ensure that the strap of her brassiére was not twisted and that there was not a single crease in the bed-sheets. Making beds could take several hours.

Overlapping with the obsessions, but probably predating them, had been an increasingly low mood. She had a marked diurnal variation of mood which was worse in the morning. Associated with these were guilty ruminations about the past and the present, suicidal thoughts, disturbed sleep and appetite.

Her diagnosis was major depressive disorder with marked obsessional features. Having not responded to antidepressant medication and electroconvulsive therapy, this patient was treated with cognitive therapy in combination with an antidepressant, clomipramine.

Cognitive therapy involved dealing with the depressive and obsessive symptoms concurrently. The obsessive rituals were treated with the *behavioural* techniques of exposure and response prevention: for example, not washing hands, except at specific times; keeping the straps of her brassiere twisted on purpose; reading the newspaper or a book without checking and refraining from examining her body for signs of cancer. Graded exposure and distraction techniques were used to facilitate taking a bath, which had become very prolonged and anxiety-provoking. At first, she could only take a bath in the dark, when checking would be impossible. Later, she was able to take a bath with the light on, within strictly limited times, and with the radio on, so that she would have something else to concentrate on. Ruminations about the meaning of phrases in the Bible or from people's communications were decreased by the self-instruction 'Stop. This is a purposeless activity which will only distress me', followed by distraction through a purposeful activity. Concurrently with the behavioural techniques, the automatic thoughts associated with the obsessive-compulsive behaviour and maladaptive beliefs were modified using cognitive techniques as described in the previous chapters.

Behavioural techniques

Specific cognitive therapy techniques for the treatment of obsessive–compulsive disorders have been described by Salkovskis (1985) and Salkovskis & Warwick (1988).

Examples of *automatic thoughts* related to obsessional behaviour were:

I must get all wrinkles in the sheet straightened, if not something bad
    will happen.
I just thought 'Oh God!' — this is blasphemous, I shall be punished.
I can't cope, I can't think rationally.
I must get the housework done in a proper order.
I must not think of other things when I'm praying.

These automatic thoughts were related to a number of *'shoulds'* which had to be discussed concurrently.

One should be clean at all times.
One should understand fully the meaning of everything one reads.
One should not enjoy oneself without some suffering.

The arbitrary nature of the 'shoulds' was stressed and the disadvantages of the 'shoulds' listed, as described in Chapter 4.

At the end of treatment, the patient was completely recovered from her depressive illness and some obsessive-compulsive features recurred only when her mood went down transiently. At follow-up, she had been able to resume work and no longer showed any depressive or obsessional symptoms.

Bulimic symptoms

Young depressed female patients sometimes present with *bulimic symptoms* which may have been occasional in the past, but which have increased in severity with the onset of depression. Typically, like obsessional symptoms, the bulimic symptoms are ego-dystonic. That is, the patient does not really want to binge, but feels compelled to do it, and then engages in compensatory behaviour, such as dieting, vomiting and purging. These patients already suffer from low self-esteem and the bulimic symptoms decrease their self-esteem further by making them feel disgusted with themselves and by enhancing their self-perception of lack of self control. Feelings of guilt and shame become predominant, making it very difficult for the patient to discuss her symptoms, so that she becomes secretive.

A 20 year old nursing student was seen at the out-patient clinic after a serious suicidal attempt. She presented with classical depressive symptoms and was diagnosed as suffering from major depression, melancholic sub-type (DSM 111-R classification). It was only after six

*sessions of cognitive therapy that she was able to discuss her eating
problems. She was moderately overweight (1 stone: 6 kg), relative to
standard height and body-weight charts, but she saw herself as
grossly overweight and as needing to lose four stones. She tried to
adhere to a very strict diet and avoid eating on certain days.
However, when problems arose, these being usually of an interpersonal nature, or when her mood plummeted, she engaged in bingeing
behaviour once or twice a day, followed by vomiting. She took
laxatives regularly.*

Concurrently with cognitive therapy for depression, a cognitive-
behavioural programme for bulimic disorder was instituted, following the guidelines described by Fairburn (1981, 1985). The patient
was seen by a hospital dietitian who explained the physical dangers of
bingeing, self-induced vomiting and laxative abuse and the
ineffectiveness of these last two measures as means of weight control.
The dietitian also prepared a detailed daily diet sheet which included
number of calories per item to encourage a normal and regular
pattern of eating. The patient was weighed weekly when she attended
for cognitive therapy.

In the treatment sessions, triggering situations for bingeing
behaviour were identified, and associated thoughts and beliefs
elicited and modified using the techniques described in Chapter 4.
Alternative behaviours for dealing with stress situations and low
mood were set up as experiments for the patient to try. The general
rationale was that if bingeing was meant to relieve bad feelings, such *Rationale*
as depression, anger and anxiety, it was not an effective strategy, as it
worked only for a very short time and then actually caused a
worsening of mood with associated automatic thoughts such as: *Automatic thoughts*

I am disgusting.
I have failed again.
What's the use, I cannot control myself.
I can't go out with friends, because I may feel like bingeing.
I cannot have a meal with the family because I can't share what they
    eat.
I shall put on weight and feel even more ugly.

The *belief systems* which had to be challenged and modified were: *Belief systems*

I am a failure in everything. I should at least be able to control my
    weight.
People look down on fat people. I'm too fat.
I cannot have self respect unless I am thin.
Everybody else is thin and successful, except me.

Her assumptions regarding thinness were part of an all-pervasive
negative view of herself and represented two *basic schemata*: *Basic schemata*

My worth depends on what others think of me.
Since I am totally worthless, the only way of keeping up with people
is to achieve better standards than they do.

It would have been counter-productive in the therapist's opinion, to treat this patient for depression only at the outset and then deal with the bulimic symptoms, as the two syndromes were interrelated in her case. Her progress through therapy showed a close parallel between the course of the two disorders. However, at the end of treatment, concern with diet remained, although the depression had remitted. The sessions with the dietitian continued and as the patient lost weight and her weight then became stable at a level which she found satisfactory, the bulimic symptoms also remitted.

*Self mutilating
behaviour*

Self mutilating behaviour

Anxious and depressed patients sometimes engage in *self mutilating behaviour*. These patients often satisfy criteria for a personality disorder on axis II of DSM III-R, as well as criteria for a major mood disorder on axis I. The personality disorder can often be characterized as 'borderline personality' or histrionic if some other definite patterns of behaviour recur in addition to impulsivity and physically self-damaging acts (borderline personality disorder) or self-dramatization and manipulative suicidal gestures (histrionic personality disorder).

A university student aged 19 was receiving cognitive therapy for a dysthymic affective disorder (DSM III-R diagnosis) of 2 years' duration, with low mood, hypersomnia, low self-esteem, fatigue and poor concentration. There had never been any evidence of a major depressive disorder (see Chapter 1) or any other disorder. In addition,

Guided discovery

he had engaged repeatedly in self-damaging acts, cutting his arms and his abdomen with a razor; he often showed intense and

Automatic thoughts

inappropriate anger; he could not bear being alone; he engaged in impulsive behaviour such as driving his motorbike in a reckless fashion; and he often felt empty and bored. His arms, from the shoulders to the wrists, and his chest and abdomen were criss-crossed with old and new scars where he had cut himself with a razor.

The patient at first could not give any explanation for his self-mutilating behaviour, of which he felt ashamed. In a cognitive therapy interview, using the 'guided discovery' method of questioning (see Chapter 3), the patient was able to make the following *connections between 'slashing' behaviour, automatic thoughts and emotions*:
Situation: Something has gone wrong — perhaps a friend is perceived as letting him down.
Automatic thought: I can't stand it.

Emotion: Low.
Behaviour: Slashing with a razor.
Situation: He obtains bad marks for an essay which he has returned late.
Automatic thought: Nobody understands me. Nobody knows how bad I feel.
Emotion: Angry.
Behaviour: Slashing with a razor.
Situation: Alone in his apartment.
Emotion: Feels empty and flat.
Automatic thought: I am not a human being. I can't feel anything any more.
Behaviour: Slashing with a razor.

The impulsive self-harming behaviour, when analysed in this way, could be modified using cognitive therapy techniques. Automatic thoughts were modified using the techniques discussed in Chapter 4. The *meaning* of 'slashing behaviour' was ascertained as being: 'so that people will know how bad I feel'. 'to get rid of tension' or 'to feel something'. Alternative behaviours which might fulfil the same ends without the cost of the current method of coping, that is disfigurement and feelings of shame and disgust, were set up as experiments which the patient could test out. Successful alternative behaviours were; engage in potentially pleasant activities, distraction, write down associated automatic thoughts and answer them.

Self-schemata related to the patient's impulsive self-harming behaviour were:

I am weak and have no self-control.
I am a worthless human being who needs punishing.

These beliefs were at the base not only of his impulsive behaviour, but also generally depressogenic. Thus, modifying them through behaviours which are inconsistent with lack of self-control and through the examination of related automatic thoughts were central to the treatment of the depression itself.

DSM-IV defined personality disorders as a disorder of perception, thinking and behaviour which is maladaptive and inflexible and exhibited across a wide range of social and interpersonal situations (American Psychiatric Association, 1994). Cognitive therapy has been adapted and modified in order to treat individuals with personality disorders (Beck *et al.*, 1990; Linehan, 1993; Young, 1990). Although the approaches may differ in detail and in the manner of conceptualization of personality disorders, they all emphasize longer treatment, working collaboratively with the patient to increase compliance with treatment, and the importance of the patient–therapist relationship as a vehicle for change. These elements are in addition to the use of appropriate cognitive and behavioural tech-

Self-schemata

Personality disorders

niques aimed at decreasing dysfunctional behaviour, improving interpersonal relationships and modifying maladaptive beliefs. As in the treatment of patients without personality disorder, the therapist's treatment is based on a thorough conceptualization of the patient's difficulties. Although it is currently premature to state that cognitive therapy is an effective treatment for a broad range of personality disorders, cognitive behavioural interventions would appear to be effective in treating some individuals who present with avoidant, borderline and antisocial personality disorders (Pretzer, 1994).

Suicidal behaviour

Suicidal behaviour

Suicidal ideation, suicidal gestures or parasuicide and suicide are more common in depressive illness than any other psychopathological group (Tsuang & Woolson, 1977). Patients with a long-standing anxiety state also show an increased risk of suicide (Gersh & Fowles, 1979). Suicide rate has remained high in spite of new safety measures, for example, less toxic antidepressant medication which reduces the fatality of overdoses and non-toxic household gas. The case of the depressed patient described in Chapter 6 illustrated the most common therapeutic approach to the suicidal patient, that is hospitalization. Hospitalization, under close nursing observation, often provides time for a crisis period to pass and for medication to start taking effect, so that suicide risk decreases. However, as hospitalization can only be implemented in extreme cases, it is useful for the therapist to have at his disposal specific techniques and strategies to reduce suicide risk. Cognitive therapy offers such techniques.

General strategy

General strategy: The cognitive therapist deals with the motive for committing suicide in a direct and detailed way. The assumption is that each individual patient has his own motives and that he has come to the conclusion that the *best* solution open to him is suicide. The therapist must redress the balance in favour of living, that is he should be able to demonstrate that dying is not the best solution for the individual. To achieve this, he has to be even more directive, warm, empathic and understanding than usual. He may even use self-disclosure or accounts of other patients, if necessary, to widen the patient's point of view and allow him to envisage other perspectives and alternative solutions.

Investigation

Investigation of the problem: The therapist asks a series of questions directly but sensitively, to evaluate the strength of the suicidal intention. How often does the patient think about suicide? What does he think about? Has he thought of specific methods of committing suicide? Has he made any preparations? Has he talked to somebody about it? Does he live alone? How successful is the chosen method likely to be? What sort of social support does he have?

Exploration of the motives: These can generally be subsumed in three classes:

- *Objective reasons,* long-term difficulties or the occurrence of a severe negative event (loss of a job, death of a friend or a spouse).
- *The desire to manipulate others,* for example to demonstrate how bad he feels, to obtain more attention from those close to him, to punish somebody, to test the love of somebody.
- *Complete hopelessness,* when the patient is trapped in a negative cognitive system — a negative view of himself, his world and his future. This is often the case with patients who have been depressed for a long time or those who suffer frequently recurring depressive episodes. Such patients are depressed about being depressed.

Therapeutic techniques:

A 45 year old accountant, married, with two children, was being treated for his third episode of depression over the last 5 years. The current episode was of 6 months' duration. He had been suspended from the high executive post he had held for 6 years in a business firm. His motive for suicide was hopelessness, with extremely negative views of himself, his current life situation and his future prospects.

The *negative automatic thoughts* associated with hopelessness were examined in detail and modified.

T: You say that your family would be better off without you. How do you reach this conclusion?

P: I'm making everybody miserable. My wife looks exhausted and it's no fun for the children.

T: How do you make your wife exhausted and miserable?

P: She has to do everything herself. I just sit there staring into space.

T: And the children?

P: I don't do things with them any more. I used to take them to school in the morning and at the weekends we would do things together, like going to a football match, the cinema and so on.

T: OK, you haven't been doing these things since you got depressed 6 months ago. In fact, that's something we need to discuss. It may be that it will help the way you feel to start doing things again, gradually — just a couple of activities every day. Sometimes, interest and energy can come back with more activities rather than less. It sounds as if you used to take a very active role in the household and your wife and children may be missing this. But have they said that they are miserable?

P: No, but then they wouldn't. They are too kind.

T: They are kind towards you?

P: Yes, they are always doing things for me and asking how I am.

T: Does that indicate that they care for you, that they love you?

P: Yes . . . (*patient is crying*)

T: If they love you, wouldn't they be more miserable without you?

P: They will get fed up with me in the long run.

T: You are assuming that this depression is going to go on for ever. The last time you were depressed 3 years ago, did you recover?

P: Yes, after 6 months I was back at work.

T: And you have kept well until 6 months ago. It's taking somewhat longer this time for you to recover. But do you think that it is probable that you will recover again, as last time?

P: I have no job to go to this time. I've brought ruin upon the family.

T: You are a highly qualified accountant. You have held very important posts. How difficult is it for accountants to get jobs these days? I keep seeing adverts in the papers for accounting posts.

P: Who will want to employ somebody who keeps getting depressed?

T: I don't know — but is there a chance? After all, you have kept well for 2 years at a time. Do you know that you will get ill again? You are having a different treatment this time. Several research studies have shown that cognitive therapy reduces the chances of getting depressed again.

The therapist gives research information to increase hope in recovery and in reduction of relapse.

P: Actually, I think that I can't cope with these high pressure business jobs. I've been getting depressed ever since I was promoted.

T: Is there anything else you could do? Have you thought of private practice?

P: Hmm . . . vaguely. I have had private clients before. Maybe I could build up this area.

T: Would you like that?

P: Yes, I did enjoy doing private work.

T: Good, you are lucky to have this option. So what are your chances of getting better and staying well, do you think now? Still 0%?

P: Well, maybe a little higher. (*smiles*)

T: Let's look at your wish of committing suicide now. What I would like to do is look at the advantages and disadvantages of living and of dying for you. Is that OK with you?

List of advantages and disadvantages for living and for dying. The therapist helps the patient through questioning, to draw a list of advantages and disadvantages. This methods allows the therapist to acknowledge and respect the patient's own reasons for waiting to do away with himself, while gently helping to redress the balance in favour of living. The reasons for dying are often the automatic thoughts which have already been elicited. For example, the patient described above made the following lists.

Advantages of dying

1 I won't be a burden on my family any more.
2 I won't get depressed again.
3 I won't have to struggle any more.

Advantages of living

1 I shall at least have a chance to get better.
2 I can try methods for staying well — do a different job, try cognitive therapy.
3 My family will be happy to see me trying.
4 I shall see my two children grow up.
5 If I get better, I can enjoy many things again. If I die, it's true I won't have to struggle any more. But I won't enjoy anything any more either.

Disadvantages of dying

1 I shall be taking an irrevocable decision when I am in no fit state to decide on anything.
2 I shall not give myself a chance of getting and staying better.
3 It would be awful for the family.
4 The family will be in a very precarious financial position.
5 *Plus* the advantages of living as listed above.

Disadvantages of living

1 It's painful to be depressed.
2 It's causing pain to my wife and childen.
3 I'm a burden for the doctors.
4 I'm ashamed to be depressed.

While patients find it easy to give reasons for dying, they need help with finding reasons for living. Every advantage and disadvantage needs to be discussed and weighed carefully, not just taken for granted or listed in an automatic fashion as a shopping list.

Therapeutic contract: The resolution which the therapist aims for at the end of the detailed discussions described above is for the patient to suspend decision about life and death until symptoms of depression have abated. He keeps copies of the answers to his automatic thoughts and the lists of advantages and disadvantages, which he can rehearse in difficult moments. A fine balance in favour of living must be reached and re-evaluated regularly until suicidal wishes have completely disappeared.

Indecision: Problems of indecision are resolved in much the same manner, by eliciting automatic thoughts and making lists of advantages and disadvantages for each alternative. Indecision is a common problem in both depression and anxiety disorders, pointing to basic schemata related to perfectionism, fear of making mistakes or of making a fool of oneself. Patients find it particularly useful to make exhaustive lists of advantages and disadvantages for each possible decision which they give a weighting to in terms of importance (see Blackburn, 1987, pp. 97–98 for detailed examples).

Difficulties encountered during therapy

The patient who does not think

Some patients insist that no thought goes through their mind when they feel depressed or anxious. The emotion just overcomes them out of the blue. As an example, they will say that they feel bad in the morning, just as soon as they have opened their eyes, before thinking about anything.

The problem in such cases is a misunderstanding of what is meant by 'automatic thought', which the patient confuses with deliberate, fully conscious thinking, about a specific subject. The therapist needs to explain the difference, with illustrations and using examples from the patient's own communications. For example, when a particular problem is being discussed during therapy, the therapist can stop and ask 'What's going through the back of your mind right now?' This may reveal thoughts which are not directly related to what is being discussed at the time, and illustrate the difference between automatic thoughts and deliberate thinking. Repeated training of this sort in treatment sessions can be followed by specific exercises, such as noting and writing down *both* deliberate thoughts *and* automatic thoughts. Any worsening of mood needs to be a cue for paying attention to automatic thinking which the patient then writes down immediately. With repeated training, such patients can usually be helped to become more aware of the automatic thoughts underlying their feelings.

The patient who does not feel

On the other hand, certain patients tend to intellectualize their problems and become adept at describing their reactions in great detail, but without taking into consideration their feelings or other people's feelings. The therapist then has to interupt the flow repeatedly and ask 'What were you feeling at the time?' or 'What sort of feelings are you having right now?' Contrary to the misconceptions which the title 'Cognitive therapy' has sometimes led to, cognitive therapy cannot progress without taking emotions into consideration *at all times*. If the patient cannot have access to his painful emotions, he and the therapist will not be able to elicit the negative thoughts which need attending to. Put simply, cognitive therapy *cannot* take place without first eliciting relevant emotional reactions. It must, therefore, be ensured that the patient records his emotions in the column so designated in the dysfunctional thought forms and that he is trained to talk about his emotions during treatment sessions. There may be a basic assumption which blocks the expression of emotions, for example 'to express emotions is weak or unmanly' or 'emotions are not important'. These assumptions would need to be elicited and modified at the beginning of treatment.

The patient who 'knows it all' and recovers in one treatment session

Occasionally, some patients who are particularly autonomous (see Chapter 2, p. 29) have one session of therapy, perhaps after several months of depression or of anxiety, and come back saying: 'This therapy really works. I've been fine all week. I don't need to come back again. I can think of a few people who would benefit from coming here'. These patients may be afraid of their privacy being encroached on, or they may feel ashamed of needing help. It is inadvisable to challenge the patient at this point or to appear to disbelieve in his miraculous recovery. The best strategy is to set an agenda which includes a review of the time since the last session and a review of original problems as listed from the first interview. It will then become obvious that some problem areas remain. The therapist can gently point this out and rehearse coping techniques. He can suggest that perhaps it would be advantageous to schedule another session in 2 weeks' time, say, to review progress. To prepare the patient for possible future disappointments, the therapist can point out that depression or anxiety sometimes follows a very irregular course, with peaks and troughs. Talking about the problems and beginning to practise certain techniques would have created hope and begun to alleviate problems. It would be helpful to try and consolidate gains on a few more occasions before the patient *does it all on his own*. Thus, by keeping the door open and suggesting rather than prescribing more treatment sessions, the therapist helps the autonomous patient to retain his sense of autonomy and to save face.

The patient who 'knows it all'

The patient who is reluctant to stop attending for treatment

Contrary to the autonomous patient, the sociotropic patient (see Chapter 2, p. 29) may become dependent on the therapist and find it

The patient who is reluctant to stop attending for treatment

difficult to terminate therapy. The cognitive therapist can avoid this common problem in psychotherapy by adhering to the structure of cognitive therapy. *First,* at the beginning of treatment, he explains that cognitive therapy is short-term and that it aims at teaching coping techniques which the patient can then apply by himself. He also gives an *estimate* of the length of treatment. *Secondly,* since progress is reviewed from time to time during the course of treatment in mutual feedback, the patient can keep the goals of treatment in mind and be aware of what has been achieved and what is left to cover. *Thirdly,* the therapist reminds the patient of the short-term nature of the treatment by comments such as 'We are now half-way through treatment' or 'I estimate that we only need to meet another four or five times'. *Fourthly,* the last session is always devoted to a review of the whole course of treatment and a rehearsal in imagination of coping techniques for potential problems. This reduces the patient's anxiety and reinforces his confidence in his self-efficacy. *Finally,* follow-up sessions at increasing intervals of time are scheduled, so that a gradual complete termination of therapy can be reached in about four sessions, at, say, intervals of 3 weeks, 1 month, 6 weeks and 2 months. The patient can then be told that if problems arise and he is having difficulties, he should not hesitate to get into contact. It is our experience that most patients are happy with just this possibility of getting in touch and they do not abuse it.

The patient who does not comply with homework

The patient who does not comply with homework

It will be clear to the reader of this book that homework assignments are an essential part of cognitive therapy. The assignments often involve written work, whether in the form of recording thoughts or making lists of pros and cons or writing down the results of a real life situation experiment or challenging basic assumptions. Some patients are not used to writing and feel shy or embarrassed from lack of practice or fear of spelling mistakes. Some patients think that their thoughts are 'too silly' to write down. The therapist should elicit the reasons for non-compliance gently and sensitively and avoid sounding like a displeased schoolmaster. Related automatic thoughts are elicited in the usual way and corrected. Practice is ensured by asking the patient to write down thoughts and answers during the session and the patient is reinforced by always considering his homework at the beginning of each session. The rationale for homework is explained very carefully and feedback about the patient's understanding elicited.

For patients who still continue to have obvious difficulties with written work, we find it counterproductive to insist on them writing things down at home. Instead, we assign behavioural tasks, ask the patient to note associated thoughts mentally and we do the detailed writing in the treatment session.

We refer the reader to the review of controlled treatment trials in Chapter 2 which clearly indicate that the combination of cognitive therapy with medication has been found to be superior to either treatment on its own for some patient groups, especially severely depressed hospital patients. It is, however, necessary to explain the rationale for the combined treatment very carefully, to avoid confusion in the patient's mind. The therapist may explain that there is no single cause of depression (or anxiety) and that 'the mind and the brain are one and the same thing', so that using both psychological and physical methods of treatment (medication) work together and ensure a better outcome. The analogy of a circle can be used, so that one can be at any one point and end up at the same point. Patients with treatment resistant depression or anxiety who have already been treated with several drugs before they are offered cognitive therapy have, necessarily, developed a biological view of their illness. They may say 'But my illness is biological. There's nothing psychologically wrong with me. All I need is the right drug'. The therapist can make a list of the symptoms of depression and/or anxiety and demonstrate that there are both psychological and biological symptoms. The *rationale* that is put forward is 'What have you got to lose? It has been helpful for some patients. Is it worth trying?'.

The combination of cognitive therapy with medication may cause problems not only for the patient, but also for the therapist. They may both be less motivated to put an effort into the therapy; the patient may feel that he is a really bad case to need two treatments; the therapist may feel that his competence is put in question if medication is prescribed.

A good understanding of depressive illness and anxiety disorders, including their biological and psychological features and causes, will help the therapist in coming to terms with a combined treatment and hence in explaining its rationale to the patient.

Conclusion

We have attempted in this practical guide to describe the rationale, strategies and techniques of cognitive therapy for the two most common conditions that psychiatrists and psychologists encounter in the clinic. We consider that cognitive therapy is *one* of the proven methods currently available to treat these disorders. Alone, or in combination with psychotropic medication, it makes us more confident in our role as helpers to treat and prevent the recurrence of these disabling disorders which affect so many of us.

We hope that our aim of making cognitive therapy simple and available has been fulfilled. In particular, we hope that the interested reader can use all or some of the techniques and methods that we describe and that he is encouraged to practise them.

From a theoretical point of view, we want to reiterate that cognitive theories provide one level of understanding the emotional disorders and one pragmatic approach to treatment which do not preclude other levels of understanding or other aetiological theories.

References

American Psychiatric Association (1994). Diagnostic and Statistical Manual of Mental Disorders, 4th edn. Washington DC.

Beck, A. T., Freeman, A. & Associates (1990). *Cognitive therapy of the personality disorders*. International Universities Press, New York.

Blackburn, I. M. (1987). *Coping with Depression*. Chambers, Edinburgh.

Fairburn, C. G. (1981). A cognitive-behavioural approach to the treatment of bulimia. *Psychological Medicine*, **11**, 707–11.

Fairburn, C. G. (1985). Cognitive-behaviour treatment for bulimia. In Garner, D. M. & Garfinkel, P. E. (eds) *Handbook of Psychotherapy for Anorexia Nervosa and Bulimia*, pp. 169–192. Guildford, New York.

Freeman, A. (1988). Cognitive therapy of personality disorders: general treatment consideration. In Perris, C., Blackburn, I. M. & Perris. H. (eds) *Cognitive Psychotherapy: Theory and Practice*, pp. 223–52. Springer-Verlag, Berlin.

Gersh, F. S. & Fowles, D. C. (1979). Neurotic depression. The concept of anxious depression. In Depue, R. A. (ed) *The Psychobiology of Depressive Disorders*, pp. 81–104. Academic Press, New York.

Linehan, M. M. (1993). *Cognitive-behavioral treatment of borderline personality disorder*. Guilford Press, New York.

Pretzer, J. (1994). Cognitive therapy of personality disorders: the state of the art. *Clinical Psychology and Psychotherapy*, **1**, 257–66.

Salkovskis, P. M. (1985). Obsessional–compulsive problems: a cognitive-behavioural analysis. *Behaviour Research and Therapy*, **23**, 571–83.

Salkovskis, P. M. & Warwick, H. M. C. (1988). Cognitive therapy of obsessive-compulsive disorder. In Perris, C., Blackburn, I. M. & Perris. H. (eds) *Cognitive Psychotherapy: Theory and Practice*, pp. 376–95. Springer-Verlag, Berlin.

Tsuang, M. T. & Woolson, R. F. (1977). Mortality in patients with schizophrenia, mania, depression and surgical conditions. A comparison with general population mortality. *British Journal of Psychiatry*, **130**, 162–6.

Young, J. (1990). *Cognitive therapy for personality disorders: a schema-focussed approach*. Professional Resource Exchange, Sarasota, Florida.

Appendixes

Appendix 1
Dysfunctional Attitude Scale
(DAS)

Rate items from 1 to 7, making sure that the most 'dysfunctional' answer is marked 7, as in the example below.

	Totally agree	Agree very much	Agree slightly	Neutral	Disagree slightly	Disagree very much	Totally disagree
1 It is difficult to be happy unless one is good looking, intelligent, rich and creative	7	6	5	4	3	2	1
2 Happiness is more a matter of my attitude towards myself than the way other people feel about me	1	2	3	4	5	6	7

Pages 211–214 show how DAS Form A is set out, including instructions to the patient on how to complete the form. The parallel form of the DAS, Form B, is less commonly used.

DAS Form A*

This inventory lists different attitudes or beliefs which people sometimes hold. Read *each* statement carefully and decide how much you agree or disagree with the statement.

For each of the attitudes, show your answer by placing a tick (√) under the column that *best describes how you think*. Be sure to choose only one answer for each attitude. Because people are different, there is no right answer or wrong answer to these statements.

To decide whether a given attitude is typical of your way of looking at things, simply keep in mind what you are like *most of the time*.

Example

	Totally agree	Agree very much	Agree slightly	Neutral	Disagree slightly	Disagree very much	Totally disagree
1 Most people are OK once you get to know them			√				

Look at the example above. To show how much a sentence describes your attitude, you can check any point from 'totally agree' to 'totally disagree'. In the above example, the checkmark at 'agree slightly' indicates that this statement is somewhat typical of the attitudes held by the person completing the inventory.

Remember that your answer should describe the way you think *most of the time*.

Now turn the page and begin

Attitudes	Totally agree	Agree very much	Agree slightly	Neutral	Disagree slightly	Disagree very much	Totally disagree
Remember, answer each statement according to the way you think **most of the time**.							
1 It is difficult to be happy unless one is good-looking, intelligent, rich and creative							
2 Happiness is more a matter of my attitude towards myself than the way other people feel about me							
3 People will probably think loss of me if I make a mistake							
4 If I do not do well all the time, people will not respect me							
5 Taking even a small risk is foolish because the loss is likely to be a disaster							
6 It is possible to gain another person's respect without being especially talented at anything							
7 I cannot be happy unless most people I know admire me							
8 If a person asks for help, it is a sign of weakness							
9 If I do not do as well as other people it means I am an inferior human being							
10 If I fail at my work, then I am a failure as a person							
11 If you cannot do something well, there is little point in doing it at all							
12 Making mistakes is fine because I can learn from them							
13 If someone disagrees with me, it probably indicates he does not like me							
14 If I fail partly, it is as bad as being a complete failure							

212

	Totally agree	Agree very much	Agree slightly	Neutral	Disagree slightly	Disagree very much	Totally disagree
15 If other people know what you are really like, they will think less of you							
16 I am nothing if a person I love doesn't love me							
17 One can get pleasure from an activity regardless of the end result							
18 People should have a reasonable likelihood of success before undertaking anything							
19 My value as a person depends greatly on what others think of me							
20 If I don't set the highest standards for myself, I am likely to end up a second rate person							
21 If I am to be a worthwhile person, I must be truly outstanding in at least one major respect							
22 People who have good ideas are more worthy than those who do not							
23 I should be upset if I made a mistake							
24 My own opinions of myself are more important than other's opinions of me							
25 To be a good, moral, worthwhile person, I must help everyone who needs it.							
26 If I ask a question, it makes me look inferior.							
27 It is awful to be disapproved of by people important to you							
28 If you don't have other people to lean on, you are bound to be sad							
29 I can reach important goals without slave driving myself							
30 It is possible for a person to be scolded and not get upset							

Attitudes	Totally agree	Agree very much	Agree slightly	Neutral	Disagree slightly	Disagree very much	Totally disagree
31 I cannot trust other people because they might be cruel to me							
32 If others dislike you, you cannot be happy							
33 It is best to give up your own interests in order to please other people.							
34 My happiness depends more on other people than it does on me							
35 I do not need the approval of other people in order to be happy							
36 If a person avoids problems, the problems tend to go away							
37 I can be happy even if I miss out on many of the good things in life							
38 What other people think about me is very important							
39 Being isolated from others is bound to lead to unhappiness							
40 I can find happiness without being loved by another person							

Appendix 2
Cognitive Therapy Scale (CTS)

This scale is used, in conjunction with the *Cognitive Therapy Scale Rating Manual* (obtainable from the Center for Cognitive Therapy, see address at the end of the scale), to assess the general and specific skills needed to apply cognitive therapy competently.

Cognitive Therapy Scale*

Therapist: .... Patient: .... Date of session: ....

Tape ID number: .... Rater: .... Date of rating: ....

Session number: .... ( ) Videotape ( ) Audiotape ( ) Live observation

Directions

For each item, assess the therapist on a scale from 0 to 6, and record the rating in the box next to the item heading. Descriptions are provided for even-numbered scale points. *If you believe the therapist falls between two of the descriptions, select the intervening odd number (1, 3, 5).* For example, if the therapist set a very good agenda but did not establish priorities, assign a rating of 5 rather than 4 or 6.

If the descriptions for a given item occasionally do not seem to apply to the session you are rating, feel free to disregard them and use the more general scale below:

0	1	2	3	4	5	6
Poor	Barely adequate	Mediocre	Satisfactory	Good	Very good	Excellent

Please do not leave any item blank. For all items, focus on the skill of the therapist, taking into account how difficult the patient seems to be.

Part I General therapeutic skills

1. Agenda

0 Therapist did not set agenda.
2 Therapist set agenda that was vague or incomplete.
4 Therapist worked with patient to set a mutually satisfactory agenda that included specific target problems (e.g. anxiety at work, dissatisfaction with marriage).
6 Therapist worked with patient to set an appropriate agenda with target problems, suitable for the available time. Established priorities and then followed the agenda.

2. Feedback

0 Therapist did not ask for feedback to determine patient's understanding of, or response to, the session.
2 Therapist elicited some feedback from the patient, but did not ask enough questions to be sure the patient understood the therapist's line of reasoning during the session *or* to ascertain whether the patient was satisfied with the session.
4 Therapist asked enough questions to be sure that the patient understood the therapist's line of reasoning throughout the session and to determine the patient's reactions to the session. The therapist adjusted his/her behavior in response to the feedback, when appropriate.
6 Therapist was especially adept at eliciting and responding to verbal and non-verbal feedback throughout the session (e.g. elicited reactions to session, regularly checked for understanding, helped summarize main points at end of session).

3. Understanding

0 Therapist repeatedly failed to understand what the patient explicitly said and thus consistently missed the point. Poor empathic skills.

*This scale is designed to provide a partial evaluation of a cognitive therapist. A separate instrument is being developed to assess, in much greater detail, the quality of the therapist's *conceptualization* and *strategy*; the evaluation will be based in part on a case summary and analysis submitted by the therapist. Furthermore, the scale is not intended to be used for the initial interview or final session with a patient.

2   Therapist was usually able to reflect or rephrase what the patient explicitly said but repeatedly failed to respond to more subtle communication. Limited ability to listen and empathize.

4   Therapist generally seemed to grasp the patient's 'internal reality' as reflected by both what the patient explicitly said and what the patient communicated in more subtle ways. Good ability to listen and empathize.

6   Therapist seemed to understand the patient's 'internal reality' thoroughly and was adept at communicating this understanding through appropriate verbal and non-verbal responses to the patient (e.g. the tone of the therapist's response conveyed a sympathetic understanding of the patient's 'message'). Excellent listening and empathic skills.

4. Interpersonal effectiveness ☑

0   Therapist had poor interpersonal skills. Seemed hostile, demeaning, or in some other way destructive to the patient.

2   Therapist did not seem destructive, but had significant interpersonal problems. At times, therapist appeared unnecessarily impatient, aloof, insincere *or* had difficulty conveying confidence and competence.

4   Therapist displayed *a satisfactory* degree of warmth, concern, confidence, genuineness and professionalism. No significant interpersonal problems.

6   Therapist displayed *optimal* levels of warmth, concern, confidence, genuineness, and professionalism, appropriate for this particular patient in this session.

5. Collaboration ☑

0   Therapist did not attempt to set up a collaboration with patient.

2   Therapist attempted to collaborate with patient, but had difficulty *either* defining a problem that the patient considered important *or* establishing rapport.

4   Therapist was able to collaborate with patient, focus on a problem that both patient and therapist considered important, and establish rapport.

6   Collaboration seemed excellent; therapist encouraged patient as much as possible to take an active role during the session (e.g. by offering choices) so they could function as a 'team.'

6. Pacing and efficient use of time ☑

0   Therapist made no attempt to structure therapy time. Session seemed aimless.

2   Session had some direction, but the therapist had significant problems with structuring or pacing (e.g. too little structure, inflexible about structure, too slowly paced, too rapidly paced).

4   Therapist was reasonably successful at using time efficiently. Therapist maintained appropriate control over flow of discussion and pacing.

6   Therapist used time very efficiently by tactfully limiting peripheral and unproductive discussion and by pacing the session as rapidly as was appropriate for the patient.

Part II Conceptualization, strategy, and technique

7. Guided discovery ☐

0   Therapist relied primarily on debate, persuasion, or 'lecturing'. Therapist seemed to be 'cross-examining' patient, putting the patient on the defensive, or forcing his/her point of view on the patient.

2   Therapist relied too heavily on persuasion and debate, rather than guided discovery. However, therapist's style was supportive enough that patient did not seem to feel attacked or defensive.

4   Therapist, for the most part, helped patient see new perspectives through guided discovery (e.g. examining evidence, considering alternatives, weighing advantages and disadvantages) rather than through debate. Used questioning appropriately.

6   Therapist was especially adept at using guided discovery during the session to explore problems and help patient draw his/her own conclusions. Achieved an excellent balance between skilful questioning and other modes of intervention.

8. Focusing on key cognitions or behaviours ☑

0 Therapist did not attempt to elicit specific thoughts, assumptions, images, meanings, or behaviours.
2 Therapist used appropriate techniques to elicit cognitions or behaviours; however, therapist had difficulty finding a focus *or* focused on cognitions/behaviours that were irrelevant to the patient's key problems.
4 Therapist focused on specific cognitions or behaviours relevant to the target problem. However, therapist could have focused on more central cognitions or behaviours that offered greater promise for progress.
6 Therapist very skilfully focused on key thoughts, assumptions, behaviours, etc. that were most relevant to the problem area and offered considerable promise for progress.

9. Strategy for change ☒ *[Note*: For this item, focus on the quality of the therapist's strategy for change, not on how effectively the strategy was implemented or whether change actually occurred.]

0 Therapist did not select cognitive-behavioural techniques.
2 Therapist selected cognitive-behavioural techniques; however, either the overall strategy for bringing about change seemed vague *or* did not seem promising in helping the patient.
4 Therapist seemed to have a generally coherent strategy for change that showed reasonable promise and incorporated cognitive-behavioural techniques.
6 Therapist followed a consistent strategy for change that seemed very promising and incorporated the most appropriate cognitive-behavioural techniques.

10. Application of cognitive-behavioral techniques ☒ *[Note*: For this item, focus on how skilfully the techniques were applied, not on how appropriate they were for the target problem or whether change actually occurred.]

0 Therapist did not apply any cognitive-behavioural techniques.
2 Therapist used cognitive-behavioural techniques, but there were *significant flaws* in the way they were applied.
4 Therapist applied cognitive-behavioural techniques *with moderate skill.*
6 Therapist *very skilfully* and resourcefully employed cognitive-behavioural techniques.

11. Homework ☑

0 Therapist did not attempt to incorporate homework relevant to cognitive therapy.
2 Therapist had significant difficulties incorporating homework (e.g. did not review previous homework, did not explain homework in sufficient detail, assigned inappropriate homework).
4 Therapist reviewed previous homework and assigned 'standard' cognitive therapy homework generally relevant to issues dealt with in session. Homework was explained in sufficient detail.
6 Therapist reviewed previous homework and carefully assigned homework drawn from cognitive therapy for the coming week. Assignment seemed 'custom tailored' to help patient incorporate new perspectives, test hypotheses, experiment with new behaviours discussed during session, etc.

Part III Additional considerations

12. Problems ☐

(a) Did any special problems arise during the session (e.g. non-adherence to homework, interpersonal issues between therapist and patient, hopelessness about continuing therapy, relapse)?

Yes   No

(b) *If yes*:

0 Therapist could not deal adequately with special problems that arose.
2 Therapist dealt with special problems adequately, but used strategies or conceptualizations inconsistent with cognitive therapy.
4 Therapist attempted to deal with special problems using a cognitive framework and was *moderately skilful* in applying techniques.
6 Therapist was very skilful at handling special problems using cognitive therapy framework.

13. Unusual factors

Were there any significant unusual factors in this session that you feel justified the therapist's departure from the standard approach measured by this scale?

Yes (Please explain below)   No

Part IV   Overall ratings and comments

14. Overall rating ☐

How would you rate the clinician overall in this session, as a cognitive therapist:

0	1	2	3	4	5	6
Poor	Barely adequate	Mediocre	Satisfactory	Good	Very good	Excellent

15. Outcome study ☐

If you were conducting an outcome study in cognitive therapy, do you think you would select this therapist to participate at this time (assuming this session is typical)?

0	1	2	3	4
Definitely not	Probably not	Uncertain— borderline	Probably yes	Definitely yes

16. The patient ☐

How difficult did you feel this patient was to work with?

0	1	2	3	4	5	6
Not difficult, very receptive			Moderately difficult			Extremely difficult

17. Comments and suggestions for therapist's improvement

*For instructions on the use of this scale, see Young, J.E. & Beck, A.T. (1980) *The Cognitive Therapy Scale: Rating Manual.* For permission to use the scale or a copy of the *Rating Manual*, please write to:
Center for Cognitive Therapy
University of Pennsylvania
Room 602, 133 South 36th Street,
Philadelphia, Pennsylvania 19104.

Appendix 3 • Weekly Activity Schedule

Note: Grade activities M for mastery and P for pleasure.

	M	T	W	Th	F	S	S
9 – 10							
10 – 11							
11 – 12							
12 – 1							
1 – 2							
2 – 3							
3 – 4							
4 – 5							
5 – 6							
6 – 7							
7 – 8							
8 – 12							

Appendix 4 • Daily Record of Dysfunctional Thoughts

This form is usually attached to a carbonized copy, so that both therapist and patient can keep a copy of recorded thoughts.

DATE	SITUATION Describe 1. Actual event leading to unpleasant emotion, or 2. Stream of thoughts, daydream, or recollection, leading to unpleasant emotion	EMOTION(S) 1. Specify sad/anxious/ angry, etc. 2. Rate degree of emotion 1–100	AUTOMATIC THOUGHT(S) 1. Write automatic thought(s) that preceded emotion(s) 2. Rate belief in automatic thought(s). 0–100%	RATIONAL RESPONSE 1. Write rational response to automatic thought(s) 2. Rate belief in rational response, 0–100%	OUTCOME 1. Re-rate belief in automatic thought(s), 0–100% 2. Specify and rate subsequent emotions, 0–100

EXPLANATION: When you experience an unpleasant emotion, note the situation that seemed to stimulate the emotion. (If the emotion occurred while you were thinking, daydreaming, etc., please note this.) Then note the automatic thought associated with the emotion. Record the degree to which you believe this thought. 0% = not at all, 100% = completely. In rating degree of emotion, 1 = a trace, 100 = the most intense possible.

Author Index